# FOREWORD

Within these pages is revealed the life and character of a noble and gracious lady—Mary Custis Lee. Possessed with courage, humility, and loyalty, the moral fiber befitting the wife of that great general, Mrs. Robert E. Lee undoubtedly in her own subtle way, was responsible for the degree of her husband's greatness.

This book, first published in 1939, was written by a dedicated historian, writer, and educator who was a longtime resident of Berryville, Virginia. Berryville, once called Battletown, is situated in the beautiful Shenandoah Valley and is a community of proud, patriotic, and industrious people whose roots are deeply imbedded in the history of our nation. Many of them are descendants of the Lee, Washington, Fitzhugh, Morgan, Meade, Stuart, and many other families who have become famous in the annals of history.

A reprint of this work is proudly presented to posterity by the undersigned, in cooperation with the Arlington House Chapter, National Society of the Daughters of the American Revolution, of which organization she is a member.

Maxine Goff Morgan<br>
(Mrs. John S. Morgan)<br>
Arlington, Virginia

August, 1973

**MRS. ROBERT E. LEE**
[Dr. George Bolling Lee and Frick Art Reference Library]

# MRS. ROBERT E. LEE

BY

ROSE MORTIMER ELLZEY MacDONALD
*Supervisor of Rural Schools*
*Clarke County, Virginia*

COPYRIGHT, 1939, BY ROSE MORTIMER ELLZEY MACDONALD

ALL RIGHTS RESERVED

439.12

Originally Published

by Ginn and Co.

Boston, U.S.A.

©

Lithographed and Reprinted

1973

by

# ROBERT B. POISAL
## PUBLISHER

Sales Offices:

| | |
|---|---|
| R.F.D. 7, Box 261 | 4541 N. 19th St. |
| Pikesville, Md. 21208 | Arlington, Va. 22207 |

DEDICATED TO
MY FATHER AND MY MOTHER

# PREFACE

A DAUGHTER of Mrs. Lee's, writing after her mother's death, said, "I want the world to know how worthy she was of her husband." But the world has not known.

Mrs. Lee lived at a time in the South when it was not considered proper for a lady's name to appear often in print. Therefore, with the exception of a few brief words in biographies of General Lee, little mention is made of her in the formal records of the times, and her name has passed almost into oblivion. It is indeed strange that she who was the inspiration in the life of the great Confederate leader should have been so neglected.

Her attitude and example during the entire period of the war were an inspiration not only to her husband but to all who came within the radius of her influence. It was those of her own household who knew her best, and it was her daughter Mildred who said, "Yes, my Mother was a hero, as veritable a one as my Father."

Those who knew her are no longer here to tell us of her; but their letters speak, and there are a few pages of memories of one who knew her in Lexington. Of inestimable value have been the carefully treasured letters written by Mrs. Lee to her immediate family and to other relatives and friends. In the Custis family Bible, which once belonged to Martha Washington, was found recorded the place of her birth.

From such trivia has this story of the life of Mrs. Robert E. Lee been pieced together: a story which tells of joy, tragedy, duty well done, and peace; a story of a heroine, the spring of whose valor was a religious faith which guided her every thought and action.

Mrs. Lee's style in letter-writing was characteristic of the times. She used dashes in place of periods, and she

## Mrs. Robert E. Lee

went from one sentence to the next without the use of capitals. To facilitate the reading of her letters, punctuation and capitalization have been supplied when necessary.

Because of the conversational tone of Mrs. Lee's letters, they cover a broad range of subjects. Therefore, letters have rarely been quoted in their entirety, rather only such portions have been quoted as at the time seemed relevant. Because of this fact, quotations from the same letter will be found scattered through a chapter and occasionally in different chapters.

The author is under obligations to many persons for their assistance; for without their co-operation this work would not have been possible. Those appealed to have been more than generous in permitting the use of private papers in their possession and allowing the reproduction of family photographs and portraits. Especial thanks are due Mrs. Hunter De Butts and Mrs. Hanson Ely, granddaughters of Mrs. Lee, and to Dr. Bolling Lee, a grandson; to Mrs. Randolph Turner and her family, Mrs. Spencer Carter, Miss Emily McCormick, Miss Betty Cocke, Mrs. James Oliver, the Honorable Henry Wickham, Mr. Edward Butler, Dr. Matthew Page Andrews, and Dr. James Smith; also to Miss Webster at Washington and Lee for papers she located and had copied. The Lee letters deposited by Dr. Douglas Southall Freeman in the Virginia State Library have been of the greatest value.

Thanks are also due for the courtesies extended in the Archive Division of the Virginia State Library, the Manuscript Division of the Library of Congress, the Virginia Historical Association, the Confederate Museum, the Virginia State Chamber of Commerce, and the Conservation Commission of Virginia.

# *Preface*

Those who read this book will join the author in her gratitude to Dr. Douglas Southall Freeman for the "Introduction" and to Dr. Matthew Page Andrews for "A Word about the Book."

The author also wishes to express her gratitude to certain publishers for the privilege granted her of quoting from their publications as follows:

For passage quoted on page 180 from *General Lee*, by Fitzhugh Lee, copyright 1894. D. Appleton-Century Company.

For passages quoted on pages 71, 79, 104, 147–148, 156, 158, 159, 160, 165–166, 178, 186, 208, 216, and 225 from *Recollections and Letters of General Lee*, by Captain R. E. Lee, copyright 1903, 1924, by Doubleday, Doran & Company, Inc.

For passages quoted on pages 206 and 282 from *A Diary, with Reminiscences of the War and Refugee Life in the Shenandoah Valley, 1860–1865*, by Mrs. Cornelia McDonald. Copyright by Hunter McDonald, 1933. Permission granted by Thomas Miller Manier, trustee of Hunter McDonald, deceased.

For illustrations on pages 209 and 243 from *The Old Virginia Gentleman*, by George W. Bagby. Dietz Press, 1938.

ROSE M. E. MacDONALD

# BIBLIOGRAPHY

BOOKS mentioned in the bibliography from which quotations are not used in the text are mentioned because in them may be found something of the culture of Mrs. Lee's generation.

BROCK, SALLY (Mrs. Richard Putnam). *Richmond during the War.* New York, 1867. Carleton & Co.

CHESNUT, MARY BOYKIN. *A Diary from Dixie.* New York, 1905. D. Appleton & Company.

CLAY, MRS. CLEMENT C. *A Belle of the Fifties.* New York, 1904. Doubleday, Page & Company.

COOKE, JOHN ESTEN. *A Life of General Robert E. Lee.* New York, 1875. Dillingham Co.

CUSTIS, GEORGE WASHINGTON PARKE. *Recollections and Private Memoirs of Washington.* New York, 1860. Derby & Jackson.

FREEMAN, DOUGLAS SOUTHALL. *R. E. Lee: a Biography.* New York, 1930. Charles Scribner's Sons. 4 vols.

HENRY, R. S. *The Story of Reconstruction, 1865-1877.* Indianapolis, 1938. The Bobbs-Merrill Company.

JONES, J. WILLIAM. *Life and Letters of Robert Edward Lee—Soldier and Man.* Washington, 1906. Neale Publishing Co.

JONES, J. WILLIAM. *Personal Reminiscences, Anecdotes, and Letters of Robert E. Lee.* New York, 1874. D. Appleton & Company.

LEE, FITZHUGH. *General Lee.* New York, 1894. D. Appleton & Company.

LEE, ROBERT E. *Recollections and Letters of General Robert E. Lee.* New York, 1903. Doubleday, Doran & Company, Inc.

LONG, A. L. *Memoirs of Robert E. Lee.* New York, 1886. Stoddart & Co.

MCDONALD, CORNELIA. *A Diary, with Reminiscences of the War and Refugee Life in the Shenandoah Valley, 1860-1865,* by Mrs. Cornelia McDonald. Nashville, 1934. Cullen & Ghertner Co.

MCGUIRE, JUDITH W. *Diary of a Southern Refugee.* Richmond, 1889.

# Mrs. Robert E. Lee

**MANUSCRIPT SOURCES**

ANDREWS, MATTHEW PAGE. Letter from Mrs. Lee to Miss Mary Meade.

BUTLER MSS. Letters from General Lee to General Butler; from John Parke Custis to General Washington; also from Mary Anna Randolph Custis (Mrs. Robert E. Lee). Property of Edward Butler.

COCKE, MISS BETTY. Letters from Mrs. Lee to Mrs. Cocke.

CONFEDERATE MUSEUM. Chilton papers, containing letters from Mrs. Lee to Mrs. Chilton.

ELY, MRS. HANSON, and DE BUTTS, MRS. HUNTER. Mrs. Lee's letters to members of her family. Property of her granddaughters Mrs. Hunter De Butts and Mrs. Hanson Ely.

MCCORMICK, EMILY. Letters from Mrs. Lee to Mrs. Lorenzo Lewis. Property of Miss Emily McCormick.

MACDONALD MSS. Letters from Mrs. Lee and her daughters to Mrs. Marshall MacDonald and from General Custis Lee to Marshall MacDonald; also letters from Marshall MacDonald and brief recollections of the Lees in Lexington, recorded by Mrs. Marshall MacDonald.

SMITH, DR. JAMES. Letters from Mrs. Lee to General Francis Smith, Superintendent of Virginia Military Institute, and to Mrs. Francis Smith.

TURNER MSS. Letters from Mrs. Lee to Mr. Edward Turner; also Diary of Thomas Turner. Property of Mrs. Randolph Turner and her children.

VIRGINIA HISTORIC SOCIETY. Letters from Mrs. Lee to Mrs. Talcott and to the Nottingham children.

VIRGINIA STATE LIBRARY. Letters from Mrs. Lee to members of her family and from Mrs. Custis to Custis Lee and to Mrs. Lee.

WASHINGTON AND LEE UNIVERSITY. Minutes of the trustees.

WICKHAM, THE HONORABLE HENRY. Letters from Mrs. Lee to members of the Wickham family.

# A WORD ABOUT THE BOOK

IN THE numerous biographies of Robert E. Lee the role of Mary Custis has been but an incidental one. Unfortunately for a faithful presentation of the Lee household, the biographers, for the most part, have presented a colorless picture of Mrs. Lee that is not in keeping with her life and character as revealed in the following pages. Here is found for the first time her full-length portrait as wife, mother, hostess, heiress of Arlington, and wartime heroine.

We now see her portrayed as a woman who by education, as well as by instinct, was wholly familiar with the historical background that pointed to the inevitability of Lee's so-called "Great Decision," regardless of the subsequent, and not infrequently erroneous, interpretations by different and differing scholars. In addition this biography shows that she was conversant with current events, which she was accustomed to discuss with her husband, keeping her counsel when, as the wife of an army officer, silence was the part of wisdom. On the other hand, there were times when she expressed her views with a certain pungency that is quite contrary to the overemphasized conception of "her quiet resignation under adversity"; in fact, the customary picture of Mrs. Lee in the Victorian cap and invalid's chair of later life is agreeably relieved by the record of her spirited *demand* for wartime protection from those she regarded as invaders of the Old Dominion's sacred soil.

From the mansion at Arlington to the cramped quarters of an army post the young bride of Lieutenant Robert E. Lee had gone, not only without a note of regret as to the marked change in her manner of living, but with pride in her expressed determination to do without accustomed services, servants, and all that appertained to them, in order

## Mrs. Robert E. Lee

to live within the limited means of her soldier husband. She was no college graduate; but, like all cultivated Virginians, she was familiar with the classics of English literature, and we are grateful to her biographer for putting it on record that the bride sent back to Arlington for her Latin grammar.

In Mrs. Lee's day there were no organized garden clubs; but wherever she went she studied gardens, wrote about them, or planted them. She long preceded the current lament over scarificed landscapes, when, upon a visit to Niagara, she deplored at length the fact that the beauty of the falls had been marred by "shops and mills" which had been built "down to its very edge" in man's inhumanity to nature. One might well believe that this woman whose picture has been so often unduly "softened," as were the rugged lineaments of Washington in the Athenaeum portrait, might have organized a militant group with politico-social reforms in view, and all this notwithstanding her ever-present thoughts of duties to her children and to her dependents—happy slaves, for whom, nevertheless, freedom was provided by her father's will and her husband's mid-war action.

One or two expressions in her letters during the awful political aftermath of the war, aptly called "the tragic era," may be unduly resented by partisans. But had Mary Custis not so expressed her personal indignation over the outrages of reconstruction, she would hardly have been human; so in the following pages her biographer correctly portrays her subject as an unspoiled heiress, an unaffected woman, and a self-sacrificing—but not necessarily or invariably a self-effacing—wife and mother.

MATTHEW PAGE ANDREWS

# INTRODUCTION

A LADY'S name, according to the unwritten code of the Old South, appeared but twice in the newspapers, once when she was married and again when she died. Literal adherence to that rule was accompanied in many instances by the loss or destruction of all family letters. The result was that the materials for the biography of a notable woman often consisted of nothing more than a few established dates and the recollections of friends and family. After a generation the preparation of even a sketch became a virtual impossibility. Scarcely a dozen Southern women of the period prior to 1860 stand out in our literature as vivid, understandable personalities. Political history is the poorer on this account and is masculinely one-sided; social history, in the more intimate aspects, cannot be written at all.

Mary Custis Lee escaped the early oblivion that overtook most Southern women. Study of the life of General Robert E. Lee included in time the publication of some of his domestic letters, in which she often appeared. From her friends came characterization of her as an interesting, talkative, cheerful, and appreciative woman. That she was cheerful and industrious during the war, and later was kind to the students at Washington College, everyone knew. Old ladies of station, when quite sure they would not be quoted, occasionally would whisper that she was a bit untidy, had no taste for household management, and usually was forgetful and tardy.

In preparing this first biography of Mrs. Lee it has been the good fortune of Miss MacDonald, or more properly the reward of her search, to find many letters written by Mrs. Lee to her children and friends and several to General Lee himself. These letters give new color and proportion to the picture of Mrs. Lee. They confirm part of the tra-

# Mrs. Robert E. Lee

dition concerning her; part of it they refute. Historically, she is revealed; psychologically, she may baffle even now.

The essential conflict in her mind was, apparently, between the diligence of her mother and the negligence of her father; between the strong piety of the one and the easygoing life of the other; between Mrs. Custis's conscientious *noblesse oblige* and Mr. Custis's unquestioning acceptance of his position as the "child of Mount Vernon," the adopted grandson of Washington. In the end the influence of the mother prevailed over the example of the father. This is charmingly illustrated in the transition from the letters written at Fort Monroe to those dated at Fort Hamilton. When the young lieutenant and his bride established quarters at Old Point Comfort, Mary Lee seemed to think—witness the letter on page 52—that she could call on her mother for everything she required. Doubtless she needed the warning Lee gave her when he said, "your dear Mother will be for giving you *everything* she has."[1] Contrast this with her report[2] on Cassy and Louis. One may be quite sure that Mrs. Lee undertook from her own sympathy and her sense of obligation to assist these unfortunate Negroes; but is it not plain that she was glad to make so full a report to a mother who would be certain to approve and to commend?

Another aspect of the letters now published for the first time is their disclosure of Mary Lee's aptitudes and interests. Her husband had thought it prudent on one occasion to caution guests who were coming to Arlington that she was not adept in housekeeping; but she manifestly was an excellent seamstress who did not balk at the drudgery of darning. She was thrifty too in the employment of her art, and gave longevity to every garment. Her next interest

[1] See page 42.   [2] See pages 91 ff.

## *Introduction*

was in society, and after that in flowers and books. Here, again, we may be sure, she was her mother's daughter.

Many revelatory passages on these and other subjects occur in Mrs. Lee's letters; but, naturally, it is for information concerning her relations with her husband that the newly published letters will be read most carefully. Did she really know him? Did she influence him? Did she share the decisions of his life and the secrets of his heart? There is danger of exaggerating the importance of these questions by implying that his was a nature more complex than hers. It was not. So far as one may judge, his was the simpler soul. For that matter, all understanding of Robert E. Lee is impossible unless one realizes at the outset that he had a clear, plain code as gentleman, Christian, and soldier, and that his adherence to this code was unquestioning, almost instinctive. As a normal, simple man, who kept a high temper in subjection, he led a consonant life with Mary Custis. There is no reason to assume that for four years their relations were otherwise than those of two young persons who loved each other in a wholesome, carefree fashion. A wellborn, handsome, but poor army officer was happily married to a rich heiress who, though not a beauty, was personable and socially pleasant. The women at the army posts found him attractive; he was full of mild badinage and of a graceful courtliness in his dealings with them; the men liked her; but neither of the Lees seems ever to have been jealous or to have had any reason to be.

The first perceptible change in their relations seems to have come in 1835–1836. After the birth of Mary, her second child and first daughter, Mrs. Lee developed a pelvic infection which apparently was not well treated. In October, 1835, when Lee returned from a long surveying tour on the Ohio-Michigan boundary, he found his wife seri-

## Mrs. Robert E. Lee

ously ill at Ravensworth, the old Fitzhugh home. He carried her back to Arlington at once, where she had a protracted and difficult convalescence. It was during this illness that she impulsively cut off her long, beautiful hair because it had become badly tangled. No sooner had she begun to mend than both her children contracted whooping cough. Ere they were well Mrs. Lee developed mumps. It was late in the summer of 1836 before the little family was restored to health. Even then Mrs. Lee had a slight limp, and by the end of May, 1837, she was confined for the third time.

These domestic troubles had their effect on Lee. A cousin who saw him in the autumn of 1836 was shocked to find him "so changed and saddened." He became dissatisfied with his service in the Corps of Army Engineers and thought of resigning to enter private work. The end of six years of married life found the Lees with the problems of parenthood outweighing their earlier joys of companionship. This change was, of course, one that comes in every marriage blessed with children; but it seems to have had a deeper effect in this case than in most other instances, because, year by year, it gave new seriousness to the life and thought of the husband.

Four more children were born to the Lees. Long absences from home increased the father's concern for the rearing of the boys. The easy life at Arlington probably seemed to him to involve danger that the two older lads might not get the proper discipline. That feeling was deepened by his knowledge that Mrs. Lee was indulgent with them. The boys themselves, as they grew, were conscious of that fact. "My mother," the youngest son wrote in late life, "I could sometimes circumvent, and at times took liberties with her orders, construing them to suit my-

## *Introduction*

self; but exact obedience to every mandate of my father was a part of my life and being at that time." It was this concern, no less than the spirit of the day, that prompted Lee to resort to preachments in the letters he wrote to his sons. He may have overdone these exhortations; but in his relations with his daughters he struck what seems to have been exactly the right pitch of affection and paternal gallantry. Perhaps it is fair to say that while he frequently urged Mrs. Lee not to indulge their sons, he spoiled their daughters. Of her method of dealing with them her letters give little information. The most curious and puzzling portrayal of mother and daughter is that given in Mrs. Lee's letter of 1856 to her daughter Annie,[1] who was then at school in Staunton, Virginia. Annie had a defect in one eye, which probably had some disturbing effect on her state of mind, and that year she had passed through what then was styled a "religious experience." Of this she had written her mother, who replied at some length. In phrases that echoed her own mother, Mrs. Lee rejoiced in the girl's confession and urged Annie to pray for the sister and the brothers, who had not at that time taken religion seriously. "Pray for your Mother," she went on, "that she may be more faithful in her prayers & example." Then she added, at the very end, this sentence: "I accept, my dear child, your penitence for all your faults towards me & freely bestow my forgiveness." Was that a wise answer to an adolescent girl who felt that she had won a spiritual battle? Mrs. Lee's letters to her sons, on the other hand, are direct and confident, as if she, who had been reared virtually as an only child, understood boys thoroughly.

The two decades of the uprearing of the children from 1837 to 1857 were busy and, in the main, happy. In Novem-

[1] See pages 117–118.

xix

## Mrs. Robert E. Lee

ber, 1857, when Lee hurried home from Texas on receipt of news that Mr. Custis was dead, he had a grim shock: Mrs. Lee had become an invalid in his absence. She considerately had not written him of her affliction, but her right hand and arm were almost useless; often she would be kept awake at night by the pain; she scarcely could move about the house. At forty-nine she suddenly had become an old woman. For the two years that followed, Lee had to remain at home in order that he might look after her and settle the neglected estate of Mr. Custis.

In this adjustment to a life far different from that of the jubilant days at Fort Monroe, religion seems to have been the most potent influence. The experience of the Mexican War, the responsibilities of parenthood, and the death of Mrs. Custis had led Lee in 1853 to be confirmed along with two of his daughters. Thereafter, every new trial seemed to be met with a new confidence. He reconciled himself to his wife's invalidism; she met patiently the racking pain. In doing this she wisely did not attempt to withdraw herself from life. On the contrary, Arlington was more than ever a center of social activity. Endless guests came to visit the girls. When the daughters were away from home Mrs. Lee often entertained her older friends and kinspeople. In the drawing room the chair of the invalid often had company about it. If the life was difficult for Colonel Lee, the effect was profound. From nursing his mother he had received part of the discipline of spirit that had carried him brilliantly through West Point. Now, in the care of his wife and in the management of a run-down plantation, he developed the self-mastery that was to be demanded for the sagacious administration of a revolutionary army of sensitive individualists.

While Lee met every demand of that hideous era of

## *Introduction*

war, Mrs. Lee displayed all the qualities that could have been asked of a woman whose life was confined to four walls. As Miss MacDonald's pages abundantly prove, Mrs. Lee showed the highest courage and the most persistent faith in the triumph of the Confederacy. If, along with that, there was a measure of vindictiveness toward the enemy, it was entirely lacking in her husband. This probably is explained by the difference between his active life and her imprisonment; between his outlook as a professional soldier and hers as a matron driven from home by an invading foe.

Most notable was Mrs. Lee's industry. She had never lost her interest in needlework, and when the wants of the army pressed, she showed amazing energy in knitting socks for the soldiers who received none from home. That was all she could do, but she did it zealously. An inspiring account of her activity during the third winter of the war is given in Mrs. James Chesnut's diary. On February 24, 1864, while half-naked soldiers were shivering on the Rapidan, Mrs. Chesnut wrote: "Friends came to make taffy and stayed the livelong day. They played cards." Two days later Mrs. Chesnut recorded a visit to Mrs. Lee. "Her room was like an industrial school: everybody so busy. Her daughters were all there plying their needles, with several other ladies. Mrs. Lee showed us a beautiful sword, recently sent to the General by some Marylanders, now in Paris. On the blade was engraved, '*Aide toi et Dieu t'aidera.*' When we came out someone said, 'Did you see how the Lees spend their time? What a rebuke to the taffy parties!'" Could there be a more charming picture of the lady in the rolling chair? Proud to show her callers a sword that had come from admirers across the seas, she and her daughters scarcely let rest for a moment the needles

## Mrs. Robert E. Lee

that were knitting for those barefooted boys in front of the foe.

Often, when one thinks of Mrs. Lee as a refugee in Richmond, one asks what her husband said to her, on his rare visits, concerning the desperate campaigns in which he was engaged. Did he confide to her his plans and admit his frustrations? Was she aware when he concluded, deep down in his heart, that the Southern cause was lost unless all Confederates exerted their whole effort? There is nothing to indicate that he told her more in the privacy of her bedchamber than he wrote her from camp. Thirty years previously at Fort Monroe, as Miss MacDonald shows in the letter printed on page 50, he seems to have formed the safe habit of keeping his professional business to himself. He did not depart from that rule during the war. To Mrs. Lee he explained what he thought it safe for intelligent, prudent Southerners to know. She seems to have passed this information to her intimates; but, so far as the records show, there is no evidence that she gossiped of the war, or speculated incautiously, or shared in the reproach of Congress and the executive. It is almost certain that she had no secrets to whisper. In so far as General Lee talked freely with anyone concerning the incompetence and the blundering he had to combat, it was with Custis, who was then a member of the personal staff of President Davis.

Miss MacDonald develops to the limit of scanty materials the story of Mrs. Lee's experiences and state of mind during the last days of the Confederacy and through the bewildering weeks that followed. Apparently by the time the family was settled at Derwent, Mrs. Lee had reconciled herself, as far as she ever did, to the outcome of the war. She could neither forget nor forgive the seizure of Arlington by the Federal government, nor could she take the

## *Introduction*

view General Lee did of the ultimate restoration of justice; but she made the best of the life she had to lead, and after she went to Lexington she found a measure of content.

Her attitude toward the post-bellum fame of her husband is even more fully disclosed by the narratives of natives and of visitors to Lexington than by the letters her biographer has collected. Of course Mrs. Lee was proud of her husband's achievements during the war and was conscious of the reverence in which he was held by Southerners. In her correspondence with her friends she dutifully recorded his comings and goings and the state of his health. Beyond this she seems to have changed scarcely at all in her own dealings with him. She still asserted a gentle but positive rule over him when he was at home, and she assumed as her special prerogative final judgment of the many likenesses of him that artists and photographers fashioned. When Edward V. Valentine, then a young sculptor, completed the model of his bust of the General, Mrs. Lee insisted on inspecting it. As she could not go to the extemporized studio, the model was carried to her home, whither Mrs. Lee summoned a few friends to serve as *amicae curiae*. General Lee himself was brought into the room and was commanded by Mrs. Lee to sit in various positions, for comparison with the bust. "To all of this," Mr. Valentine later wrote, "the General submitted . . . without a murmur."

Who can doubt that Mrs. Lee enjoyed this display of her authority over the man who had commanded tens of thousands? May there not have been also a certain conscious, if forgivable, self-gratification in her willingness to have him wait on her? One day, for example, a lady came to call with her small son in attendance. During the course of the chat, which probably was not marked by brevity,

# Mrs. Robert E. Lee

the lad wandered about the lower floor of the house and, after the manner of boys, lost his hat. When this fact was discovered, as the guest prepared to leave, Mrs. Lee ordered the General, politely but positively, to find the missing headgear. Needless to say, the visitor was shocked to think that the "great man of the South" should be sent on so petty a mission. Secretly Mrs. Lee may have enjoyed the incident. General Lee, then as always, played his part as a dutiful second in command at home. Faithfully he humored Mrs. Lee during those last years and maintained that it was his special privilege to wheel her about.

There is distinct psychological interest in the "last scene of all." As the General lay dying Mrs. Lee sat by his bedside, his hand in hers, for hours on end. About 9.30 A.M., on October 12, 1870, he breathed his last. She was led away from the room to her own chamber, where she spent the remainder of the day. Before it ended she wrote to a beloved cousin a long letter in which she described fully the illness and passing of her husband. The letter was full of subdued emotion, but it was entirely coherent and was penned with manifest self-control. How came she to write that day? How could she? Was it because she wanted an outlet for her feelings, or was it because she felt herself duty-bound to communicate immediately, after the manner of her generation, the details of a deathbed? One may do no more than surmise; but in the picture of the gnarled-fingered old matron in the white cap, bent over her writing while the bells tolled and the whole town wept, one may have the secret of Mary Custis Lee—family obligation, courage, interest in life and in death, resignation, calm faith.

DOUGLAS SOUTHALL FREEMAN

Westbourne, Richmond, Virginia

# MRS. ROBERT E. LEE

# CHAPTER I

# *Child of Arlington*

THERE may have been those who thought of Mary Anna Randolph Custis as a lonely little girl, for she was the only child of Arlington House. However, looking back on her childhood, she never thought of herself as having been lonely; for if there were no brothers and sisters with whom to play, there were numbers of cousins who spent weeks at a time at Arlington. The most frequent visitor was cousin Angela Lewis of Woodlawn. The deepest affection existed between Mrs. Custis, Mary's mother, of Arlington and her sister-in-law Nelly Custis, Mrs. Lawrence Lewis, of Woodlawn. Frequent trips were made between the two plantations. Roads were bad and difficult of travel for carriages; so when the sisters, bringing their little girls, did come to visit each other, their visits lasted several days.

Not so far away and situated on a much better road was Tudor Place in Georgetown, the home of Britannia Wellington Peter, another first cousin near Mary's age. From a greater distance came Marietta Turner, whose home was Kinloch, Fauquier County, Virginia, and Mary Goldsborough, a cousin from

## Mrs. Robert E. Lee

Shoal Creek, near Cambridge, Maryland. The visits of Marietta Turner and Mary Goldsborough were not so frequent, and they were therefore of longer duration. There were many other friends and cousins who came to play under the great oak trees on the Arlington lawn and to sleep in the trundle bed in the nursery; but it was these cousins, whom Mary cherished all through her life, that were to prove their love and loyalty to her when the name of Lee connoted tragedy.

Those who knew this little girl thought of her as a child born to an enviable position, with the brightest of futures assured. Little did they realize that if the history of her life were some day written in music, it would be a great symphony of blended joys and sorrows—the joyous tempo of childhood and girlhood changed into one of care and trouble, of tragedy in which were received wounds that could never be healed, even in those last days of tranquillity. Such a symphony would represent the great thundering of battle, conflagration, surrender, desolation, and finally the heart sob of a family in exile, with no home to call their own; but through it all would run the theme of the sublime character of Mary Custis Lee.

Her life history was to be interesting and romantic, but tragic. As Mary Custis, idolized daughter of Arlington, and then later as Mrs. Robert E. Lee,

## Child of Arlington

*Arlington, the Lee Mansion, Virginia*
[James Sanders]

mistress of Arlington, she was to taste of life's brightest promises. As the wife of General Lee, she was to drink to its dregs the cup of tragedy.

Mary Anna Randolph Custis was the daughter of George Washington Parke Custis, the grandson of Martha Washington and the adopted son of General Washington. He had inherited from his father, John Parke Custis, among other broad acres a tract of land just across the Potomac from the "Federal City," as Washington was then called. Upon the

## Mrs. Robert E. Lee

crest of the forest-clad hills he built a mansion, from plans in all probability drawn by himself. Bricks were burned on the place, timber was cut from the 1100 acres. He named the estate Arlington, thus perpetuating the name of the ancestral home of the Custises, situated on the Eastern Shore of Virginia. Lossing, a visitor at Arlington in 1853, described the building as a mansion occupying

> a very commanding site upon the brow of an elevation more than three hundred feet above the tide-water of the Potomac, and half a mile from its shore. The building is of brick and presents a front, the center and two wings, of one hundred and forty feet. The grand portico, which has eight massive Doric columns, is sixty feet in front and twenty-five in depth. It is modeled after the Temple of Theseus at Athens. In front, sloping towards the Potomac, is a fine park of two hundred acres dotted with groves of oak and chestnut, and clumps of evergreens; and behind it is a dark old forest, with patriarchal trees bearing many centennial honors and covering six hundred acres of hill and dale. Through a portion of this is the sinuous avenue leading to the mansion. From the portico a brilliant panorama is presented—the Capitol, the Executive Mansion, Smithsonian Institution, the growing, magnificent Washington Monument, and almost every house in the Federal City may be seen at a glance from this point, while between them and Arlington flows the bright flood of the Potomac.

The atmosphere of the house indicated culture and refined comfort; whereas the immensity of the

## Child of Arlington

estate, the beauty of the lawns, the broad and well-kept drive, and the abundant provision everywhere for the comfort of both man and beast showed the indelible traces of the genial and hospitable gentleman.

But the Arlington estate on which George Washington Parke Custis took up his residence when a young man bore no resemblance to the Arlington described by Lossing. The house in which he then went to live had been built in the early part of the eighteenth century. It was an unpretentious dwelling containing four rooms and located near the bank of what was called Little River, about a mile to the east of the present mansion, and was surrounded by a grove of stately oaks. Not far below was a magnificent spring which was to become famous as the Custis Spring. This small dwelling was but a temporary abode; for within a year after the death of Mrs. Washington young George Washington Parke Custis began the erection of Arlington House.

The mansion was started in 1802, when Custis was twenty-one years of age, but because of lack of ready money the work of construction proceeded slowly. Young Custis, according to the standards of the day, was considered a very wealthy man; but he was land poor and slave poor.

On July 7, 1804, when Custis was twenty-three years old and his home was not yet completed, he was married in Alexandria to Mary Lee Fitzhugh,

## Mrs. Robert E. Lee

sixteen-year-old daughter of William Fitzhugh of Chatham, that lovely estate which crowns the hills across the Rappahannock from Fredericksburg. Chatham, built in 1750 by William Fitzhugh, was famous for its hospitality. It was the center of the social life of Fredericksburg and the surrounding neighborhood. "Here the gentry gathered from all the great houses in Tidewater to dine, to drink, to dance, to meet their cousins, to arrange marriages, and to watch the fleetfooted Regulus, Kitty Fisher, Brilliant, and Volunteer."

Four children were born to George Washington Parke Custis and Mary Lee Fitzhugh. Their first child, born in Alexandria on May 15, 1805, lived only a day. Martha Elizabeth Ann Custis, the second child, who was born at Alexandria on May 15, 1806, lived not quite a year, dying in Alexandria on March 10, 1807. The third child, Mary Anna Randolph Custis, was born at Annefield, Clarke County, Virginia, on October 1, 1808. Their only son, Edward Hill Custis, was born at Annefield on October 14, 1809, and died on October 19, 1810, at Ravensworth, Fairfax County, Virginia. Only one child survived, Mary Anna Randolph Custis. This little girl was destined to have her life visibly interwoven with the tragic era of American history.

By the will of his grandmother, Martha Washington, young Custis became the proud possessor of

# Child of Arlington

*Annefield, Birthplace of Mrs. Lee*

the priceless relics from Mount Vernon—furniture and pictures, plate and china, and, more precious still, personal effects of Washington. It was not the silver, china, or furniture which interested little Mary, but the "family pictures of every kind," as Mrs. Washington had stated in her will. About many of these portraits her father had stories to tell her. There was the portrait of her great-great-grandfather, Colonel Daniel Parke. He always appeared to the little girl as a most glamorous figure. He was born in Virginia, but was educated in England. Colonel Parke was aide-de-camp to the Duke

## Mrs. Robert E. Lee

of Marlborough at the battle of Blenheim in 1704. When the great battle had been fought and won, it was Colonel Parke whom the Duke of Marlborough selected to bear the tidings to the queen of England. Riding by night and by day, crossing the English Channel in a fishing skiff during a violent storm, he bore to Queen Anne the report of the victory, written by Marlborough on a tavern bill. The queen rewarded the gallant messenger with a miniature of herself, set in diamonds. This miniature, as Mr. Custis pointed out to his little daughter, could be seen suspended on a chain which hung around the neck of Colonel Parke in the portrait of him painted by Sir Godfrey Kneller.

It was Frances, the eldest daughter of Colonel Daniel Parke, who appears in the records as "beautiful in form and feature and one of two heirs to a great fortune," who in 1706 married John Custis of the Arlington estate, situated on the Eastern Shore. The marriage proved anything but a happy one.

Frances Parke is reputed to have had a violent temper and a sharp tongue. For weeks at a time she and her husband communicated with each other only through the servants, after this fashion: "Pompey, ask your master if he will have tea or coffee, and sugar and cream?" To which Mr. Custis would reply, "Tell your mistress I will have coffee as usual, with no cream."

# Child of Arlington

*Martha (Dandridge) Custis
(Afterward
Mrs. George Washington)*

*George Washington
in the Uniform of Colonel of
Virginia Militia*

[Courtesy of Washington and Lee University]

It was said that on one occasion Mr. Custis surprised his wife by inviting her to go for a drive. Her acceptance may have surprised him. Reaching the waters of Chesapeake Bay he did not stop, but drove the horses into the water. "Where are you going, Mr. Custis?" asked his wife, more from curiosity than from alarm. "To hell, Madame," he is said to have answered. "Drive on," she said; "any place is better than Arlington." This he did. When the horses were forced to swim, and Mrs. Custis had drawn her feet up on the seat, he then headed the

## Mrs. Robert E. Lee

horses for shore, saying, "I believe you would as lief meet the Devil himself, if I should drive to hell."

"Quite true, Sir," tradition says she answered; "I know you so well I would not be afraid to go anywhere you go."

After this the two signed an agreement to keep the peace. Mrs. Custis lived only a few years longer. She left a son, Daniel Parke Custis, who, upon the death of his father a few years later, inherited a considerable property, with the proviso that, under pain of disinheritance, he should have erected over his father's grave an English marble stone bearing an inscription at once so unchivalrous and so vindictive as to give it place among the annals of Virginia as a crime against good breeding and good taste.

Over the mantel at Arlington House hung the portrait of little Mary's great grandmother. She was Martha Dandridge, the belle of Williamsburg, who at the age of sixteen had married Daniel Parke Custis. Children came to this couple; but only two survived, a boy and a girl, John Parke Custis and Martha Parke Custis. After eight years of married life Daniel Parke Custis died, leaving Martha Dandridge Custis a widow at the age of twenty-five. Within two years she married Colonel George Washington, who thus became the stepfather of John Parke Custis and Martha Parke Custis.

*Forebears of Mary Custis Lee*

Colonel Daniel Parke     George Washington Parke Custis
Frances Parke     Daniel Parke Custis

[Colonel Daniel Parke by courtesy of Frick Art Reference Library and Dr. George Bolling Lee, and the others by Frick Art Reference Library and Washington and Lee University]

## Mrs. Robert E. Lee

John Parke Custis at the age of nineteen married Eleanor Calvert, who was sixteen. She was the daughter of Benedict Calvert of Mount Airy, Maryland. There were four children born of this union. The youngest, a boy named George Washington Parke Custis, was born at the seat of his maternal grandfather, Benedict Calvert, on April 13, 1781. He was only a few months old at the time of his father's death. John Parke Custis was serving as an aide to Washington at Yorktown during October of 1781.

A violent attack of camp fever obliged him to leave his post for Eltham, a place not far distant. General Washington hastened thither as soon as possible, but was met at the door by Dr. Craik, who informed him that all was over. The chief bowed his head and in tears gave vent to his deep sorrow; then turning to the weeping mother, he said, "I adopt the two younger children as my own."

Thus Eleanor Parke Custis and George Washington Parke Custis became "the children of Mount Vernon," and the portrait of Washington, in which he is shown as a colonel of the Virginia militia, hung near the portrait of his wife in the home of his adopted son, and little Mary Custis learned to call them Grandpapa and Grandmamma.

The portrait loved best by the little girl was the

## Child of Arlington

very beautiful one of Nelly Custis. Aunt Eleanor she called her. Of this aunt she wrote many years later:

Nelly Custis was considered one of the most beautiful women of the day, to which her portrait at Arlington House, by Gilbert Stuart, bears testimony. All who knew her can recall the pleasure which they derived from her extensive information, brilliant wit, and boundless generosity. The most tender parent and devoted friend, she lived in the enjoyment of her affections.

There was another portrait which greatly interested Mary. It was known as "the Custis children." The portrait showed John Parke Custis, aged six, and Martha Parke Custis, aged four, as little manikins arrayed in all the finery worn by their elders, after the fashion of the day. There were rainy days, days when there was no one with whom to play, or days when her father was too busy to tell her stories, that little Mary would wish that the Custis children might step from their frame and become her playmates for the day.

As the little girl grew up, she learned from her father many stories about the early days of our country; for the mind of Mr. Custis was richly stored with memories of the past. She was an eager listener to the stories he would tell her not only about Mount Vernon but also about the days when he lived in New

## Mrs. Robert E. Lee

*"The Custis Children," John Parke Custis and Martha Parke Custis*
[Washington and Lee University and Frick Art Reference Library]

York and Philadelphia as the adopted son of the first President of the United States.

Among the valuables inherited by Mr. Custis from his grandmother were the family papers. These were a source of greatest interest to him. Frequently his little daughter, coming into the library,

[16]

## Child of Arlington

would find him deep in the reading of them. If by chance he might be perusing one that he felt would be of interest to her, he would read it aloud to her. Thus she learned much of the early history of the United States. One of more than passing moment was written by Mary's grandfather, John Parke Custis, to his stepfather, from Williamsburg on May 29, 1778:

It is with much pleasure I inform you of the safe arrival of a French fifty gun Ship in Hampton Road yesterday. I have just parted with the Cap. at the Governor's. He has brought the most valuable cargo that has arrived since the war. Cloth & Linen sufficient for fifteen thousand Men, four thousand Suits ready made, a great number of soldiers Blankets; Some military Stores. The first cost of the cargo is five millions of Livres. Our Bay has been clear for some time, many vessels have arrived, but the one I have just mentioned is the most important.

Our Assembly has been setting for some Time and have not been idle. We should have been able to have finished our Business by this Time, but I am ashamed to inform you that the Senate never made a House untill the Day before Yesterday. We expect to break up in a Day or two. Three Bills have passed the House of Delegates for reinforcing the Army. One for raising 2000 Volunteers to serve one year. To induce Men to enlist We have given 30 dollars Bounty and exemption from Militia Duty for as long a time as they shall serve, and their persons from Taxation for the same time. A Second for raising 350 Horsemen to serve untill the end of the Campaign. They have no bounty

## Mrs. Robert E. Lee

but the same priveleges with the foot, the State is to equip them. I fear we shall not be able to get Horses and accoutrements. The men are very fond of the Scheme, many have equipped themselves, and I hope will shortly join you. The third is to recruit the regiments. We have offered 150 dollars to Him who enlists for the war & 100 to Him who enlists for three years; they are exempt from Taxation, and enjoy all the privileges with the others. They are to be furnished with the following articles: Ossabrugs @ 1/6 pr yd., Hats 7/6, Shoes 20/, Stockings 2/, Rum 8/pr gallon, Whiskey 5/. Whatever else they want is to be furnished at 120 per cent on the final cost, and a suit of clothes every year gratis. I think we have now offered the most generous Terms and if they Do not enlist they must be drafted. I cannot be more particular at this time, as the House is sitting and the Post will be gone before we break up. You will be kind enough to excuse the inaccouracies, and believe Me your most affectionate—

J. P. Custis.

P.S. I presume before this reaches you Mamma will have left Camp. If she has not, be pleased to give my Love & thanks for her affectionate Letter of the 20th inst. Nelly will write to her on a supposition she is at Mt. Vernon. Nelly tenders her affectionate regards to you.

The atmosphere of Arlington was an ideal one in which to rear a child; for although it was a luxurious home, here was found a very simple, straightforward loyalty to family, to church, and to God. Religion was a vital and ever-present reality

## Child of Arlington

in this home. Sunday was a day for serious study and constant repression; for the Episcopalians of that period, except in point of doctrine, were almost as strictly Sabbatarian as the stanchest Scotch Presbyterians. The day began at Arlington House with family prayers, and after supper the family and any guests who might be there, as well as the house servants, gathered for evening prayer in the family sitting room. Before meals there was grace. On Sunday, promptly at ten o'clock, the carriage was at the door to take the family to church—usually to Christ Church, Alexandria, but sometimes to the chapel of the Episcopal Theological Seminary. After church the family went home and had dinner; then little Mary Custis might have a short walk with her father, after which she was expected to learn a hymn and the Collect for the day. While she was thus occupied, Mrs. Custis devoted herself to the religious instruction of the servants. She knew the terms of her husband's will, which provided for the gradual emancipation of all his slaves, and she therefore devoted herself to the teaching of the Negroes, both on Sunday and on other days, to prepare them for their freedom. Mr. Custis belonged to the best type of Virginia planter, to whom the sale of a slave was abhorrent; hence he was called upon to support an army of retainers, whose natural increase was a liability rather than an asset.

## Mrs. Robert E. Lee

When she was through with her Sunday school for the servants, Mrs. Custis was ready to hear Mary say a hymn, the Collect for the day, and the catechism.

Mrs. Custis was a most unusual woman, her wonderful disposition drawing to her both old and young. She dedicated herself to those gentle offices, quiet duties, and daily graceful ministries of love so becoming to her station.

The place of a mistress on a great plantation was not only one of honor and distinction but also one of heavy responsibility. Mrs. Custis was the most important personage about the home. From early morn until morn again the most important and delicate concerns of the plantation were her charge and care. From superintending the setting of the turkeys to combating disease, there was nothing which was not her responsibility. She was mistress, manager, doctor, nurse, counselor, seamstress, teacher, housekeeper, all at the same time. She was at the beck and call of everyone, especially her husband, to whom she was guide, philosopher, and friend. Mrs. Custis's life was therefore one long act of devotion—devotion to God, to her husband and child, to her servants, to her friends, and to the poor.

Arlington was a home of unbounded hospitality, where Mr. Custis played the part of the charming host. Though deeply interested in the current events

## Child of Arlington

of the day, he identified himself more with the past. He was a man of even temper and remarkably buoyant spirits, with a kindly feeling not only for his friends but also for his servants. It was natural that one who had been brought up in the hospitable atmosphere of Mount Vernon should carry on the family traditions, and that Arlington House should become the center of the social life of its environs.

Mr. Custis not only shared his home with his friends but also was anxious that others who might care to do so should enjoy his broad domain. There was a charming spot at the foot of a wooded slope near the bank of the Potomac. Not only did Mr. Custis give permission for this to be used as a picnic ground, but he had a wharf built as a convenient landing for the little boat which ran between neighboring cities and Arlington Spring, as the picnic ground came to be called.

When Mary Custis was fifteen one of the most pleasant incidents in the history of Arlington House occurred. In 1824 General Lafayette visited the United States on the invitation of Congress. He had visited Mount Vernon in 1784, when George Washington Parke Custis was only three years of age. Though Mr. Custis's memory of Lafayette was dim and shadowy, he had not forgotten the many interesting things which had occurred during that visit. Now he was to have as a guest under his roof

## Mrs. Robert E. Lee

one whose reverence for the memory of Washington equaled his own. He was anxious to honor him.

Lafayette arrived in Washington on October the twelfth. After the official reception accorded him there, he journeyed over to Arlington. In honor of the Revolutionary hero, Mr. Custis had the war tent of General Washington pitched on the lawn, and there, according to tradition, General Lafayette stood to receive the respectful homage of friends and neighbors of Mr. Custis.

*General Lafayette
by Charles Wilson Peale*
[Washington and Lee University and Frick Art Reference Library]

The following Saturday General Lafayette was the guest of the city of Alexandria. The *Alexandria Gazette* of October 19 says of his reception:

Saturday was a beautiful day—the air was mild, and the slight fall of rain the day before had laid the dust. At an early hour the streets assumed an appearance of activity. The gathering of troops, the sound of martial music, the delighted children, all gave the appearance of preparations highly pleasing, for it was that of joy and gratitude.

## Child of Arlington

All along the line of march the "windows of the houses were filled with ladies, who, as they waved their handkerchiefs, told the General that he was welcome." Among these ladies were Mrs. Custis and Mary. Mrs. Custis may have had eyes for the "splendid barouche" in which rode General Lafayette and for the carriage which followed, in which rode Mr. Custis and the son of General Lafayette, George Washington Lafayette; but Mary Custis had eyes only for young Robert Edward Lee, who was one of the marshals in the parade.

## CHAPTER II

# Courtship and Marriage

IN 1810 there came to Alexandria from the beautiful estate of Stratford, which for many years had been his home, Henry Lee, known to fame as "Light-Horse Harry" Lee. Lee established his home in a "small, but trim and comfortable house on Cameron Street"; comfortable, yes, but lacking the beauty and charm of his former home. The steps led from the brick sidewalk to the front door, which opened into a hall bearing no resemblance to the broad and spacious hall at Stratford. Instead of a lawn of broad acres and a lovely flower garden with box-bordered walks, there was only a small side yard in which the younger Lee children played.

It was from Shirley, that beautiful plantation on the James, that Anne Carter had gone as a bride to Stratford. She must have found a sharp contrast between her present life in Alexandria and the rich ease of her girlhood and her early married life; yet it did not embitter her.

The youngest of the Lee children, Robert Edward, was "going on three" at the time of the removal of the family to Alexandria. He was only eleven at the time of his father's death, and he became both son

# Courtship and Marriage

*Shirley*
[Virginia State Chamber of Commerce]

and daughter to his invalid mother, a heavy responsibility on the shoulders of one so young. There were occasional long holidays, when young Robert went with his mother to visit at Ravensworth, the home of his cousin William Henry Fitzhugh. At Chatham, the former home of William Fitzhugh, father of William Henry Fitzhugh, the constant entertaining called for had proved a strain on both the nerves and the income of its proprietor. In the latter part of the eighteenth century he had sought refuge in Fairfax County on his plantation, which he called

## Mrs. Robert E. Lee

Ravensworth. Here in the house which he built he reproduced Chatham. Until this house was finished his home was in Alexandria, and it was in his town house that his daughter, Mary Lee Fitzhugh, was married to George Washington Parke Custis. Ravensworth was inherited by his only son, William Henry Fitzhugh, who had married Anne Maria Goldsborough of Myrtle Grove, Talbot County, Maryland. Near by, at Arlington, lived his only sister, Mrs. Custis.

*Mrs. George Washington Parke Custis*
[Dr. George Bolling Lee and Frick Art Reference Library]

Calling, among relatives, was almost unknown; but visits of several days and often of longer duration were frequently made, as if to justify the trip, which had been made over bad roads. Very often Mrs. Custis and little Mary might be found staying at Ravensworth at the same time that Mrs. Lee and young Robert were there. There were likely to be other guests too; and while the mothers sat and sewed and talked of the many things of interest to the mistresses of great plantations, the children

## Courtship and Marriage

played on the great lawn such games as hide-and-go-seek and puss-wants-a-corner. So it may be said that little Mary Custis and Robert Edward Lee grew up together, and those who watched remembered that from the first he put her in a place by herself.

Though an only child and the "object of absorbing and tender love" of her parents, Mary Custis was unspoiled. Her charm of manner, her wit, her thoughtfulness of others, all combined to make her a toast in any social gathering in which she might be. She enjoyed society and was as popular in Washington as in Virginia. Of what she did she was likely to write her friends, and because she told of the things in which they were interested, her letters were eagerly looked forward to by her young friends and family. There was sometimes a teasing note, as one may see in a letter to her cousin Frances Parke Lewis, who had married E. G. W. Butler:

It is long since I received my dearest Parke's mournful letter which affected me deeply—& I am still more alarmed to learn from Aunt Lewis that she has not heard from you for 3 weeks. Sincerely do I trust that you are not more unwell. Why does not Mr. Butler write if you cannot & quiet our fears? But I still hope it is only some mistake in the Post Office and that you are quite restored in health and spirits & with this joyful idea I will endeavor to cheer you with some account of the late gay scenes I have witnessed.

Maria's wedding took place on the anniversary of your own April 4th. There were about 90 persons & the bride walked with much dignity through the midst of them with her attendants—Virginia & Mr. Trimble, Capt. Smith & Ann Mason—whose entrance was beyond description. The evening passed away merrily & the next night we beheld C. Macomb led to the altar. She looked beautiful in her bridal veil, her attendants were Alexandrine & Eilbeck Yecco Mason . . . Sophie Baligny . . . & Selina Robertson . . . They all wore worked bobbinet dresses over satin. They were very gay . . .

We went to a beautiful supper at Mrs. Rush & every thing in elegant style & Mrs. Rush herself so charming. . . . Catherine Mason will go to Mexico in the winter & Maria Cooper is to live at Old Point.

I expect to go to the E[astern] Shore in a few days, if nothing happens to prevent; the girls are so charming & so very anxious to have me with them that I cannot resist the opportunity afforded me by Aunt Maria's going over. . . . I am very anxious to see more into poor Washington's prospects . . .

The Miss Carters have gone down to Shirley on their way to Philadelphia. Their brother Charles Henry is said to be much smitten with Elizabeth Tayloe & Mr. Shirley Carter with Miss Ella Wickham. I suppose you have heard of the duel between Mr. Shirley Carter & Mr. Wickham in which Mr. C. would not fire at the brother of his love.

The Miss Carters have not been so much admired as was expected, except by the foreigners. I am afraid they are rather *heartless*; at least I did not *love* them, on a better acquaintance though I admired their accomplishments.

. . . We have been trying to persuade Aunt Lewis to come and stay with us, for I think she injures her health by staying so much at home; but she seems to think her

## Courtship and Marriage

first journey must be to Cincinnati. I hope indeed she will go; the change of air and scene will be so beneficial to her & then to see you & her darling grandson will be ecstasy. . . . Mother sends a great deal of love & many kisses to your babe . . .

Farewell & believe me,

> Your devoted cousin & friend,
>
> Mary Custis.

We have just received a package from Woodlawn containing 3 of your letters & announcing your restoration to health, which we are delighted to hear. I will write you from the E.S.

When Robert was nineteen he entered West Point. On his brief leaves of absence he might usually be found visiting where Mary Custis was a guest. But the love affair of the young couple did not receive the wholehearted approval of Mr. Custis. Mary Custis had received a fine classical education and had the accompanying advantages of wealth and position. In the eyes of her father a West Point cadet without means of his own did not seem a suitable match for the heiress of Arlington. However, the young couple found allies in both Mary's mother and her father's sister, Mrs. Lawrence Lewis of Woodlawn. If Robert realized Mr. Custis's opposition, he did not let it deter him from coming to Arlington nor from managing to be found in whatever neighborhood Mary might be visiting.

# Mrs. Robert E. Lee

*West Point at the Time Robert E. Lee Was a Cadet There*
[Photograph by United States Army Signal Corps]

It was first love for both Robert and Mary, and it was destined to be a lasting one. Mary Custis was a very popular girl, and many suitors found their way to Arlington. Among those in public life in Washington who crossed the river to call on Mary Custis was Representative Sam Houston, chairman of the Congressional Board of Visitors of the United States Military Academy. But Mary Custis was so indifferent to the claims of fame as to prefer the quiet youth who had graduated from West Point at the age of twenty-one and was now known as Second Lieutenant Robert E. Lee, Corps of Engineers. The consent of Mr. Custis was finally won; and on June 13, 1831, just two years after his graduation

## Courtship and Marriage

from West Point, Robert Edward Lee and Mary Anna Randolph Custis were married. Thirty-three years later, during the siege of Petersburg, facing the Army of the Potomac, he wrote to his wife, "Do you recollect what a happy day thirty-three years ago this was?"

The wedding day having been decided upon, preparations at Arlington went apace. All the seamstresses numbered among the servants on the plantation were put to work, for the trousseau was to be made by hand with stitches so fine as to be almost invisible. According to the custom of the times, friends were busy embroidering yokes and sleeves for chemises and nightgowns. Petticoats seven yards around were tucked by hand from hem to waist. Dainty nightcaps were made from sheerest linen lawn. But Mary gave little thought to such utilitarian preparations; these were the care and responsibility of her mother.

If she gave but little thought to her trousseau, however, she was very much engrossed with the gay preparations for the wedding and just whom Robert would choose for his groomsmen. It was easy for her to name the bridesmaids; for they were to be those who were her playmates in childhood days. There were Angela Lewis, from Woodlawn; Britannia Peter, from Tudor Place in Georgetown; Catherine Mason, whose father's plantation was

## *Mrs. Robert E. Lee*

Analostan Island; Marietta Turner, from Kinloch, Fauquier County; and there were her two cousins Mary Goldsborough and Julia Calvert from Maryland. Robert chose for his groomsmen his brother Smith Lee, his cousin Thomas Turner, and Lieutenants John P. Kennedy, James A. Chambers, Richard Tilghman, and James H. Prentiss.

The published notice of this event was short:

Married June 30, 1831, at Arlington House by the Reverend Mr. Keith, Lieutenant Robert E. Lee, of the United States Corps of Engineers, to Miss Mary A. R. Custis, only daughter of G. W. P. Custis esq.

Fortunately others who were present at the ceremony have left a more detailed account of the wedding:

The stately mansion never held a happier assemblage. Its broad portico and wide spread wings held out open arms, as it were, to welcome the coming guests. . . . Its halls and chambers were adorned with portraits of the patriots of the Revolution and of the "Father of His Country." Without and within, history and tradition seemed to breathe their legends upon their canvas as soft as a dream of peace.

Tall candles lighted the rooms. Everywhere there was laughter and merriment; lovely damsels, dressed as was the fashion of the day, with curls framing their faces, coquetted with the gentlemen old or young.

## *Courtship and Marriage*

The young bride came down the stairs with her father. The butler gave a signal to Mrs. Lawrence Lewis, who was seated at the piano; softly the strains of music began to fill the room. The young lieutenant and his best man entered the drawing room by a side door; the bridesmaids and groomsmen had formed an aisle through which the bride entered the drawing room on the arm of her father. It is not difficult to imagine the picture made by the charming young bride and the handsome, stalwart young officer of the Engineer Corps as they stood before the floral altar in the large drawing room and exchanged their vows. The marriage service of the Episcopal Church was read by Mr. Keith, and Mary, in tones too faint to be heard by any but the groom, promised to "love, honor, and obey" Robert, and he promised to cherish her "until death us do part." Never were the words of the marriage service more truly a vow. Born to the manor, bred to the purple, Mary never forgot that she was just a woman, happy in merging her identity in that of her famous husband. Marietta Turner, writing many years afterward of the wedding, says:

The night of the wedding at Arlington happened to be one of steady rain, and much fun arose from the appearance of the Rev. Mr. Ruel Keith, who arrived drenched to the skin and, though a tall man, was compelled to conduct the nuptial service in the clothes of my cousin George

## *Mrs. Robert E. Lee*

Washington Parke Custis, a very great gentleman but a very small man so far as inches were concerned. I, as one of the bride's-maids, stood with Lieutenant Chambers, while my brother Thomas was assigned to my beloved Britannia Peter of "Tudor Place." It was the thirtieth of June, 1831, and though mid-summer rain denied the company the enjoyment of the gardens, which commanded an unparalleled view of the Potomac and the city of Washington, the evening was one to be long remembered. My cousin, always a modest and affectionate girl, was never lovelier and Robert Lee, with his bright eyes and high color, was the picture of a cavalier. The elegance and simplicity of the bride's parents presiding over the feast, and the happiness of the grinning servants, untainted by any disloyalty and unreproved by their master and mistress, remain in my memory as a piece of Virginia life pleasant to recall.

In accordance with the custom of the times the wedding party remained at Arlington, for this was before the days of wedding journeys. The week was filled with merriment and festivities. There were horseback rides along the country roads. In the evening musicians from "the quarters" came to furnish music, and in the drawing room young couples danced the Virginia reel to the music of the banjo and the fiddle. Every evening before the gentlemen retired, punch was served from a bowl which had belonged to General Washington. In the bottom of the bowl was a painting of a ship, the hull resting on the bottom and the mast reaching to the brim.

## Courtship and Marriage

It was a custom at Arlington that on one evening the gentlemen drink the height of the mast—a custom strictly observed and a punch bowl never emptied.

The young lieutenants, their leave ended, were obliged to say good-by; the bridesmaids lingered a few days longer. Early in July the bridal pair started a round of visits to their relatives. First they paid a visit to Ravensworth, the home of Mary's uncle William Henry Fitzhugh; then they proceeded to Woodlawn to see Mary's adored Aunt Eleanor, doubly dear, not only because she had interceded with her brother on behalf of the young couple but also because she had been largely instrumental in securing Robert his appointment to West Point.

After paying a few visits to some of Robert's relatives they returned to Arlington. Thereafter preparations were begun for their departure to Fort Monroe, where Robert was to return to duty early in August.

## CHAPTER III

# The Wife of an Army Officer

AT FORT MONROE there began for the Lees the simple life of a young lieutenant and his wife; for Mary Lee brought no independent fortune to her husband. She was anxious to prove that she, who had known nothing but the greatest luxury, could live on her husband's salary without financial aid from her father. Their quarters were in the house of Colonel Talcott, for accommodations were limited at Fort Monroe. Colonel Andrew Talcott had married Harriet Randolph Hackley, who was a cousin of Mary Custis Lee's.

Mrs. Custis was anxious to send some furnishings from Arlington. This Mrs. Lee thought unnecessary, replying to her mother's offer, "We have got as much in our little room as it will hold"; but she thanked her mother for the oilcloth she had sent her with which to cover the washstand. Mary Lee must have found the quarters cramped. They could not under any circumstances be called spacious—to the child of Arlington House they must have seemed small indeed. But if she found them uncomfortable she made no mention of it in her letters to her mother.

# The Wife of an Army Officer

*Fort Monroe, Virginia*
[Photograph by United States Army Signal Corps]

The young couple were radiantly happy, but the very light seemed to have gone out at Arlington; for Mr. and Mrs. Custis had lavished all their affection on their daughter, their lives had revolved around hers. For Mrs. Custis the parting was especially hard. A few days after Mary left, her mother wrote:

I have dictated I cannot tell how many letters in the silent hours of night, as well as in the leisure which the comparative solitude of our house now gives. I will not attempt to tell you how I felt at your departure. I hastened to turn from my own loss to a contemplation of your hap-

## Mrs. Robert E. Lee

piness. United to the man of your choice, you could I am sure with him find enjoyment in far less favorable circumstances than those in which you are now placed.... I am glad Robert comes of such a *loving* family. I have no fear of an excess of love when guided by wisdom; it seeks the best interest of its object.

Lieutenant Lee had many friends at Fort Monroe. These were all eager to extend courtesies to his bride, and a round of entertainments was given in their honor. Mary quickly adapted herself to the life of an army post, making friends of all who met her.

"The only objection I have to this place," she wrote her mother, "it is so public that you can never go out alone ... but I must add that I have a husband always ready to go with me when his duties permit."

Sunday was a lonely day. Only occasionally were services held, and these in a vacant room by a visiting clergyman, as there was no chaplain at the fort at this time. Mrs. Lee, writing to her mother, regretted that there "are no seats provided in the room . . . for the blacks, consequently they never go"; this she considered "a great omission." But if there were no services, there was her "morning's reading," which "consists generally of Doddridge and my Bible"; and Cassy, her maid who had come with her from Arlington, must be "got down to her Bible lesson."

# The Wife of an Army Officer

Mrs. Custis had written Mary of a projected trip to Ravensworth and then over "the Ridge" to visit her cousins the Meades. The trip was to be made in the old Mount Vernon coach. Hearing of this, Mary wrote, "The old vehicle I trust will take you up safely." The trip was evidently made in safety; but the old coach had been well shaken in its trip over the mountains and was pronounced too ramshackle for the return trip to Arlington. So the coach was left at Annefield and became the playhouse of the Page children.

Bishop Meade, a brother of Mrs. Page's, on a visit to Annefield was quite horrified to see the use to which the President's coach had come, and he asked of Mr. Custis permission to put it to what he considered a much more worthy use. Bishop Meade, in *Old Churches and Families of Virginia*, says:

It so happened, in a way I need not state, that this coach came into my hands . . . after the death of General Washington. In the course of time, from disuse, it being too heavy for these latter days, it began to decay and give way. Becoming an object of desire to those who delight in relics, I caused it to be taken to pieces and distributed among the admiring friends of Washington who visited my house, and also among a number of female associations for benevolent and religious objects, which associations, at their fairs and on other occasions, made a large profit by converting the fragments into walking sticks, picture frames, and snuff boxes. About two-thirds of one of the wheels thus produced one hundred and forty dollars. There can be no doubt but that at its dissolution it yielded more to the cause of charity than it did to its builders at its first erection. Besides other mementoes of it, I have in my study, in the form of a sofa, the hind-seat on which the general and his lady were wont to sit.

The days passed quickly, and Christmas drew near. The Lees began to make plans to return to Arlington for the holiday season. Mary, who had never spent a Christmas away from Arlington, had no thought of being separated from her parents at this time.

Travel in Virginia in those days was something like a pilgrimage with stations along the way, the plantations of friends or relatives. The stay at a plantation might be only for the night; but more frequently it was for days, which sometimes lengthened into weeks. Thus in planning their trip to Arlington the Lees included in their itinerary visits to several relations. Embarking on a James River boat, they made their first stop at Shirley, the home of the Carters; then they proceeded to Baltimore for a visit to the Marshalls. At last they reached Arlington, where master and mistress and the many servants greeted them eagerly and affectionately. Great were the preparations which had been made for the reception of the young mistress, for such the servants continued to regard her.

## The Wife of an Army Officer

Mary luxuriated in the love which surrounded her at Arlington. The months at "the Point" had been happy months, but Mary had missed her mother dreadfully. She had begun to realize that the home of an officer in the army could not be long in one place. In writing to a friend soon to be married she said: "I am a wanderer on the face of the earth. I suppose you will remain . . . near your Mother? What happiness! I am with mine now—the past and the future disregarded."

As the time of the expiration of Lieutenant Lee's leave of absence drew near, Mrs. Custis was loath to part with her daughter and begged that she might stay a little longer, at least until the weather moderated. The life of luxury at Arlington, with someone to anticipate his wife's every wish and with servants eager not only to do her bidding but to find things to do for her, and the very evident loneliness of Mrs. Custis induced young Lee to consent to the wishes of Mr. and Mrs. Custis; so he made the trip back to his post alone.

It continued to be a cold winter. The river was frequently filled with ice, which made the arrival and departure of the boats uncertain. Mary lingered on, setting no date for her return home; and Robert, growing more impatient, wrote to her early in May, "I can't consent to your remaining longer than the first of June."

## Mrs. Robert E. Lee

There had been many things to see to that spring, for it had been decided that the Lees would go into quarters of their own. Mrs. Custis was so eager to contribute to the furnishings of the new home, and Mary was so enthusiastic over her mother's offer, that Robert wrote:

I know your dear Mother will be for giving you *everything* she has; but you must recollect *one* thing, and that is, that they have been accustomed to comforts all their lives, which now they could not dispense with, and that we in the commencement ought to contract our wishes to their smallest compass and enlarge them as opportunity offers.

Servants were to be selected from those belonging to Robert. He wrote that he did not wish Nancy brought, since he remembered her as a "bad cook and washer." "Mary can come or stay in Georgetown." However, he wished Mrs. Lee to bring the servants she liked, but thought "two good servants" as much as they should require.

From Arlington Mary brought flowers for her garden, sharing them with Mrs. Eustis, who, Mary wrote her mother, "was much pleased with the flowers, some of which I sent her and the rest I have put in our yard here, and they are doing very well."

In her "new habitation" Mrs. Lee busied herself making "cotton curtains for the back room." She was also "commencing a little painting for Mary

# The Wife of an Army Officer

Goldsborough." She busied herself in her garden, and in the autumn she wrote her mother that it was "quite warm here, but few of the trees have commenced to change colour. There are many beautiful chrysanthemums in bloom all over the Point, but not as fine as mine & the garden we have left looks beautiful now—so many roses in bloom."

She missed the sound of the church bells each Sunday morning. "The beat of the drum summons us to church." "The only music we hear Sunday morning is the band on the parade ground."

During the first months of Mrs. Lee's married life she had proved herself a rather dilatory letter-writer, often disappointing her mother when the mail would arrive with "nothing from Mary." From Ravensworth her mother had written her shortly after her marriage:

> Your Aunt Maria sent down for your letter, but we are disappointed. Smith thinks that the mail bag was possibly sent up to Washington and had not come down when Charles called. Of course, I greatly desire to hear how you are and everything which your letter was expected to contain, but will not yield to any fear.

If Mrs. Lee was an unsatisfactory correspondent at that time, she proved herself a most satisfactory one upon her return to "the Point." Her letters now were charming and gave to her parents every detail of her daily life.

## *Mrs. Robert E. Lee*

I walk every morning before breakfast on this beautiful beach & inhale the sea breezes which are said to bring health along with them. Of course all the bathing is over. ... I have got through very little work except mending up some of Robert's old clothes—a coat of his I have darned & new lined the sleeve. You ought to see how nicely it is done.

Among the accomplishments which Mrs. Custis had taught her daughter was that of being an accomplished needlewoman. So now Mrs. Lee was tracing patterns on flannel petticoats and embroidering them with great care. Friends were sending patterns for baby sacks and wrappers; for those were the days when the exchange of patterns was among the amenities, and every good housewife had her pattern box. Mrs. Custis, shopping in Alexandria, was selecting lovely dainty material to be made into baby dresses. The seamstress at Arlington House was busy stitching rows of tucks in the voluminous skirts in accordance with the fashion in baby clothes at that time. Mrs. Lee writing to her mother in August says, "I have begun to work at night while Robert reads to me." On September 16, 1832, her son was born at Fort Monroe and named George Washington Custis for her father. Mr. Custis heard with delight the news of the birth of his first grandson. He thought of him as one day master of Arlington; but the fortunes of war were to rule otherwise.

# *The Wife of an Army Officer*

Mary Lee was undoubtedly much more interested in her family, in study, and in serious reading than she was in society. Though always a gracious hostess to such guests as her husband felt should be invited to their home, she cared little for formal society. The summer following the birth of her son was centered in little Custis, though she rarely called him Custis, using such pet names as Bun, Bunny, Boo, Boose, Bouse, and Dunket. But if she did not care for formal society, she was always eager for visits from friends and relatives; therefore, when her aunt, Mrs. Lawrence Lewis, failed to make a promised visit, Mrs. Lee wrote to her mother:

Tell Aunt Eleanor it was very peculiar of her to give up her trip, for there are many opportunities every boat. It is the last difficulty that need have stopped her. I think she had much better come here or go & see Rosalie, for it is bad both for the health and spirits to stay forever in one place. The bathing is now delightful, and Bunny is too sweet. He is the most restless little creature you ever saw and very mischievous. I calculated that you and Aunt Eleanor would take the whole trouble of him when you came down.

Mrs. Huger, the wife of one of the officers, had set the fashion in a new and elaborate style of sunbonnet, and the ladies at "the Point" were eager to follow a style which would protect their complexions in such a becoming way; but there were no stores at

# Mrs. Robert E. Lee

which the necessary material could be bought unless one went to Norfolk. So Mary writes to her mother, who is coming to make them a visit:

If you should get this in time, and you come through Alex<sup>a</sup> [Alexandria], will you get 2 yds of some material to make me a bonnet to wear about here. Mrs. Huger has one she got made on the Point, of coloured muslin. It takes 2 yds of the muslin, which is pretty wide; but of gingham, which is narrower, it would take 2 1/2 yds. I should like either yellow, purple, or pink. You know that it does not require *very fine* muslin. If you do not see any you think would answer, as you have but little time to select, get me a piece of coloured french chintz or some plain pink cambric, not too deep but a pretty shade; but do not get any if you are hurried, because I can wait 'till you get to Norfolk. Tell Father he must bring Tom down and come prepared to stay much longer than a week. I hope that we shall be able to find some crabs for him. Tell Aunt Eleanor that she has missed the greatest treat by not getting to see this sweetest Bun. You must not fail to come on Saturday, Grandmother. Little *Dunket* will go to meet you if it is not warm.... Now make up your mind to pay me a long visit, for you know that I shall not be able to leave here much before Christmas. Remember me to all the servants. I forgot to send the book I got for the children, but will keep it now "till we go up." Will you bring down a Latin dictionary, as I brought a Greek one by mistake.

Already she was making plans to return to Arlington for Christmas, though it was still some months distant. This was to be a joyous Christmas

# The Wife of an Army Officer

at Arlington; the young heir was to be brought home, and his grandfather was planning a celebration worthy of the event.

Mrs. Lee had sent urgent invitations to the members of her family and to Robert's relatives to visit them at Fort Monroe. She was eager to show them what a big boy young Custis had become; she was proud of her housekeeping; and she was anxious to let them see the home that she and Robert had made. Among those who accepted her invitation that summer was Lorenzo Lewis, of Audley, and his wife, Esther Maria, with their young son George Washington Lewis. Apparently there was great congeniality between these two young women, which in the years to come was to grow into an understanding friendship. Just now they were two young mothers, each adoring her first-born, with a pleasant rivalry as to their precociousness and intelligence.

Mrs. Lee writing to her mother says: "Little Wassy is exceedingly fond of him [Custis], always kissing him, but is so rough that Bouse [Custis] does not like him half so well as he does Martha, who is much more gentle." In September Mrs. Lee wrote to her mother:

> Esther and Loren [Lorenzo] have staid much longer than they at first anticipated—Lorenzo very much engaged in killing birds to stuff.... Mrs. Huger returned on Saturday—looks better.... She brought me a very

## Mrs. Robert E. Lee

nice silk dress which I had written for & a cape & gave me the very welcome information that all stiffening was quite out of fashion; so I shall be quite *a la mode* myself.

... Bouse's [Custis] socks only arrived yesterday & were very welcome, as his were entirely *hors-de-combat*. He is the sweetest little fat creature you ever saw & obeys his Father most implicitly. If he wakes up in the night and cries & Robert speaks to him, he stops immediately.... I think he has lost much of his dove appearance & has much more of the lion about him now, though he is a very good-natured fellow. If his energies can only be well directed, they may be the means of much usefulness. But I already shrink from the responsibility. It requires so much firmness & consistency to train up a child in the right way & I know that I am so remiss in the government of my servants & so often neglect to correct them when they do wrong. I must endeavor with God's assistance to be more faithful.

But Mrs. Lee's interests were not all centered in family affairs. Among her other interests was the Colonization Society, to which the Arlington family had been large contributors. Mr. Gurley, secretary of the society, and his wife were frequent visitors at Arlington. Their home was in Washington. It was said of him that he "is a most interesting man, and in his life a perfect Christian."

Mrs. Lee continues her letter to her mother with the inquiry: "Did you see the piece in the *Intelligence* eulogizing Mr. Gurley's eloquence? I can well imagine if he was in his best vein that it was very great."

# The Wife of an Army Officer

Though Mrs. Lee enjoyed entertaining her friends in her own home, she cared little for the round of parties which seemed so essential a part of the social life of an army post at that time. In a letter to her mother she says:

> We have been quite satiated with tea drinking lately, almost every evening an invitation some where. Except that we generally get some nice cake and fruit, they [the parties] would be rather stupid. I suppose it is my fault, but there are not many persons here very interesting.

However, if she did not find tea-drinking interesting, she found an absorbing interest in her son. She writes:

> It has been quite cool for several days, so much so that I have put on Bouse's flannel petticoat.... I asked Bouse just now what I should say to Grandmother; he replied "loodle, loodle." He is not as bad now as he was when I last wrote.... He is a great fidget, & I am obliged to put a chair at the head of the stairs to keep him from going down, as his principal amusement now is crawling out of the door.

The difficulty which had existed at this time between the line and the staff brought the President of the United States, Andrew Jackson, and Brigadier General Gratiot to "the Point" for a tour of inspection. The post had been all aflutter, both politically and socially. Writing to her mother, Mrs. Lee says:

## Mrs. Robert E. Lee

The President and General Gratiot—all the great folks are to leave tomorrow.... I shall be truly rejoiced when they all go, and we shall have a little quiet, and Robert will have a little time to be at home. What the consultations at the Rip Raps have resulted in, except that they are to be finished next summer, I do not know, for Robert is not very communicative on the subject. The President inspected the fort yesterday on horseback and paid me a visit of a few moments & in the evening the ladies came over to take leave. I carried Bouse in to see the President, who took him in his arms and held him some time. Bouse looked at him with a fixed gaze, put his hand over his nose, but did not pull it hard, and put his fingers in his eyes. The old man gave him Rachael's picture to play with, which delighted him much, and then presented him with a half dollar & told me to put a hole in it and put it round his neck; said he was a fine boy & a good boy and that I must take off his shoes and let him run about barefoot.... Do give my love to all at Chantilly. How I should love to be there. I do pine for a sight of those blue mountains. You must have felt very lonesome traveling up by yourself. I wish indeed Father had gone.

*Andrew Jackson*
[From a painting by Rembrandt Peale. Courtesy of John Lewis, Philadelphia]

# The Wife of an Army Officer

The Lees had both been brought up in a religious atmosphere and considered a strict observance of the Sabbath essential. Churchgoing on Sunday was taken for granted, and some mention of the sermon was usually made in Mrs. Lee's letter to her mother; so while writing of inspection, teas, and the President's visit, she takes time to say:

Dr. Ducachet preached two excellent sermons last Sunday. The one in the morning was particularly addressed to young officers. It was an eloquent, learned, and earnest discourse from the text "There is a lion in the way," answering all the arguments against religion and most affectionately urging all to embrace it. It was a faithful sermon, and the one at night more so, from the text "What shall it profit a man if he gain the whole world and lose his own soul?" on what he gives in exchange for his soul. I was glad to see the house crowded and some very attentive hearers, particularly among the soldiers. I hope some good may have been done.

Saying something in each letter of her homecoming at Christmas, she writes:

Tell Aunt Eleanor I expect she will be so enchanted with Bun that she will do nothing else but work for him & play with him.... Judy [the baby's nurse] says, "Tell Nurse she will be surprised to see what a fine boy we will bring up with us."

"Nurse" evidently held a warm place in the affection of her young mistress; frequent mention of

## *Mrs. Robert E. Lee*

her was made in Mrs. Lee's letters. At one time Mrs. Lee was greatly worried about Nurse's eyes and suggested to her mother that she be taken to Baltimore to see Dr. Smith. There were often commissions which she asked Nurse to execute for her—"Tell Nurse if she can buy me any dried apples *cheap*, I should like to have some." Again she writes to ask Nurse to try to find some dried peaches for her, as she wishes them for a very sick woman at "the Point."

Writing to her mother, she says:

> I received the contents of your basket in fine order. The fruit was not at all injured or bruised. Do bring me some more currants & gooseberries when you come down, if they are still in season. Mr. Smith told me there was a refrigerator on board the boat, so you could put anything you wished to preserve in that & will you let George make some nice biscuits for me, for I never can get Meniday to make any good ones. Bring me also some green apples, if they are large enough to coddle & pears to bake, for as usual we get nothing of that sort here. Those cuttings you sent all died. Bring me some more, as this is a good time to raise them & be sure to bring the books for the school.

But there were also packages sent from "the Point" to Arlington whenever opportunity offered. Such opportunity came when "old Mr. Chevallie" was "going up on the Potomac." The young housekeeper, anxious that her mother have a sample of her

# The Wife of an Army Officer

housekeeping, sends by this gentleman a loaf of bread which is "only tolerable, being made of our common flour. I would have had two loaves made for you out of our best flour, if I had thought of it. . . . I also send two bunches of asparagus, as yours does not seem to be as good as usual."

Mrs. Lee had written her mother that she was happy to tell her there was "a spirit of usefulness abroad at 'the Point.' The Miss Archers & some others of the young ladies have become teachers in the school . . . and they have formed themselves into a *Working Society*; meet every Wednesday." The proceeds from their labors were used to purchase books for the use of the Sunday-school scholars. As the members of the society had expressed their intention of getting Mrs. Custis to purchase some books for them, Mrs. Lee asked her mother to be on the lookout both in Washington and in Alexandria for suitable books. At the same time she says:

> I send you $2 of our Society money with which I want you to get, as far as it will go, some first and second reading books & some of a very small catechism called *Brown's Catechism* commencing with
>
> > "Who made you? God.
> > Who redeemed you? Christ.
> > Who sanctifies you? The Holy Ghost."
>
> I believe you know it, we had it at Arlington.

## Mrs. Robert E. Lee

She was greatly interested in the Sunday school, which, she says, is now quite large: "Today I commenced there with my black class of 6, 3 of whom read quite well." It was a matter of regret to her that her own servants seemed unable to finish their work in time to get off to Sunday school. But she taught them their Bible lesson on Saturday and heard them say the lesson on Sunday. She was also busy teaching them to read. "Margaret and Meniday get their lessons every week & Dick has gotten through the first reader."

In November Lieutenant Lee wrote to a friend, "Mrs. Lee and her little limb are at Arlington"; but it was not until near Christmas that he was able to join them there, and then only for a short time. It was an exceedingly severe winter; ice made navigation of the Potomac extremely uncertain and at times impossible. Lieutenant Lee decided to make the return trip overland on horseback. It was therefore impossible for Mrs. Lee to return to Fort Monroe with him.

Though it was a severe winter and travel was difficult, it did not prevent visitors from coming to Arlington, and young Mrs. Lee delighted to show her young son to the many friends and relatives who came to spend a day or maybe a week. Life at Arlington House was very luxurious, and for Mary Lee perfectly carefree. However, as the weather moder-

## The Wife of an Army Officer

ated, she began to make plans to return to Fort Monroe. After she had made the trip back home, life took on the routine interrupted by the journey to Arlington. She found great happiness in being with her husband in their own home. It was the evenings especially to which she looked forward; for she was happy in the company of her husband, "who spends his evenings at home instead of frequenting the card parties which attract so many, but this is *entre nous*." Seated before the open fire she would sew, while by the light of the lamp her husband would read to her. "I have been reading some of Zenelow & going over my arithmetic, and at night we have read *Patroness*, one of Miss Edgeworth's novels & *Belinda*, which I thought were considered very fine; but we find much that is faulty both in style and sentiment, though some very good precepts." The evening reading always ended with a chapter from the Bible followed by a prayer. Thus in this little home the young couple carried out a tradition of both their families and started a custom which they followed through all their lives.

Though she would not admit it to her husband, Mrs. Lee was often homesick for the hills which surrounded Arlington. She "longed for a little rural scenery, but ought not to complain of what I have not when I have so many comforts and especially that of a tender and affectionate husband."

## Mrs. Robert E. Lee

All her letters were filled with the growing charms of her young son, now not quite two years old. She says of him: "Booty really talks very well & calls everything by its proper name. . . . I have fixed a cart for him out of a basket top & he rides a wooden goat which some one gave him. . . . I think they have diverted him a little from his books. I mean to teach him his letters before you come down, if possible."

The Lees remained at Fort Monroe until the autumn of 1834, when they were both made happy by the orders which directed Lieutenant Lee to report to Washington for service as Assistant to the Chief of Engineers. Reporting in Washington, Lieutenant Lee set out to find a house into which to move his family; but it seemed impossible to find one suited to their needs. Therefore, to the great delight of Mr. and Mrs. Custis, the Lees decided to make their home at Arlington. This arrangement was physically hard on Lieutenant Lee, who rode to and from his office each day. But such inconvenience as it may have caused him was far outweighed by the charm of the life at Arlington. Mary Custis Lee's marriage had made no difference in her status at Arlington. She remained the "young mistress," adored by the servants. They were all eager to do things for her; and Cassy, her maid, whom she had taken from Arlington, found little left to do. It was Nurse who decided

## The Wife of an Army Officer

the attentions to be paid by each one, and it was Nurse who selected the small colored boy who was to be a playmate for Custis.

It was a charming family group to which Lieutenant Lee returned each evening from his duties in Washington. There was always an hour of play with little Custis before he was taken off to bed by his nurse.

It was a joy to Mrs. Lee to see the growing affection of Mr. Custis for her husband. She realized that her father had forgotten any antagonism that he might have felt toward her marriage. She saw that now there was mutual respect and growing appreciation between her father and her husband. Lee had a genuine love for Mrs. Custis; her warm heart, unaffected piety, and sincerity impressed him more and more. Many years later he wrote of her: "She was to me all that a mother could be, and I yield to none in admiration for her character, love for her virtues, and veneration for her memory."

There were always guests at Arlington House, cousins and friends from the vicinity coming for a day and those whose homes were farther away coming usually for a month at least. The Lawrence Lewises were among the most frequent and always the most welcome; for there was the deepest affection and understanding between Mrs. Custis and her husband's sister.

## *Mrs. Robert E. Lee*

Though living so near the capital of the United States, Mrs. Lee, great-granddaughter of Martha Washington, now felt little interest in the social life of official Washington. But she eagerly followed the discussions of her father and his friends on the political situation of the country; for, as was the custom of the times in Virginia homes, the government and its policies, as well as foreign affairs, were freely discussed around the fireside in winter and on the broad veranda or under the trees on the lawn in summer. The Virginia gentleman considered no group complete without the ladies of his household; hence the Virginia woman became imbued with the science of politics. It was partly this association and partly heritage which made Mary Custis Lee a keen student of politics and gave her a greater understanding of that momentous decision her husband was to be called upon to make. Had she been less well informed, less understanding, he could not have discussed with her, as he did later, the clouds which he saw arising. It was because she had become accustomed to facing questions of moment with him that she could make his decision her decision in his great renunciation.

Mr. Custis, a man of no small culture, was a delightful conversationalist and raconteur. He made Lee's army associates who came to Arlington most welcome, and they were charmed with "the shabby

## The Wife of an Army Officer

appearing gentleman who welcomed them." They found the atmosphere of this splendid mansion friendly and leisurely.

It seemed as if the Lees were scarcely oriented to the pleasant mode of life at Arlington when, in the spring of 1835, Lee was sent on a mission to make a survey of the boundary line between Ohio and the territory of Michigan. When Lieutenant Lee bade his wife good-by, he thought it would be for only a few weeks; but the mission took the entire summer. Though Mrs. Lee was in wretched health at this time, she made little mention of it in her letters to her husband. It was during his absence that their second child, Mary, was born. Mrs. Lee was seriously ill, and her recovery was very slow. Her mother was greatly alarmed over her condition, as was also her Aunt Maria Fitzhugh. After a family consultation it was decided that a change to Ravensworth might be beneficial. It was therefore at Ravensworth that her husband found her upon his return. Mrs. Lee, though ill, had been able to write to her husband; but she had minimized her condition and had forbidden any member of the family to tell him the true circumstances. He was therefore shocked and greatly alarmed on his return, and thought that she should go back to Arlington. Mrs. Lee had willingly agreed to go to Ravensworth; but now that her husband had returned and was on duty in Washington,

## Mrs. Robert E. Lee

it would be possible for him to be with her at Arlington. So the day after her husband's arrival she returned to Arlington.

In November Mrs. Lee wrote to her cousin Mrs. Andrew Talcott:

> I have been too sick to answer your kind letter before, my dear Harriet & it is only for the last week I have been able to sit up at all.... I have not gained strength sufficient to *stand*. You may suppose, after a confinement to my bed almost four months, I am much reduced & fear it will be some time before I shall be able to walk.... My little Mary Custis has become very engaging & promises to be quite a beauty. She is a clear brunette with brown hair, very fine large black eyes, a *perfect* little mouth & respectable nose & is perfectly fat & healthy....
>
> When you or the Capt. write again, will you mention the price of the silver comb, for as I have lost all my fine suit of hair I may as well dispose of it. I scolded Robert for getting it, as I had a very good one.

Early in the summer Lieutenant Lee took Mrs. Lee to one of the mineral springs of Virginia. These springs were considered a panacea for all ills. They certainly proved beneficial to Mrs. Lee, who returned to Arlington greatly improved in health.

Little Mary was a special delight to her father; but it was Custis who always held first place in the affection of his mother. She was inclined to spoil him; and her father, who thought of his grandson as the future master of Arlington, indulged him far

## The Wife of an Army Officer

more than he should have done. It was his father only who corrected him.

Mary was not yet two years old when a little brother was born who was given the name of his great-uncle William Henry Fitzhugh, of Ravensworth. The Lee family was addicted to the use of nicknames; and this little boy, who bore the proud name of William Henry Fitzhugh, soon became "Rooney," by which name he was known even many years later when he represented his native state in the Congress of the United States.

When Mrs. Lee married an army officer she realized that there would be no permanent home for her and that she frequently would be separated from her parents. But she had not realized that her husband's profession might sometimes call him to perform duties in places where she could not be with him. Therefore, it was a great disappointment to her when she realized that she could not go with her husband on his receiving orders to go to St. Louis. However, she said nothing to dampen his ardor; for she understood how irksome had been the assignment in Washington, and she knew it was because of his anxiety about her that he had made no effort to be ordered elsewhere.

Travel to the West was extremely difficult. It seemed most inadvisable for Mrs. Lee to make the trip at this time. Rooney was only two months old,

# Mrs. Robert E. Lee

and the eldest child, Custis, not quite five. The father's parting charge to little Custis was to "look after his mother." The little fellow took his father's words very seriously, and felt that quite a responsibility had been laid on his shoulders. Custis had been dreadfully indulged by his grandfather, and he missed the firmness with which his father had managed him. He was inclined to be willful; but in his most difficult moods he could be managed by a gentle reminder that his father had left the family in his care.

Shortly after her husband had left for the West, Mrs. Lee, with the children and nurses, set out for a round of visits to relatives and friends. Some time was spent at Ravensworth, where Custis found that he must share honors with Rooney, who bore the name of the master of Ravensworth. From Ravensworth the family set out for the "upper country," stopping for a short while at Chantilly, the home of the Stuarts. In the "upper country" there was a long visit to Kinloch, whose master, Thomas Turner, had been the guardian of Robert after his father's death. Because of the happy days which Robert had spent there as a child, he had always the deepest affection for the place. Later, when Custis and Rooney were older, he would frequently take them for visits there.

From Kinloch, Mrs. Lee and the children went over "the Ridge" to Audley, the home of her cousin Lorenzo Lewis. Wherever they went, there were

# The Wife of an Army Officer

likely to be other guests, coming either to spend the day or maybe the night, all eager to see Mary and her children. Custis, a handsome and most engaging child, was soon quite spoiled by the attention he received, and evidently acquired, among some members of the family, the reputation of being unmanageable. Rumors of this having reached his father, he wrote Mrs. Lee:

> Our dear little boy seems to have among his friends the reputation of being hard to manage, a distinction not at all desirable, as it indicates self-will and obstinacy. Perhaps these are qualities which he really possesses, and he may have a better right to them than I am willing to acknowledge; but it is our duty, if possible, to counteract them and assist him to bring them under control ... you must assist me in my attempts, and we must endeavor to combine the mildness and forbearance of the mother with the sternness and perhaps unreasonableness of the father. I pray God to watch over and direct our efforts in guarding our little son, that we may bring him up in the way that he should go.

As pleasant as had been the round of visits, Mrs. Lee was glad when she and her little brood were once more at home. She easily fell into the daily routine, sewing for the children, reading not only the English classics but also the French; nor did she neglect her Latin. She wrote charming letters to her husband, keeping him in touch with the daily life at Arlington. There were always guests, and they brought news

## Mrs. Robert E. Lee

and interesting bits of gossip about friends and relatives. Such news as she felt would be of interest to her husband found a place in her letters.

Christmas was drawing near. Never since their marriage had the Lees been separated at this time. Now they both hoped that nothing would prevent the work in St. Louis from being finished in time for Lieutenant Lee to return to Arlington for Christmas. Finally, the hoped-for letter came, saying that the work for the year was completed and that he would shortly be on his way home. Plans for Christmas were already under way, but now they took on a happier note.

Lee made the trip home by way of Wheeling and the old Cumberland Road on to Frederick; from Frederick over the new Baltimore and Ohio Railroad, the cars being drawn by horses part of the distance. It was his first trip by this new method of transportation. This being a little more rapid than the former method of travel, he was able to reach home in time for Christmas.

The winter months were spent partly on duty in the Engineer's Office in Washington and partly on leave at Arlington. Thus Mrs. Lee was relieved in a measure from the entire responsibility of the training of the children. Her husband realized how heavy had been this responsibility, and he was now anxious to relieve her in every possible way. Thus Custis be-

# The Wife of an Army Officer

*A Train Such as Lee Traveled On*
[From a painting by Herbert D. Stitt.
Courtesy of the Baltimore and Ohio Railroad Company]

came his charge entirely, and he was "firm in his demands and constant in their enforcement, insistent in their execution."

During the winter it was brought home to Lieutenant Lee that the training of the children should not be the entire responsibility of Mrs. Lee. He had missed his wife and children while he was on duty in St. Louis, and the question of their accompanying him when he returned to duty there the next spring had been frequently mentioned in his letters to Arlington, for he "felt it was highly proper to be as much as possible" with his wife and children.

## *Mrs. Robert E. Lee*

Both Mr. and Mrs. Custis had discouraged the thought of their daughter's making so long and hard a trip. Mrs. Custis even suggested in one of her letters that Lieutenant Lee resign from the army and make Arlington his home. But he replied that he had "thought much on the subject of our coming out here next spring and have yet seen no impropriety in the step." He agreed that while it would be ideal to "locate ourselves at Arlington," yet "we cannot live where we please."

Mrs. Lee had inwardly rebelled against the separation from her husband. Now she was eager to go with him and was in no way daunted by the inconveniences she was told that she would find at a frontier post. Houses, her husband told her, would be hard to get and badly arranged, and rents were high. It would be necessary to take their own servants, as the "people there did not wish regular work."

The winter passed happily at Arlington, for the family circle was now complete. There was always the "children's hour," between the setting of the sun and the lighting of the candles. Mr. and Mrs. Custis were seated on one side of the fire, which lighted the room with its great flames and cast grotesque shadows on the ceiling. On the other side of the hearth sat Lieutenant Lee and his wife, with little Rooney in her arms. Mary was seated on a little

# The Wife of an Army Officer

*Baltimore at the Time of the Lees' Visit*

stool at her grandmother's feet. Custis sometimes sat beside his grandfather, but more often by his father. All listened with interest to the stories which the father would tell the children of his life in the West. They thrilled Mrs. Lee, even as they did the children, and as the storytelling hour lengthened she became more and more desirous of sharing her husband's experiences. Mrs. Custis, knowing how sheltered had been the life of her daughter, still doubted the advisability of her making the trip. But now she kept her thoughts to herself, feeling that, after all, it was a question for the Lees to decide. So when Lieutenant Lee returned to St. Louis in the spring, he was accompanied by Mrs. Lee and the two boys,

## Mrs. Robert E. Lee

*Mrs. Robert E. Lee, 1838,*
*by William E. West*

*Robert E. Lee, 1838,*
*by William E. West*

[Photographs by United States Army Signal Corps]

Custis and Rooney. Mary remained with her grandmother. Kitty, one of the servants from Arlington, went as nurse.

It would have been an adventurous journey for anyone at that time; but for Mary Lee, reared as she had been, it was an adventure indeed.

The start was made from Washington in the cold and blustery days of March. The first leg of the journey was by train to Baltimore. While in Baltimore, Lee agreed to sit for his portrait, which was painted, Mrs. Lee wrote her mother, by "William E. West & his picture is a very admirable likeness & a fine painting. . . . He wishes me to sit also, but I think I would prefer Sully. . . .

# The Wife of an Army Officer

*Philadelphia, Where Mrs. Lee Found the Market "Well Worth Seeing"*

"Now, my dearest Mother, I have determined to sit for my picture & Robert has agreed to remain 'till Monday week."

From Baltimore the next destination was Philadelphia. From there Mrs. Lee wrote her mother:

It rained almost all day Saturday, so that I could not go out shopping & on Friday I was engaged all day. I went to market Saturday before breakfast, tho' it was very showery. Cousin Hackley told me it was well worth seeing. I never saw wooden ware kept in such beautiful order. The tubs of milk & butter were as white as snow & the butchers & butcher's boys, of which I suppose there were more than 50 in the market, had all long linen shirts most beautifully white put on over their clothes. There were a few flowers, but not many fresh vegetables, except salad & kale. All the

## Mrs. Robert E. Lee

*Pittsburgh at the Height of Travel by Water*[1]

morning after breakfast I was expecting Mrs. Coxe, when ever the sun shone out, to take me to the Fairmount Waterworks & the Gerard College; but she thought the weather too bad to venture & I had not time to make any other arrangement as company came in & I found it was time to go there where I had promised to spend the day. Esther looks thin & the children badly.... As soon as they are quite well, she is going to Arlington. Mrs. Coxe was very kind ... she has a delightful house & the Doctor showed us some of the curiosities of his cabinet. The bad weather has entirely prevented my seeing much of the city. It is very neat & regularly built; but the streets are very narrow & there is nothing imposing in the air of the buildings generally. But I cannot give anything more than my first

---

[1] Redrawn from *History of Travel in America*, by Seymour Dunbar, copyright 1915. Used by special permission of the publishers, The Bobbs-Merrill Company.

# The Wife of an Army Officer

impression, for I have seen very little of it. We went to see the splendid service of plate presented by the stock holders of the U. S. Bank to Mr. Biddle. It cost 18 thousand dollars & is indeed splendid.... I will write from Pittsburgh. ... Tell Father, Robert & I have been waiting for some less hurried moment to write to him.... We shall leave here in the cars tomorrow at six o'clock & reach Harrisburg at 3 & there take the Canal for Pittsburgh, which we shall reach in about 3 days. Our stay there is I suppose uncertain. ... Love to all at home & many kisses to my little darling.

At Pittsburgh it was necessary to wait a week for a steamboat which would take them down the Ohio River to Louisville. Lieutenant Lee, writing of the trip, says: "Our journey was as pleasant as could be expected in a country of this sort.... The boys stood it manfully and indeed improved on it, and my Dame, taking advantage of frequent opportunities for a nap, ... defied the crowding, squeezing, and scrambling."

At Louisville Mrs. Lee had a glimpse of the charming social life of the city, attending a wedding and several other entertainments.

The little boys had been so fascinated by the steamboat trip that, when once settled at St. Louis, they took up steamboating for their favorite game, in which they initiated their young playmates, the Beaumont children. "They converted themselves even into steamboats, rang their bells, raised their

# Mrs. Robert E. Lee

*St. Louis as the Lees Saw It*
[From a lithograph in *Das Illustrierte Mississippithal*, by George B. Douglas]

steam (high pressure), and kept on so heavy a pressure of steam, that I am constantly fearing that they will burst their boilers," wrote their father.

It was not until early in June that the Lees found comfortable quarters, with meals, at the home of Dr. William Beaumont, an army officer and the leading professional man of the town.

Mrs. Lee brought her daily life to Arlington in her frequent and chatty letters to her parents. Irregular mails and slow transportation made Arlington seem far away indeed. Their quarters were far from luxurious; but if Mrs. Lee felt any inconvenience she made no mention of it in her letters.

# The Wife of an Army Officer

She was happy in being with her husband, in sewing for her children, and in gathering wild flowers; nor did she neglect her painting. In her books she found companionship, her Bible being her daily companion. She missed her small daughter, but she knew that the little girl was well and happy at Arlington. Writing to her mother, she says:

We are much more comfortable now. Our rooms have been whitewashed & painted—quite cool & pleasant, looking out on the water; and being small, they require less furniture.... We have two small closets, in one of which I have arranged my books & shall now commence the Life of Washington, as I feel more settled. I have been reading some beautiful poetry of Coleridge, Shelley, Wordsworth, some French books lent me by Mr. Cabané & other little things, among them Goldsmith's Life & poems. Custis has read considerably in that book Mr. Dana gave him, "Todd's Lectures to Children," & seems quite interested. He gets a spelling lesson by heart every day & has improved very much in his writing; but it is very hard to induce him to sit down to his lessons, tho' I think he is on the whole slowly improving. I am so anxious to have that portrait of daughter. Do get Mr. W$^{ms}$ [Williams] to paint it at once & send it to me, as there will be many opportunities when Congress rises.... I should like very much if he would take one of you of a small size which I could carry about, and I would like him to take you without your cap, which he could do very well in this warm weather. You don't know what a comfort it would be to me to have these pictures to look at.

## Mrs. Robert E. Lee

Knowing her mother's great love for flowers, she writes her:

Mrs. Shreeve has a beautiful yellow honeysuckle of a kind I never saw before, of which she is going to give me a root when I go home. The prairie flowers too are very fine. I shall endeavor to procure some seed when I go to the Rapids. Mrs. Bliss is coming out here to join her husband & we shall probably go up with her. I received a *Statesman* & an *Intelligence* not long since, but have not had a *Churchman* for some time.... Give my love to Aunt Eleanor.... Tell her I think Cincinnati is by far the handsomest city we have seen in the West & I should judge the most desirable residence in every respect.

Army acquaintances who had been ordered from Washington to this far-distant post were eagerly welcomed; for frequently these newcomers had called at Arlington before leaving for the West, and they could bring Mrs. Lee news of her parents and daughter. They were often bearers of purchases which Mrs. Lee had commissioned her mother to make for her.

A letter written to her mother in August gives a very vivid picture of the life that the Lees were leading:

I received your letter of the 2d August this morning, my dearest Mother. I had been anxiously expecting to hear from you, for it takes a letter such an age to arrive

# *The Wife of an Army Officer*

here that it is old before it comes. . . . Mr. Miller . . . told me that any letter or package sent to Williams, the silversmith who lives in Washington not far from Gadsby's, he would take charge of with pleasure & even said he would ride over to Arlington if he had time. . . . The things I wrote for are of no immediate consequence, so do not trouble yourself about them. I am afraid that money must turn out like the cruse of oil to answer all the purposes to which it is appropriated, but you know there will be more forthcoming soon. . . .

Mee [Mary] must keep up her spirits & think of me out here almost devoured alive with moschetaes, for they are as thick as a swarm of bees every evening. . . .

I went out to Capt. Shreeve's to breakfast not long since & there was the most splendid cornfield I ever saw. The stalks stood as close as possible & he said it would produce from 60 to 80 bushels the acre; but all the soil here is like a rich alluvial deposit, yet rich as it is I would rather a thousand times live in Old Virginia or somewhere near it. . . . Mr. Rooney is better & walks all about with his feet turned out & arms spread forward & is the most mischievous & cunning little fellow you ever saw. . . . Excuse this very stupid & unconnected letter, for Rooney is playing around me pulling my pens, paper & ink & is now trying to throw his Papa's hat out of the window. He has got on the little pink dress you sent & looks very sweet in it indeed with his little rotund figure & turned out legs.

Kitty is much disappointed at not hearing from any of her friends. . . . You must remember me to all the servants particularly. I wish I had some of the little ones here to amuse Rooney the time Kitty is washing; for I find it rather tiresome to nurse all day such an unsettled brat,

# Mrs. Robert E. Lee

tho' his Father has come to the conclusion that there is not such another child in all Missouri & that he would not exchange him for the whole state.... I have some idea of trying Custis at school this fall for one quarter, to see if it will stimulate him; but he is always so led away by his companions that I am a little afraid....

Have you heard any thing further about our Union Bank? I think it is time another payment was forthcoming. There is plenty of silver out here, we never see a bank note of less than $5.

The portraits of Lee and his wife, which had been painted in Baltimore by West, had arrived at Arlington, and Mrs. Lee wrote her mother:

I am glad you like my portrait better. I did not like either of them altogether, but I had only a moment to look at them after they were finished. You must take the opinion of strangers generally as you are too partial a judge.... You have no idea how much company yours is for me & the likeness grows upon me.

Mrs. Lee's letters to her mother showed how broad her interests were. She expressed some surprise at the selection of Mr. Kemper as Bishop of Maryland, when "they had Drs. Wyatt & Johns to select between." Of the new church which was building in St. Louis she says, it "will be spacious and handsome & filled to overflowing notwithstanding the Unitarian is considered the fashionable church."

## *The Wife of an Army Officer*

She never lost interest in her friends. She writes:

You say nothing further of my poor Susan. Do write me something about her & that fated family. All my letters to Mary for two years have been of condolence & I have not the heart to write her another. The morning of her life has indeed been overcast with the deepest gloom & what has become of Mr. Coolidge the wretch who could not appreciate the treasure which should never have fallen to his lot?

Mrs. Custis had been ill during the summer, but she was quite recovered when she wrote to her daughter in September. Her letter clearly shows her character. She says:

Mr. & Mrs. Keith returned from their excursion about a week ago and came over to see me. They gave me quite an interesting account of their journey, and at parting he read the 103rd Psalm, so applicable to my situation, and prayed with that fervor of devotion for which he is remarkable, not for me only but for you and yours. I felt as if I wished you could enjoy the privilege of hearing him rather than myself. I hope that you have not been entirely without pastor's visits. . . . After Mr. Keith left me, I read over the psalm again and went on involuntarily to the next, 104—did it ever strike you how forcibly the power and goodness of God are depicted in that psalm? . . . He said in his prayer, to account for this wonderful dealing of Providence, "we thank thee that thou hast raised her up, that she may glorify thy name. Oh! give her grace to be more and more useful in her generation, a comfort to

## Mrs. Robert E. Lee

her friends." ... O! my child pray for me that I may not be spared in vain.

It was not until January that Captain Lee—for he had received his commission as Captain of Engineers—completed his work in St. Louis and was ready to return to Arlington. Mrs. Lee wrote to Mrs. Talcott:

He [Mr. Lee] has stopped work here & is now settling up his accounts and then we should be at leisure to go either home or to New Orleans, but in this country it is impossible to travel by land with young children & the navigation is all closed, so unless some sudden change should take place in the weather, we shall have to remain here in quiet. . . .

This is quite a large place and I have found some very fine & agreeable people but I am getting too old to form new friends and would rather be among those I know and love.

So the family was forced to remain in St. Louis for the winter, the first that the Lees had spent away from Arlington since 1834.

It was the first of May when the family finally started East. The trip from St. Louis to Wheeling was made by steamboat and required over a week. At Wheeling a private stage was engaged, and very hard travel it proved; but Captain Lee and his family arrived at Arlington on the night of May 11, the trip having been made in eleven days, which was considered quite a feat. The captain, however, could

# The Wife of an Army Officer

*Travel by Stagecoach*

not linger, as the orders which awaited him required him to return to the West, and he left on May 25.

These continued separations were hard on the Lees, though they both realized how fortunate Mrs. Lee was in having the home of her parents to return to. He writes, "I must tell you how distressed I was to leave you and the dear children and Mother and all to go so far away into a comparatively wild country, with none to protect you and none to comfort me."

A fourth child, Anne Carter Lee, was born on June 18, 1839. She was several months old before her father returned to Arlington, but her mother's letters had pictured all her charms to him.

Captain Lee was very insistent in his letters to his wife that she and the children should go to a more bracing climate, if only for a few weeks. So when Anne Carter Lee was a little over one month old, Mrs. Lee completed her plans to go to Kinloch,

## Mrs. Robert E. Lee

and on July 27 Edward Carter Turner, master of Kinloch, records in his diary: "At night Mrs. Custis and Mrs. Lee (her daughter) with a squad of children, negroes, horses, and dogs arrived." Thomas Turner, the father of Edward Carter Turner, had been the guardian of Robert E. Lee, and young Robert had spent many happy days at Kinloch; now his wife was as welcome there as he. Several weeks were spent at Kinloch. With cooler weather the family returned to Arlington.

Mrs. Lee consoled herself in her husband's absence by constantly talking to Custis about his father, telling him that when he grew to be a man she hoped that he would follow in his father's footsteps. Custis took his mother's words literally, but could not see why she should wait until he was a man. Lee returned to Arlington early in December. Taking Custis with him for a walk on a day when the ground was covered with snow, he found that Custis had dropped behind. Turning to look for his son, Lee saw that the little fellow was walking in the tracks made by him, imitating his every movement. When Mrs. Lee heard of the incident, she told her husband of the emphasis she had laid on Custis's following in his father's steps. "Then," said Captain Lee, "it behooves me to walk very straight, when my son is already following in my tracts." To which Mrs. Lee rejoined, "I pray that he always will."

# The Wife of an Army Officer

In July Lee bade his family good-by and went again to take up his work on the Mississippi, and Mrs. Lee was left with the responsibility of four children. With Custis now eight years old, Mary six, Rooney four, and little Anne in her cradle, Mrs. Lee found her hands very full.

The children were always up early, and taken out under the trees to play by their Mammy and the nurses who were under her. When the breakfast hour arrived, the three older children joined their mother and grandparents at breakfast. After breakfast there were family prayers, and then the two older children would have their lessons, with their mother as their teacher. Both children were anxious to write to their father, anxious too to read his letters to them; therefore they were very willing pupils during the short time their lessons lasted.

While the lessons were going on little Rooney was likely to be found with his grandmother in the flower garden; for it was a fancy of hers to gather the roses while the dew was still on them. This garden, which was Mrs. Custis's pride, was south of the house. It might well have been called a memory garden; for in it were flowers which had once grown at Mount Vernon, and plants from Shirley, from Chatham, from Gunston, and the gardens of many other friends. She and her friends, as was the custom of the times, were always exchanging flowers with

## Mrs. Robert E. Lee

one another. "Cousin Julia Stuart," whose home was at Cedar Grove, had written Mrs. Lee:

> I wish while you are gardening you would raise me some young roses or any pretty flowers. You always have so many pretty varieties of flowers at Arlington. Have you not the Cherokee rose? If you have and it is not too much trouble, I wish you would raise me one of that kind, I have heard it was beautiful. . . . Flowers will be an amusement to me. I intend to rival your Mother in that department.

The house was always full of company. Among the visitors were likely to be boys and girls of the ages of the Lee children. So when lessons were over, the children were free to play under the watchful eye of Nurse.

It was then that Mrs. Lee and her guests would gather with her mother on the portico—some to sew, some to embroider the patterns which they had traced on some fine bit of linen or mull. If the boy who had gone on horseback to Alexandria for the mail should bring among the letters one from Robert, Mrs. Lee would stop her work and, after reading her husband's letter through, would read to her friends such portions of the letter as she felt might be of interest to them. They were interesting letters, and all were eager to hear them.

There were other guests, men in public life, who came across the Potomac from Washington, or

# The Wife of an Army Officer

officers of the army—all had something to say of the name Captain Lee was making for himself. It was the army men who told her that her husband's work on the Mississippi was regarded as a brilliant performance. While Mrs. Lee was naturally proud of these encomiums, it was her father who realized more fully than she that her husband now had a recognized reputation in the Corps of Engineers.

With the spring came the news that her husband had been ordered to superintend the work in New York Harbor and that he wished his family would join him there. The house which had been assigned to Captain Lee was in wretched repair, and he wrote that it would require a considerable amount of renovating before it could be made habitable. Though her departure was delayed, the days were busy ones for Mrs. Lee. When the Lees left Fort Monroe, their furniture had been brought to Arlington and stored there; now it was got out and the carpenters at Arlington began repairing and covering such pieces as Mrs. Lee selected to take to Fort Hamilton. These were supplemented by certain pieces which her mother gave her from Arlington; other pieces were ordered to be made by Green, a well-known maker of furniture in Alexandria. The furniture was all to be shipped by boat from Alexandria, and Mrs. Lee was anxious that it reach New York by the time the house was ready for occupancy.

## Mrs. Robert E. Lee

There were five children now, Eleanor Agnes being the baby and only a few months old.

Mrs. Lee was still far from strong. So during this summer she took but little part in the social life of Fort Hamilton; but on Sunday she and her husband, with the older children, could always be found in the little garrison church. Wherever the Lees went they always identified themselves with the Episcopal Church; hence upon their arrival at Fort Hamilton they had immediately been transferred from Christ Church, Alexandria, to Saint John's at Fort Hamilton.

Both Captain Lee and his wife had been most insistent that Mrs. Custis come to them for a visit, for they had both felt anxious about her health. In July they were both made very happy by hearing that she was really coming to make them the much-desired visit. Captain Lee wrote her minute instructions as to route and baggage, advising her to travel with as few parcels as possible and urging her to put everything into a trunk and have the trunk plainly marked, so that it might be readily identified. Such things as she might need for her trip, he wrote her, could be carried in a carpetbag.

Among the inducements offered her mother was a description of the drives around Fort Hamilton. She wrote, "We have got a very nice little carriage, one of the nicest and most convenient of its size."

# The Wife of an Army Officer

With the coming of winter, work in New York Harbor was discontinued and Captain Lee was ordered to report to Washington. The children were jubilant when they knew that they were to reach Arlington in time for Christmas. There was no less joy on the part of their grandparents when they heard the news.

The servants all entered into the preparations. They brought in cedar and pine with which to decorate the house. They called it "bringing in Christmas." The piece of the Yule log saved from the year before was put into the fireplace in the drawing room ready to be lighted by Mr. Custis, as he had seen his foster father light it so many years ago at Mount Vernon.

In the woods and at the woodpile the axes rang, so that there might be no dearth of wood. Arlington was heated with open fires, which must not go out; so the wood must be piled high, ready for the housemen to carry in. When, on the twenty-second day of December, the Lees arrived at Arlington, they found the air filled with Christmas.

Early spring again found the Lees at Fort Hamilton; but they returned to Arlington early in the autumn in order that the sixth child might be born under the roof of its grandparents. The baby, whose birthday was October 27, 1843, was named for his father, Robert Edward. During the winter Lee was

## Mrs. Robert E. Lee

on duty in Washington; so the family remained at Arlington until spring, Captain Lee going over to his office every morning and returning in the evening to the life he loved so well. But, with the coming of another spring, came also his orders to return to Fort Hamilton, and the family made their trek.

In June President Tyler visited the Brooklyn Navy Yard, his visit being the occasion of quite a military display. Mrs. Lee, writing to her mother, says:

> I went to Brooklyn today to witness the reception of President Tyler at the Navy Yard. The officers here with their families were invited to join with the Naval Officers in welcoming him. I thought the procession a rather poor one & there seemed to prevail among the crowd but little enthusiasm, tho' there was a plenty of hurrahing at the Navy Yard where he made a speech.

The officers and their families were all invited to the commandant's house for refreshments; but the house was so crowded that many stayed out under the trees. "Then we all proceeded down to the wharf. The boats and crews, collected there from all the ships in the harbor, were ready for our reception & we embarked & escorted the President over to Castle Garden, forming quite a pretty regatta."

Mrs. Lee was made very happy that summer by the promise of a visit from her aunt Mrs. Lawrence Lewis, who was coming to New York with two of

# The Wife of an Army Officer

her grandsons and their father, Mr. Charles Conrad. Preparations were made for the arrival of the dearly loved Aunt Lewis, "the sheets were well aired"; but, greatly to the disappointment of Mrs. Lee, her aunt, accompanied by her son-in-law and two grandsons, remained only a day. She found the boys "have grown very much." Evidently the visitors had stopped in New York to do some shopping and "They got felt hats for the boys trimmed with black velvet & steel bugles, I believe their own choice."

Mrs. Lee too had been on a shopping trip, looking for "something to wear—but all too dashing for me." She was more fortunate in millinery and wrote, "Just bought a very pretty bonnet of drab coloured satin lined with pink; drab is the most fashionable colour & would suit you trimmed with same—mention this because I thought you must get one—want you to have a pretty one."

Having failed in her efforts to get her mother to come to Fort Hamilton, Mrs. Lee was urging her now to visit some of her relatives. It will "do you good, just leave your cares at home & go."

Although it was now six years since the *Great Western* had established steam navigation across the Atlantic, her arrival still made news. The Lees, returning from spending the evening with some friends, "Heard afar off in the stillness of the night the rolling of immense paddles in the water." They

## Mrs. Robert E. Lee

"stopped on the bank to listen & presently a gun & then a rocket announced the arrival of the *Great Western*." There was always eager inquiry as to what news the *Great Western* had brought. On this trip "the *Great Western* seems to have brought but little news, except that Queen Victoria is enjoying herself in the society of her kingly visitors."

Wherever Mrs. Lee might be, her deepest interest was in the things which interested her family. She had for a long time been a most liberal contributor to the American Colonization Society. Colonization was a topic often discussed at Arlington; but she found at Fort Hamilton that

Colonization is a subject never mentioned in this part of the world; neither do I hear much of the subject of abolition. Politics are just now the order of the day. We were in Brooklyn last week & there was a tall hickory pole planted at every corner. Flags spread all over the streets & [there was a] procession more than a mile long, partly civil & partly military, in which were carried three coons & a bust of Henry Clay crowned with dahlias.

The American Colonization Society had been established in 1817 for the purpose of purchasing sufficient territory in some suitable locality on the western coast of Africa and to provide for the removal to such place of those persons of color who wished to emigrate to the land of their forefathers. It was neither sectional nor sectarian in its origin. Some of

# The Wife of an Army Officer

the most eminent men from both the North and the South aided in its establishment and were large contributors to its support.

When the Lees returned to Arlington, Custis was entered at Fairfax Institute, a near-by boarding school for boys, the two older girls having lessons with their mother. When Mrs. Lee returned to Fort Hamilton in the early spring, Mary and Anne remained at Arlington with their grandparents, and a governess was procured for them. Custis remained at Fairfax Institute until the close of the session. As the time for his trip to Fort Hamilton drew near, his mother wrote to Mrs. Custis:

... You wrote to me of Boo's wardrobe, which part of your letter I neglected to answer. He had better bring on his two new pairs of gambroons, his plaid jacket, also his new blue cloth one. He will not need his cloth pants. His brown linen jacket. One of his coats, the nankeen, would be best, as it is so cool here; and if he has room in his trunk, all the old suits that are made to button on to the jacket, as I can make him wear them and then he can leave them for Rooney. In that case he would not require all his shirts. I hope Rosie has made those two new shirts I cut out for him. He had better travel in his cap, as it will be more convenient, and bring all his clothes to you, when he comes, to put away; also his old cap, which need not be thrown away. He has some old nankeen pants, which will do to wear under his coat. He must bring on his cloak also. He had better bring on his night drawers and a pair of those drawers with bodies to wear with his

## Mrs. Robert E. Lee

old clothes; you will find them all in my closet. I think I showed Rose where I put them.

Mrs. Lee was freer now than at any time during her stay at Fort Hamilton. There was time to make calls, time to spend a day with some friend living near by. Of a day spent at Morrisania, with her cousin Martha Jefferson Morris, she wrote her mother:

We rode out to Morrisania a few days since and passed the day. . . . It is a beautiful ride. We crossed over at Hell Gate and saw Blackwell's Island, some beautiful country seats embowered in trees. Morrisania is beautifully situated, though from long neglect the grounds are much out of order. Pat [Martha Jefferson] is much interested in improving them and has some beautiful flowers; she will save some seed for you, and some dahlia roots. All mine died last winter, but I will try and keep some for you this fall. The interior of the house is very handsome, the wall all wainscoted and adorned with splendid mirrors; but there is not a great deal of old furniture remaining, and Mrs. Carey says that Mrs. Morris got rid of nearly all the plate and handsome things in various ways. There is a set of gold knives and forks and spoons remaining, which Mrs. Carey showed me. She is very fat and seems to be very happy in Pat and Gouverneur; the latter appears to be very amiable and unpretending. Pat looks very thin and pale. They sent a great deal of love and pressed me very much to bring you there this summer to stay a week. Ah, if you would only come, we could do a great many pleasant things.

# The Wife of an Army Officer

Mrs. Custis was always deeply interested in the welfare of the servants at Arlington. She had written Mrs. Lee to ask her to look up Cassy, one of the Arlington servants, who had married and was now living in New York. Writing to her mother of her efforts to locate Cassy, she says:

I received your letter concerning Cassy a day or two since, my dearest Mother, and would gladly have gone at once myself to see into the state of things, but you know what a wilderness New York is and there are many parts of the city into which it is not safe for a lady to go without risk of being insulted, and as Robert could not go with me, I wrote yesterday to Lily, telling her you had heard that Cassy was there; that her Mother was very anxious for her to come on; and that you had written to me to assist her, if necessary, with money to pay her expenses on to Arlington; and that I wished Cassy to come down here to see me, as there was a steam boat running direct here from New York every day; that if Cassy could not come, Lily must write immediately and tell me all about her plans and wants. I hope she will come tomorrow, or that I shall hear, and I will leave my letter open to tell you the result. . . .

Wednesday. Cassy came down on Tuesday and spent the night here, and went back this morning in the steam boat. She looks pretty well and says her own health is much better, but that Louis has been so sick ever since Xmas, he has not been able to work; that he is a perfect skeleton; that when they left Hudson, they were obliged to sell all their best things, keeping only their bed-clothes and common clothes, to pay house rent and Dr's bills; that they have been in New York some time and staid first with

# Mrs. Robert E. Lee

*Broadway in 1836*
[Courtesy of the New York Public Library]

Lily and then with Betsey, who were both very kind to them; that now they had rented a room for 4 dols a month, for which Lily lent them the money to pay in advance; that she had got a little washing which had enabled them to get along, but that Louis was still too sick to work.... She said that she was very anxious to go to Arlington, but that she could not leave Louis, and he did not want to go home unless "he could go as he ought to do." It seems there is a good deal of pride in the matter. She says I must tell her Mammy, she does not wish all the servants to know that they are not in prosperity. I told her that was all nonsense, to tell Louis from me, that I thought the best thing he could do would be to go at once to the District; that the journey would be of service to him; and that he could lodge as cheaply in Washington as New York, till he was well enough to get employment; and that Cassy could stay

# The Wife of an Army Officer

with her Mother till then, where he could see and hear from her; that they could in all probability get passage in a packet to Alexandria for about $10, which sum I would send them as soon as I heard they had decided to go. She is to write and let me know as soon as they determine what to do. I gave her a little money, some few things, as many as she could carry back with her. Robert says he knows it is no part of your wish that Louis should go on; but I told him that it was impossible for her to leave him in his present state, and I thought he could probably do much better in Washington than in New York. As soon as I hear Cassy's decision, I will inform you. If they cannot go, I will advance her some money to repay Lily. She says the letter you got was sent by Eddison, who is now steward on one of the packets, and that she told him to ask her Mammy to send her some money, if she had any to spare. I told her I would send her money to take her on as soon as I heard from her, which would be all she needed before she reached Arlington.

Though entertaining in her home at Fort Hamilton was much more difficult than at Arlington, the latchstring was always out for any of their friends who might be in that vicinity; and Mrs. Lee was greatly disappointed when any friend failed to come to see them. So she was both pleased and disappointed, when in writing to her mother in September, she says:

I received your letter last night, my dearest Mother, and I was rejoiced to learn you were so much better. You

# *Mrs. Robert E. Lee*

have no doubt ere this received my letter. I should have written again had I known that you were still at Arlington; but I supposed you must have left home, and waited to hear where you were. We have had a great change in the weather. It is almost cool enough now for a fire. It is delightful to me, though everyone else is shivering. Mrs. DePeyster and her daughter Sara have been staying with me for a week past. They leave tomorrow, and Mrs. Hackley and Capt. Talcott are coming down to stay for a few days.

We see by the paper which announces all arrivals in New York, that Cassius and Phillippa arrived at the Astor House on Saturday; but I fear they have passed on, tho' I had hoped they would at least have apprised us of their arrival that we might have sent Custis on by them.

Both Mrs. Lee and her husband were anxious that there should be no delay in Custis's entering school that autumn, and they had been anxiously on the lookout for an opportunity to send him with someone, for Custis was considered too young to make the trip alone. So Mrs. Lee explains:

We have been waiting the last ten days for an opportunity, and if they [Cassius and Phillippa] have gone, know of none earlier than next Friday. Capt. and Mrs. Clarke are going to Baltimore, and the Captain will proceed the next day to Washington; so that if he [Custis] does not go before, Lawrence can find him at Miss Polk's Saturday morning. If any change should take place or any further delay, I will write to Father, as he will be at home to receive the letter. I shall also probably decide upon my movements before I write again; but do not let me keep you near home, as in all events I cannot come before the first of October, and when Custis does get there, he must go immediately to school.... I have fixed all of Boo's [Custis] clothes that he will require this fall and have bought cloth for a winter suit for him, so he will need nothing at present.

Hearing that her mother had finally got off for a visit to Ravensworth, she addressed a letter to her there, with messages to the family:

Remember me most affectionately to all at Ravensworth. I hope Aunt Maria has got reconciled to her dress or disposed of it. I have a cap to send by Custis both for her and yourself, and a new pattern.... I have a cardinal for Annie cut out like daughter's, which will answer for this winter; next year I will present them both with something prettier. I also have two dresses for my "Wig" [Agnes] who is the sweetest little thing in the world and a great pet of "Papa's."

I hope that you will go to Kinloch or at least to see Marietta, if you cannot get farther.

I am sorry to hear you are so tormented by moschetaes, we have but few here....

I have Catherine still with me, and she is a great comfort ... but I fear when her husband arrives I shall have to give her up, as it will induce too much intercourse with the soldiers, which at present is entirely broken up.

I have enjoyed excellent health this summer and have been very active in the house ... taken little exercise out of doors, except my afternoon rides.... If it continues cold, we shall have to stop bathing, which will be a great dep-

## Mrs. Robert E. Lee

rivation to me.... You never told me the amount of my dividends, I have some idea of laying it out in blankets if I meet with any great bargains here.

With the coming of November Mrs. Lee made her farewell calls and began her packing preparatory to the yearly trip to Virginia. But the trip was delayed by an accident to Rooney. While exploring the barn, he climbed to the hayloft and, finding a chopping knife, decided to experiment. The result was that the tips of two of his fingers were cut off. The accident was the cause of great anxiety to his parents, as it was feared that the fingers would not knit after they had been sewed on by the doctor. Captain Lee, writing to Custis of the accident, says, "He may probably lose his fingers and be maimed for life." It was most important that Rooney should be kept perfectly quiet, lest by tossing in his sleep he might disturb the dressing or break the ligaments. Each day his mother sat beside him, reading to him and telling him stories. At night it was his father who watched beside him. Thus with careful nursing the little boy's fingers were saved.

It was some time, however, before the family could leave for Arlington, as Captain Lee was unwilling that Mrs. Lee should make the trip except under his escort, and he was unable to secure leave until after Christmas. This was a great disappointment to all the children, and poor little Rooney felt

# *The Wife of an Army Officer*

that he was responsible. At his dictation his father wrote a letter to Custis for him, telling Custis all the details of his accident, not sparing himself, telling also of his great disappointment that they would not be at Arlington for Christmas. He closes his letter with "Anny, Wig, and Rob are well. Anny & I say our lessons to Ma in the mornings." Thus Mrs. Lee now added to her regular duties that of teaching her children. She was ambitious for her children and greatly interested in their progress at school.

Though it was a great disappointment to all the family not to be able to be at Arlington, they spent a very happy Christmas at Fort Hamilton, and on Christmas evening Mrs. Lee wrote to her mother:

Your letter has just arrived, my dearest Mother, very opportunely, for I had intended to write to you tonight & give you some account of our Xmas, which has been a day of great enjoyment to the young ones, as their Papa filled their stockings with various presents & they received various ones from the Stauntons. I have felt sad that we could not all be together, but thankful that our young ones were all well & Rooney well enough to accompany us to Col. Staunton's, where we dined. The ground is covered with snow, but not deep & the weather quite mild. I took Annie & Wig to church, which was beautifully decorated with evergreens & Mr. Cander gave us a very good sermon & then administered the communion.

The children were awake at 4 o'clock this morning discussing the contents of their stockings & could not be in-

## Mrs. Robert E. Lee

duced to sleep again, so that I feel pretty tired tonight. Tell daughter her Papa has got for her a very pretty book called the Christmas Annual. I wish the old Boo had his box of tools; but they will have to wait for me I expect. . . . Hope to come on soon; I cannot now say on what day, for Robert seems unwilling to trust me alone & has no idea when he will be able to leave. . . . I am ready packed.

Lee was able to make arrangements early in January to accompany Mrs. Lee and the children to Arlington. His leave was short, and it was therefore necessary for him to return almost immediately to Fort Hamilton. There he received the news of the birth of his seventh child, Mildred Chiles Lee, born on February 10, 1846.

Before Mrs. Lee had completed her plans to return to Fort Hamilton, there came rumors of trouble with Mexico, and in May war was declared. Since there was the possibility and the hope on Lee's part that he would be ordered to Mexico, it seemed advisable for the family to remain at Arlington.

Many army friends came over to Arlington from Washington. From these Mrs. Lee learned of the great excitement in Washington. On every side there was talk of preparations, appointments, and expeditions. Twenty thousand volunteers had been called for from the Southern states. Of all this Mrs. Lee wrote her husband. She knew that he hoped to be among those sent. But he wrote her

# The Wife of an Army Officer

that it was uncertain whether the Engineer Corps would be given duty in the field. In the meantime he could only wait; hoping, however, for a part in the Mexican campaign. Knowing that this campaign would give him the opportunity for which he had wished, Mrs. Lee was greatly delighted when a letter from him said that he had received orders relieving him of duty at Fort Hamilton and directing him to proceed via Washington for service in Mexico.

Lee quickly followed his letter. After a few days at Arlington he set out for Mexico. It was with mingled emotions that his wife and the household at Arlington bade him adieu. Of her anxieties his wife made no mention to him. She spoke only of her pride in him.

The family at Arlington now had only one interest—the war in Mexico. Everyone was eager for news. Army friends stationed in Washington often found their way over to Arlington. They enjoyed discussing the Mexican situation with Mr. Custis, whom they found well informed. From these visitors the Arlington family heard much of what was going on in Mexico. But it was Lee's own letters which were most eagerly looked for and read with the greatest interest. The children were all told of what their father was doing in Mexico, and petitions for his safety were earnestly voiced at both morning and evening prayers.

## Mrs. Robert E. Lee

In August Mrs. Lee went to Audley. Audley was now the home of her Aunt Eleanor, who, after the death of her husband, Lawrence Lewis, had left Woodlawn and gone over the Ridge to make her home with her son, Lorenzo Lewis. It was while Mrs. Lee was there that Lorenzo Lewis died. Mrs. Lee shared the nursing with his wife, and it was Mrs. Lee whom he asked to write his will. He had asked that his oldest son, Washington, a cadet at the Virginia Military Institute, be sent for. This was done, but the boy was unable to reach home before his father's death. It was Mrs. Lee who wrote him in detail of his father's illness and things of which he had talked. Writing of the slaves she said: "Let no motive of worldly interest induce you to act an unkind or ungenerous part towards them. I well know what a trial they are, but think we are little disposed to make allowances for their peculiar ignorance and debased condition. . . ."

The campaign in Mexico lasted twenty months. Mrs. Lee kept anxious vigil at Arlington. Though her husband wrote nothing of the danger he was in, nor of his narrow escape from death, still much of this was naturally reported to the War Department in Washington; and, as such rumors will, they finally reached Mrs. Lee through various sources. Her anxiety was tempered with pride, for all the dispatches mentioned Lee's distinguished service.

# The Wife of an Army Officer

Finally the anxious days were past, and the news came to Arlington that Lee was on his way home, after an absence of a year and ten months. Great were the preparations made for his reception. The carriage was sent over to Washington to meet him at the station; but by some mischance the coachman missed him. Thinking there had been some misunderstanding about the time of his arrival and being most anxious to get home, he secured a horse and started on horseback for Arlington, while the coachman still waited.

From every window the children and Mrs. Lee watched to see if there were any sign of the carriage approaching. Only a lone horseman was seen wending his way along the driveway, which curved in and out under the great oak trees; but they had no eyes for the horseman, so anxiously did they look for the carriage. Then, as they looked, they saw that the dog, which belonged to Captain Lee, had rushed out and was now leaping wildly about the horseman and barking furiously but in a most joyous manner. Then, and then only, did they realize that the horseman was Captain Lee. In a moment Mrs. Lee was on the portico and in her husband's arms. The children were gathered in the hall to greet their father; but this soldier seemed a stranger to them, and they were shy in their first greetings. However, any embarrassment they might have felt

## Mrs. Robert E. Lee

soon wore off, and they were eager to be with him wherever he might be.

The summer passed happily. Each evening after Captain Lee had returned from Washington and supper was over, the family would gather on the portico. There was little talk of war at this time. Lee was the questioner, and he wished to hear of his family and his friends. He begrudged the two years it had been necessary for him to spend away from his children. Now he wanted to catch up on those years. So he asked the children many questions, and they told him of the things they were interested in and what they had been doing during his absence. And Mary Custis Lee, as she sat and watched her husband and children, had only thankfulness in her heart. She thought, indeed "my cup runneth over" with joy and gladness.

Lee had discouraged any attempt to gain promotion for him by importuning the President. But general orders, issued August 24, 1848, by the War Department, raised him to the rank of colonel, in recognition of his service in Mexico.

After a few happy months at Arlington, interrupted by various short trips which he was ordered to make, Lee was finally ordered to Baltimore. The house occupied by the Lees on Madison Avenue was not a large one; it seemed quite small compared with the spaciousness of Arlington. The children, whose

## The Wife of an Army Officer

playground had been the broad lawn under the spreading oak trees, found the yard on Madison Avenue cramped indeed. The older children, however, were very happy in Baltimore, for there were numerous young cousins who were always anxious to have the Lee girls join them in some form of entertainment. Thus the girls soon found themselves admitted to a large circle of charming young people.

As always when the Lees established themselves in a new home, they immediately connected themselves with an Episcopal church. In Baltimore Mount Calvary was the church of their choice, being also the church attended by Judge and Mrs. Marshall, the brother-in-law and sister of Colonel Lee.

In Baltimore, where they had many friends and relatives, the Lees took a much more active part in the social life than they did in Washington. The younger children were now old enough to be left in the care of their nurse, who was a much stricter disciplinarian than was Mrs. Lee. The younger children were always full of interest when they knew that their father and mother were going out to some evening entertainment. They loved to see their mother dressed in some lovely shimmering evening dress; but it was their father in full-dress uniform who intrigued them most. They often begged to be, and were, allowed to stay up until their parents were

## Mrs. Robert E. Lee

dressed and ready to leave. Robert, the youngest son, cherished a memory of his father on these occasions:

. . . always in full uniform, always ready and waiting for my Mother, who was generally late. He would chide her gently in a playful way and with a bright smile. He would then bid us good-by, and I would go to sleep with this beautiful picture in my mind, the golden epaulets and all—chiefly the epaulets.

Custis was now a cadet at West Point. He had been there about a year when Mrs. Lee experienced her first anxiety about any of her children. The report came to Colonel Lee that an inspector had found liquor in the boy's room. His mother would not believe that her son could be guilty of infringement of regulations. Colonel Lee was not sure. But the mother's steady belief in her son was an inspiration to the father in this trying time. He, better than Mrs. Lee, realized what the consequences would be if it were proved that Custis had hidden liquor in his room. It was the mother who comforted the father at this time, and they spoke of their anxiety to no one. Mrs. Custis, who had been visiting the Lees in Baltimore, wrote to Custis after her return to Arlington in October:

I feared at one time that you might think me neglectful in not writing to you during the period of your difficulty at West Point, but it was not till late in August, a few days

# The Wife of an Army Officer

to my leaving home, that I heard anything about it; and then, as everything was settled, I concluded not to mention the subject to you, as I had not had the power to do it at the time you most needed sympathy. When I met your Mother at Audley, she said nothing on the subject, wishing I suppose to spare me the pain of knowing anything about it; but an, I suppose, unintentional allusion while in Baltimore induced me to ask a few questions. I had from the first moment felt sure you had nothing to do with the forbidden article, but a careless handling of it. Yet the consequences even of that slight deviation were so serious (and but for your previous good conduct and the kindness of your friends and the Secretary might have proven even more so) that I often felt deeply for you and your parents, especially your Father who had doubtless expected you to come out like himself *blameless.* He never once adverted to the subject in my presence, so that I knew how painful it must be to him. Your Mother was consoled by the idea that there was nothing sinful in your conduct on that occasion—may she never have to mourn for the sins of her eldest born. . . .

Your grandfather is urged with a spirit of improvement lately. He is making new steps to the Portico (the old ones having so decayed as to be unsafe); intends paving it with hexagon brick tiles, which are now being burned in one of the vast brick kilns in Washington; then he is going to put a new roof on the stable, which is more needful than the other, though all are most desirable. You will hardly know the old place when you get back. If its living tenants could renovate so easily, they too might seem changed; but there is one thing they cannot change in—affection for their grandson.

## Mrs. Robert E. Lee

In December she wrote: "The Portico steps are finished at last. Charles and Arthur are engaged in repairing the floor." The tiles were to be laid as soon as Mr. Custis could haul them. At that time he was "crippled for means of hauling," as he had lost one of the oxen the previous summer and had sold the other for beef.

Agriculture was a subject of great interest at Arlington; so Mrs. Custis considered it would be of interest to her grandson that "there is a great talk of an 'Agricultural Bureau' at Washington to improve the Science of Agriculture."

Mrs. Custis had been disappointed that Lee had not "changed soldiering for farming," as she had urged him to do. If he had done so, her granddaughters "might avoid the dangers of city life." "Rich people in town," she wrote, "seem to me to live to no purpose but to show fine furniture and fine dress."

Annie and Agnes were spending the winter at Arlington. They were much happier there than in Baltimore. Their grandmother wrote Custis: "We are to have a governess in January for Anny and Agnes—there is only one subject in which they are dilligent, cutting up paper into babies & dresses & articles of furniture, strewing them—leaving a trail."

From Baltimore Mrs. Lee wrote Custis in December:

## The Wife of an Army Officer

It is my turn my dear boy to write, tho' I have but little of any interest to communicate to you. Your Papa gave me a fine account of you. One report of you *I like not*, that you *cannot help* getting demerit marks. I will quote the reply of the peasant to Kossuth: "Nothing is impossible to him that wills it," only adding that in resisting evil we all need the aid of a higher Power, the author of all our good resolutions and desires, to enable us to accomplish them. This assistance we can all obtain by prayer, earnest prayer; and why should we not pray to One who is always more ready to hear than we to ask? Why should we slight our highest privilege? Look into your heart, my son, and see if it is often lifted up to Him who made it and who has bestowed upon you so many blessings, far more than you deserve.

I have been trying very hard to persuade your Grandpa and Grandma to come and spend Xmas with me, but as yet without success. If they will not, we shall go down there. We shall all think of and wish for you, when enjoying ourselves together. It seems a pity that in this short life we should be so much separated from those we love; yet all is meant to teach us that this earth is not our home, that only in heaven are we to look for perfect bliss. There parting and sorrow are alike unknown.

Milly says I must tell you that Rob is sick and she and Angelina are quite well, the latter having recently been restored by having the upper half of her cranium cemented on. . . . Your affectionate Mother.

But Mrs. Lee was unable to persuade her parents to come to Baltimore for Christmas; so the Lees went to Arlington, and Colonel Lee wrote Custis:

# Mrs. Robert E. Lee

We came home on Wednesday morning (December 24). It was a bitter cold day, and we were kept waiting an hour in the depot at Baltimore for the cars, which were detained by the snow and frost on the rails. We found your Grandfather at the Washington depot, Daniel and the old carriage and horses. Your Mother, grandfather, Mary Eliza, the little people, and the baggage I thought load enough for the carriage; so Rooney and I took our feet in our hands and walked over.... The snow impeded the carriage as well as us, and we reached home shortly after it. The children were delighted at getting back, and passed the evening in devising pleasure for the morrow. They were in upon us before day on Christmas morning, to overhaul their stockings. Mildred thinks she drew the prize in the shape of a beautiful new doll; Angelina's infirmities were so great that she was left in Baltimore, and this new treasure was entirely unexpected. The cakes, candies, books, etc., were overlooked in the caresses she bestowed upon her, and she was scarcely out of her arms all day. Rooney got among his gifts a nice pair of boots, which he particularly wanted; and the girls, I hope, were equally well pleased with their presents, books and trinkets.

Your Mother, Mary, Rooney, and I went into church; and Rooney and the twins [who were visitors] skated back on the canal, Rooney having taken his skates along for the purpose....

I need not describe to you our amusements, you have witnessed them so often, nor the turkey, cold ham, plum pudding, mince pies etc. at dinner. I hope you will enjoy them again, or some equally as good.

I had received no letter from you when I left Baltimore, nor shall I get any till I return, which will be, if nothing

# The Wife of an Army Officer

happens, tomorrow a week, 5th January, 1852. You will be in the midst of your examinations. I shall be very anxious about you. Give me the earliest intelligence of your standing, and stand up before them boldly, manfully; do your best and I shall be satisfied.

It was in the spring of 1852 that Colonel Lee received orders to "proceed to West Point towards the close of the month of August, and on 1st of September next relieve Capt. Brewerton of the Superintendency of the Military Academy and of the command of the post of West Point."

Arriving at West Point Mrs. Lee found the superintendent's house both handsome and commodious. The social life was charming, and, best of all, the family was now able to see more of Custis. Fitzhugh Lee, a nephew of Colonel Lee's, was also a cadet there at this time, besides a number of other relatives and friends. Saturday being a half holiday for the cadets, they were then free for social engagements. Mrs. Lee, knowing this, made Custis feel that she wished him to bring some of his friends home with him every Saturday evening for supper.

Almost immediately Mrs. Lee busied herself with plans for the garden and wrote her mother:

We are now busy gardening. I should be glad to have any seed you have. They can be sowed very late here. I have been planting some flower roots today. We have a very good and industrious gardener & by the time you come,

## Mrs. Robert E. Lee

my flowers will be in full perfection & West Point in full beauty. Would I could be with you this spring to assist you in your labours; but as it seems to be decided I am to stay here, you must come on to me as soon as possible. Do not be any later than the middle of July.... Cloudy today, fine time to plant out my roses.... The garden occupies part of our mornings. I have been taking all of the flowers out of the green house & putting them in the grounds.

Always fond of wild flowers, she was anxious to find those growing around West Point; so she "took a long walk up the mountain ... in search of wild flowers. Everywhere" she found "rocks upon rocks sublimely piled & the flowers peeping from among them with scarcely any soil to sustain them.... Tomorrow we propose mounting to the top of the Crows Nest, a very high mountain in this vicinity."

Annie and Agnes had remained at Arlington with their grandparents, a governess having been engaged to teach them. Mrs. Lee wrote her mother:

Milly & Rob go to school; but their school is so near, the weather does not keep them at home.... They are getting on well & seem pleased with their school.

The female department is taught by a young woman, the wife of the teacher, who is a graduate of one of the Northern colleges. There are only 4 girls & about 10 boys. ... Children send love to Annie & Wig.

Mrs. Lee had spent some time at Arlington after leaving Baltimore and before going to West Point.

# The Wife of an Army Officer

Her mother had been very reluctant to part with her, and this had seemed natural; but Colonel Lee had realized that it was largely due to the failing health of Mrs. Custis. He had even urged Mrs. Lee to remain for a time with her mother; but to this Mrs. Custis would not consent, believing that whenever it was possible a wife's place was with her husband.

Without warning there came the news that Mrs. Custis was very ill. Though Mrs. Lee started immediately, she did not reach Arlington until after the death of her mother. It was a terrific shock; but, always thoughtful of others, Mrs. Lee set herself to the task of comforting her father. It was an added sorrow that her husband's official duties prevented his coming to her; but as soon as possible after the commencement exercises at West Point he joined Mrs. Lee and his family at Arlington.

Colonel Lee had for Mrs. Custis the deepest affection. He spoke of her as "mother," saying, "She was to me all that a Mother could be, and I yield to none in admiration for her character." Now shortly after her death he wrote to Markie [Martha] Williams, "The blow was so sudden and crushing that I shudder at the shock and feel as if I had been arrested in the course of life and had no power to resume my onward march."

## CHAPTER IV

# *Mistress of Arlington*

AFTER a service of three years at West Point Colonel Lee was ordered in April, 1855, to Louisville, to take command of the Second Cavalry. Mrs. Lee and her daughters returned to Arlington, as it was impossible for Colonel Lee to take his family with him to his new post.

At Arlington, heretofore, Mrs. Lee had always had the companionship of her mother. She had never known the place without her. To all who came to Arlington at this time the place seemed indeed bereft without the presence of one who had come there as a bride fifty years ago and who had been its only mistress. Mrs. Custis had been a woman not only of exceptionally fine character but also of great charm and sweetness.

Though Mary Custis Lee had been petted and idolized by her parents and her husband, there was nothing selfish in her character. Her thought was always for the happiness of others. Now, though she missed her mother sadly, she tried to keep her feeling of loneliness out of her letters to her husband.

# Mistress of Arlington

When Mrs. Lee bade her husband good-by, she had no idea when he would be able to return home, and she knew that it would be impossible for her to join him. She was therefore greatly surprised and delighted when she received a letter from him apprising her of the fact that he had been ordered to New York for a short duty, which would enable him to return home for a brief visit in January. The visit was indeed short. He had hardly arrived, when he received his orders to rejoin his regiment in Mexico, and he left on February 12, 1856.

*Colonel Robert E. Lee, 1855*
[Courtesy of the Honorable Henry Wickham]

The separation from her husband became increasingly hard for Mrs. Lee. Not only was her health wretched, but as mistress of Arlington she had many responsibilities and many important decisions to make. Of much of this she would have been relieved by her husband's presence. She was devoted to her father, but it worried her that he was so dilatory about his affairs. There were many questions on which Mr. Custis wished his son-in-law's opinion, and these were referred to him by Mrs. Lee in her correspondence. But mails were slow and very irregular. Frequently a long time would elapse before her letters would reach her husband and his advice be received.

Repairs were greatly needed at Arlington. Some of these she would authorize; but there were others which entailed a greater expense than she cared to assume the responsibility for.

There was also business to attend to for her husband, when it was necessary for her to be the intermediary between him and the banks. She wrote him most minutely of bonds paid, coupons clipped, and money deposited, as well as her own drafts against his bank account; but she felt that her statements must appear confused indeed when compared with the clear way in which he kept his accounts.

An added anxiety was the condition of Rooney's health. He had been at Harvard, but had returned to Arlington upon the advice of his physician, who had attended him in a prolonged attack of bilious fever.

Colonel Lee felt that Arlington was not a healthy place in the summer, and he had written Mrs. Lee urging her to go either to the springs or to the mountains. Eager to regain her health she wrote to him in July:

I shall go either to Bath or the Warm Springs & think of taking with me Rooney, Mary & Rob, who seem most

## Mistress of Arlington

to require some renovation.... Annie & Agnes will remain with their Grandpa. Rosalie Stuart left us this morning at half past 5 to go down the river in the steam boat. I let Precious Life [Mildred] go with her ... thought the little trip would be of great service to her. Julia had urged them all to go. They are at their summer retreat, which they say is perfectly healthy. Rooney, Annie & Wig [Agnes] rode in with them.

The Warm Springs were selected by her; but she returned to Arlington in August because, as she wrote her husband, "the time was so nearly approaching for Rooney to return to College & I did not feel able in my helpless state to travel without him, that I determined to come home.... Mary & Rob got off at the Ravensworth depot to make a little visit. Aunt Maria sent her carriage to meet them."

Rooney, who "had a warm and affectionate heart," was still an irresponsible youth and a cause of some anxiety to his father, who felt that his son was not applying himself properly to his studies at Harvard. Writing to Mrs. Lee he said, "It is time [for him] to begin to think of something else besides running about amusing himself & I wish him to do so at once." Rooney was undecided whether he should return to Harvard or go to the University of Virginia. His father was willing to leave the decision with him, but in either case his "standing must be better than normal." For his father felt that "we

## Mrs. Robert E. Lee

have to pay for all we get in this world whether knowledge or pleasure & if we get the value of our labour it is all we can ask."

In making plans for the children's schools that autumn it was decided that Agnes and Annie should return to Staunton, where they had attended the Virginia Female Institute the year before. Mrs. Lee was still undecided about the best arrangement for Rob, who was now thirteen; but finally wrote her husband, "I had thought of sending Rob to Saint James, but think he had better go to Mr. Lippitt's for one more term."

With Rooney at college, Annie and Agnes at boarding school, Rob away all during the week, and Mary off on frequent visits, Mrs. Lee felt "bereft" of her children. She wrote her husband, "I generally take my breakfast in my room & after I have arranged all my work for the day, come down stairs and remain until bed time." With her lameness, it was increasingly hard for her to go up and down the stairs.

There was little intercourse with Washington because, as Mrs. Lee wrote Mrs. Talcott, "the river is still full of ice which is aground & there is a large gap in the bridge." This was the "long bridge" and the only means of approach to Washington from Arlington.

With the arrival of Martha [Markie] Williams at Arlington on one of her frequent visits, Mrs. Lee

## Mistress of Arlington

heard that "Washington is exceedingly gay," and to Mrs. Talcott she wrote:

> Everybody is *agog* for the inauguration. I never felt so little interest in a new President, for I never admired Mr. Buchanan. . . . Mr. Peabody, as you will see by the papers, is creating quite a sensation in Washington. He is indeed a most liberal man. Mr. Cochran is entertaining him munificently & Mrs. Elisha Riggs is to give him a grand party. I am quite out of the world now; the bridge is broken & do not expect to get to Washington until it is mended.

Loving mother that she was and most anxious for the spiritual welfare of her children, she wrote to her husband "of the joyful news that has filled my heart with thankfulness & my lips with praise. I yesterday received letters from both of our dear little girls at Staunton." It was Annie's letter which was the cause of such joy to her mother; for, as she wrote her mother, she "had suffered much from a sense of sin and unworthiness, but had now found comfort and peace in believing. . . ."

To Annie her mother wrote:

> It is very late my precious little daughter, but I cannot let another day pass without telling you the real happiness your letter afforded me, *you* for whom I have felt so anxious, to hear that God had sent his spirit into your heart & drawn you to himself. Remember what He says, "Those who seek me early shall find me." The promises of God

are sure & cannot fail. Therefore *seek* Him with all your heart.... You must pray for your sister & for your brothers who are out of the fold of Christ. Think what a happiness to your Mother to be able to present *all* her children at the *throne* of God & to be able to say, "Here I am Lord & the children Thou hast given me." Pray for your Mother that she may be more faithful in her prayers & example.... I accept, my dear child, your penitence for all your faults towards me & freely bestow my forgiveness.

A lover of nature in all her aspects, Mrs. Lee was likely to make some allusion in her letters to flowers, birds, sunsets, or views. She writes: "yesterday I spent at Riversdale.... The flowers were magnificent."

Because of a late spring she says, in a letter written in May: "The woodbine is only now in bloom. It often blooms by the first of April & the roses are not yet out."

Pets also found mention in her letters, especially the cats. To one of her daughters she writes: "Tom Tita is the proud father of two kittens, one like him, who were produced in the garret where he pays them frequent visits.... We have named one Cyclopie, as she has the misfortune to be possessed of only one eye."

Colonel Lee's sister Mildred, Mrs. Edward Childe, had died in Paris in the summer of 1856. The following year Mr. Childe brought his children back

## Mistress of Arlington

to America. They were all frequently at Arlington. In making her plans for the summer Mrs. Lee had offered to take Mary Childe with her to the springs, and she wrote Colonel Lee, "Brother Childe & family are to meet at Relay House & go with me & leave Mary under my care while they circulate about."

The trip to Bath was delayed; but Mrs. Lee finally left, taking with her Mary Childe and Mary Anne, her maid. Only Annie went with her mother, the other daughters remaining to entertain the number of young people gathered at Arlington. From Bath Mrs. Lee was to go to Capon, and it was agreed that any of her daughters desiring to do so should join her there. She was delighted with the new pool, over sixty feet long, which she found at Bath. This was for the use of the gentlemen; but "the ladies have a large one, too." Though an excellent swimmer, Mrs. Lee found it impossible to teach Mary Childe and Annie. This task was taken over by "a pretty young girl of sixteen."

Earlier in the spring Mrs. Lee had written her husband telling him that much to her surprise General Winfield Scott had secured for Rooney an appointment as second lieutenant in the 2nd Infantry. It had greatly surprised her that Rooney did not care for it, though he would have liked an appointment to the cavalry. Rooney had left the decision in the hands of his mother. This she did

## Mrs. Robert E. Lee

not wish to make without first consulting his father. But the decision had to be made; and though she wrote to her husband of Rooney's appointment, it was not possible to wait for his reply. Mrs. Lee knew that Rooney was dissatisfied at Harvard. Realizing that her son had a "warm & affectionate heart, but too careless & reckless a disposition," she felt that army discipline would be of great value to him. She therefore advised him to accept the appointment, which he did.

*General Winfield Scott*

Shortly after Mrs. Lee's arrival at Bath she heard from Custis (now stationed in Florida), whom she had not seen for two years, that he had been ordered to California. He was ordered to New York to take a steamer sailing from there, and would therefore be obliged to go without seeing his mother. This was a source of great distress to her. Fortunately for her sake he was unable to reach New York before the steamer sailed, arriving there one day too late. Since it would be some time before he could get another steamer, he decided to return to Arlington for a short

# Mistress of Arlington

visit to his grandfather. From there he went on to Bath to join his mother. She was greatly shocked to see how unwell he was, especially as there had been no intimation of his ill health in his letters to her or to any member of the family. Telling her husband of this, she wrote:

> The morning after he arrived, I *clandestinely* without his consent, which I knew I should not obtain, wrote a very polite note to Genl Totten, begging he might be allowed a little time to recruit his health and visit his friends. The Genl immediately sent me, by telegraph, the desired permission & orders to sail for California the 5th of August. So we have all been made very happy by his presence here for nearly two weeks.

There were a number of people at the springs; but Mrs. Lee took little part in the social life, finding her enjoyment in her children. She was anxious about her husband, to whom she wrote:

> I do so long for tidings of you & yet always feel afraid to hear. May God in his mercy preserve & keep you now and ever. Life is at the best a fleeting current; whether it glides smoothly on or rushes in a turbid course, its end is the same, the great ocean of eternity.... May God prepare us all.

It was while at Bath that Mrs. Lee received the news of Rooney's engagement to his cousin Charlotte Wickham. She felt that their youth and near rela-

## Mrs. Robert E. Lee

tionship was a detriment; but, as she wrote her husband, "a virtuous attachment is often a great safeguard to a young man."

From Bath Mrs. Lee went to Audley, the home of Mrs. Lorenzo Lewis, where she stopped for a short time on her way home. Her visit was short; for her father had for some time been looking forward to attending the agricultural fair which was to be held in Louisville, Kentucky, that autumn, and she felt that she should be at home before he left. Then, too, she must decide on the school which Rob was to attend, for she felt that he should now be at boarding school. Several schools had been considered. Finally she wrote:

> I have just sent my poor little Rob to school at Mr. Ambler's in Fauquier. . . . They are about to move the College of St. James to Baltimore & I think, after it is all permanently arranged, it would be best to send him there. Mr. Ambler is very highly recommended, having taught several years, & it [his school] is in the country just at the Blue Ridge mountains, a fine healthy situation near a church & among religious & moral people.

Always enjoying visits with her cousin Esther Lewis, Mrs. Lee regretted that it had been necessary to cut her visit short. "I should have liked very much," she wrote, "to have prolonged my stay up in the country; but tho' Father did not go to Louisville, he has been so unwell ever since I returned &

## Mistress of Arlington

is now quite sick with an attack of Influenza. The Doctor came over to see [him this] morning & has ordered him some medicine."

Among Mr. Custis's activities as a farmer was that of breeding sheep, in which he had been very successful. To foster improvement in sheep and to encourage woolen manufacture at home, he had, in 1803, inaugurated an annual convention for the "Promotion of Agriculture and Domestic Manufactures," which really marked the beginning of the woolen manufacturing interests of the country. These meetings were known throughout the country as the Arlington Sheep-Shearing. They brought together from all parts of the country an assemblage of men interested in the industry and others prominent in public affairs. All were the guests of Mr. Custis. The master of Arlington had never lost his interest in farming and the breeding of sheep, and for some time he had looked forward to the trip to "the great West."

Upon her return from Audley Mrs. Lee found her father very unwell, and it was quite evident to her that he would be unable to make the trip. Finally there came a bright October morning when the genial master of Arlington bade his body servant, who came to kindle the fire, to tell Mrs. Lee that he would not be able to join her at breakfast. Mrs. Lee, coming to her father's room upon receiving his mes-

## Mrs. Robert E. Lee

sage, was alarmed at his condition. She immediately dispatched a messenger on horseback to Alexandria for the doctor.

Mrs. Lee, writing afterward of her father's illness, said of him:

> Fully impressed with the belief that he could not survive the attack, the terrors of death seemed mercifully withdrawn and with the gentleness and trust of a child did he await its approach. . . . He requested that his pastor be summoned, to whom he avowed his belief and hope in the only atonement offered for sinners, with clasped hands joined in prayers for the dying, then gently sank to rest in the seventy-seventh year of his age.

During the four days of her father's illness Mrs. Lee had been too occupied with him to write her husband of the serious nature of his illness; and even had she done so, it would have taken ten days or more for a letter to reach him. She had especially wished that Custis might have come to the grandfather who adored him; but Custis was on his way to duty in California, and Rooney, who had accepted the commission as Lieutenant of Infantry, was already on his way to Texas. So in the second great sorrow of her life Mary Custis Lee was alone.

The announcement of Mr. Custis's death reached Colonel Lee in a letter from Mrs. Fitzhugh, followed by one from Mrs. Lee. Mrs. Lee spoke of her father as one "who was always only too kind & indulgent

## Mistress of Arlington

to me and mine." She uttered no regrets, but spoke only of her joy in his belief. Nor did she ask her husband to come to her. It was not until October 21 that Colonel Lee received the news of his father-in-law's death. Fortunately he was able to secure leave, and three days after he received the news he was on his way home, reaching Arlington on November 11, 1857.

It was a sad home-coming. The shadow of "the old master's" death still hung over the plantation. Mr. Custis had been a man of a most hospitable nature; nothing could exceed the easy grace and politeness of his manner. In the life of the builder of Arlington might be seen one of the brightest instances of a country gentleman. Of her father Mrs. Lee wrote that she "never received an unkind word. He was endowed with an even temper and remarkably buoyant spirit; and towards his family, his servants, his friends, and the world, there was a constant outflow of kindly feeling from his warm and generous heart."

Though he was devoted to his father-in-law, of far greater distress to Lee than his death and an even greater shock was the condition of Mrs. Lee's health. Not wishing to add to her husband's anxieties, she had kept from him the seriousness of her condition, for she knew how it would distress him. She had written a friend, "I almost dread his seeing my crippled

## Mrs. Robert E. Lee

state." So she had kept the knowledge of her condition from him, and now, totally unprepared, he found his wife a sufferer from arthritis, frequently unable to sleep at night because of the intense pain, her right hand and arm helpless.

By her father's will Mary Custis Lee was left a life interest in Arlington and its contents, and also in other property; all of which at her death was to go to Custis Lee, "he my eldest grandson taking my name and arms." To Rooney Lee went the "White House," a plantation in New Kent County. Romancoke was willed to the youngest grandson, Robert E. Lee. To each of his granddaughters was left a legacy of $10,000.

*Mrs. Robert E. Lee, Arlington, 1858*

Never a very efficient farmer, Mr. Custis, in his later years, had become a very negligent farmer. He was an easygoing master, requiring little of his slaves. At the time of his death the Arlington plantation of eleven hundred acres was sadly run down.

## Mistress of Arlington

As executor Lee felt that his presence at Arlington was necessary if he was to give proper attention to the affairs of the estate. He therefore requested an extension of his leave. This granted, he settled down to the life of a farmer, a life he had often longed to lead; but he now found that it had been easier to build some fortification or to administer the affairs at West Point than it was to bring order out of chaos at Arlington.

He missed his army life, and Mrs. Lee, though happy to have him at home, feared that his prolonged absence from duty might affect his career. But General Scott, commanding general of the army, assured her that Colonel Lee's career would in no way be affected. Though it was three years before Lee returned to his regiment, he was not on leave during this entire time; for he was frequently called to serve on a court martial or assigned to duty at the War Department in Washington. On October 17, 1859, he was ordered to Harpers Ferry to take command of the forces which had been ordered there to quell the insurrection.

During the time that Lee was on leave at Arlington, Rooney was married to his cousin Charlotte Wickham. The wedding took place at Shirley, which had been the home of Lee's mother, Anne Carter, and which had been the scene of her marriage to "Light-Horse Harry" Lee. Because of her

## Mrs. Robert E. Lee

health Mrs. Lee was unable to attend the wedding. The Lee girls were there and also their father, who always cherished the warmest affection for Shirley. The affair was a pleasant interlude for Colonel Lee; for here he found gathered a number of his nearest friends and relatives. It was a wedding typical of Virginia at that period. The guests lingered for a week or more. Colonel Lee stayed on, thoroughly enjoying the young people. This week at Shirley marked perhaps his happiest in a time of depression. Upon his return to Arlington he found Mrs. Lee most anxious to hear all the details of the wedding: who the bridesmaids were, what they wore, with what groomsman each one walked, what the wedding supper consisted of, what cousins were there. She was eager to hear it all, and she found in her husband a most satisfactory raconteur.

During Mr. Custis's lifetime, at intervals of many months, he had contributed to the *National Intelligence* a series of articles which he called "Recollections." Because of the fact that he was the grandson of Martha Washington and the adopted son of George Washington, the "Recollections" contained many interesting and minute details of the family life of Washington. For some years he had been urged by his friends, who realized the value of these reminiscences, to rearrange and revise the "Recollections" and to publish them in a more

## Mistress of Arlington

permanent form. Being of a dilatory nature he had put it off from year to year, and it had never been done. Shortly after his death Mrs. Lee set herself to the task of doing what her father had been urged to do. For two years she occupied herself with this task. She thoroughly enjoyed the work, not only because of her devotion to her father but also because of the many letters she received commending her efforts. These letters were a source of great gratification, speaking of her father, as they did, in the most commendatory terms. The book, published in 1860, is known as *Recollections and Private Memoirs of Washington, by his Adopted Son, George Washington Parke Custis, with a Memoir of the Author, by his daughter*. This work, says Mrs. Lee, was "actuated by filial affection and a feeling that these recollections of the Father of his Country by his adopted son should not be lost." At the time that Mrs. Lee started the editing of the memoirs she realized that the arthritis from which she was a sufferer was spreading. She did not wish to sit and think of what the future might hold for her, nor did she wish to burden her family and her friends with her anxieties about her health; for in her character was found a heroic unself-pitying courage. But she knew that she must have occupation. Occupation for her hands she had in plenty; but there must be occupation for her mind. The writing of the *Memoir*

## Mrs. Robert E. Lee

of her father and the editing of his *Recollections* supplied the needed occupation for her mind. Colonel Lee was justly proud of this work by his wife, which came from the press and reached Arlington about the time he left there to rejoin his regiment in Texas.

Shortly after Colonel Lee left for his post, Mrs. Lee went for a visit to her son Fitzhugh (Rooney) at his plantation, the "White House." From there she wrote to E. G. W. Butler, who had married her cousin Frances Parke Lewis, and whose home was now in the Parish of Iberville, Louisiana:

I hope ere this, you have seen my book & that it has made a favorable impression upon you. I had a letter from the Printers, Derby & Jackson, when it was first issued, saying that they would thankfully receive any aid from me that might assist in its circulation, as they knew I had many personal friends who would be interested in it & whom, of course, they knew nothing about. I had written to Parke that if Mr. Mittenburger wanted any copy, he had better apply to Derby & Jackson; so I hope that every thing has been conducted with proper etiquette & that the work has met with a kind reception in New Orleans. It certainly ought to be most valuable as a reliable production, for you know my Father had a most retentive and unerring memory & no one living could have had such opportunities of knowing all about Washington.

Speaking of her visit, she says:

I reached this place yesterday morning for the first time in 35 years. I hope now to be frequently here, as my son &

## Mistress of Arlington

daughter propose to make it their home. It is a fine rich country, but not very picturesque.... I left Custis in charge of the girls at Arlington while I came down here. He is, I fear, quite a confirmed bachelor tho' only 26.

Writing to her daughter Agnes, she says:

The servants were all delighted to see me. Tell Nurse that they make so much over me, that I do not know what to do.... They call me Mistress & always ask after Papa as *old* Master.

It was during her visit to the "White House" that her first grandchild was born and named Robert Edward Lee for his grandfather. Rooney having written his father of his namesake, Colonel Lee replied:

So he is called after his grandpapa, the dear little fellow. I wish him a better name and hope he may be a wiser and more useful man than his namesake. Such as it is, however, I gladly place it in his keeping, and feel that he must be very little like his father if it is not elevated and ennobled by his bearing and course in life.

Though Mrs. Lee's letters were now filled with pleasure over her grandson, she did not neglect to write Annie about things she wished done at Arlington. Stain was to be made from walnut juice, to be used on the doors. Annie was to "get directions" and find if "the walnut bark must be boiled." She was anxious about the servants who were sick. "If they are not better, send them to the Doctor...."

## Mrs. Robert E. Lee

During the three years of Lee's stay at Arlington he and Mrs. Lee had visited the Hot Springs, the waters of which had proved most beneficial to Mrs. Lee, and she had shown marked improvement under the watchful care of her husband. In the summer of 1860, having heard the healing qualities of the waters of Saint Catharine's in Canada spoken of in the highest manner, she decided to make the trip there. Accompanied by Markie Williams and Agnes and escorted by Custis, the party left Baltimore and reached Niagara after two "long and tiresome days' journey." Writing early the morning after their arrival while the other members of the party were yet asleep, Mrs. Lee felt that she was not yet prepared to express an opinion "of the famous Niagara," not yet having seen all the beauties; but she "was disappointed in the first *coup d'œil*. Man has done all in his power to mar its sublimities by building work shops & mills down to its very edge."

Later she adds: "I have looked out at the falls this morning; still lament they were not left in a wild state. How grand it must have been when the Indians wandered on its shores."

Annie, now twenty, had been left in charge of the establishment at Arlington; but her mother could not refrain from writing her instructions as to the many things which she wished done in the house and on the grounds. Billy and Ephraim were to wash

## Mistress of Arlington

a bag of wool and Nurse must see to its being properly dried and put away. "When Sally and Patsey have done knitting, they can pick it." George was to pick the tomatoes, and Nurse, with someone to help her, must put them in cans. She also wished all the empty bottles filled with catsup.

To young Robert his mother sends a message that she depends "upon him and uncle Charles to attend to outdoor concerns, the garden and the park & to keep the children at work." Annie is reminded that the plants are to be watered and that Ephraim must spread the vines and tie them up. For the strawberry bed Daniel must furnish Ephraim with plenty of manure. The cellar is to be kept locked "as the wine there is a tempting article."

After a stay at the hotel in Saint Catharine's, which she found "intolerably stupid," they went to "a sweet little vine covered cottage," where they were very comfortable. The manner and customs of the people she found quite different from any she had ever encountered before; but of greater interest were the numbers of runaway slaves to be seen in Saint Catharine's, and they, she understands, are becoming a great problem to the authorities. "Tell Nurse I have seen no acquaintances among them."

Though they were far from home and in another country, the family custom was adhered to, and on Sunday the party were found worshiping in the

## Mrs. Robert E. Lee

Church of England and praying "for the Sovereign lady, Queen Victoria."

It had been decided before Mrs. Lee left home that Mildred was to go to boarding school that winter, Mrs. Powell's in Winchester having been the one selected. It was necessary that the preparations for her going be made before Mrs. Lee's return to Arlington; so Annie was written to, to inspect Mildred's wardrobe. If cotton was needed out of which to make underclothing,

> send to Perry for his everlasting cotton, which is thick. ... It is $12\frac{1}{2}$ cts. per yd. If you want any other cotton, write for his *best* for $12\frac{1}{2}$ cts. & let Mical pay for it out of the market money. You had better have her dresses & gowns made also & see if you or your sister have anything that will do for her, as there will be no time when I return to make anything for her.

Mildred, even then a most independent young spirit, wished to be the one to decide what were her needs. This her mother realized. She regrets that Annie should have so much responsibility and hopes that Mildred "will be reasonable about her clothes & not give you unnecessary trouble." Mrs. Lee was anxious to be at home before it was time for Mildred to leave for school; and, feeling that she had given the waters at Saint Catharine's a fair trial without any appreciable benefit, she decided to leave for home. The return trip was made by New York,

## Mistress of Arlington

where she left Markie Williams and Agnes and hurried home. Traveling all night, she was greatly disappointed on arriving at home to find that Mildred, having found an agreeable escort to Winchester, had not waited for her mother's return. "Perhaps," she wrote, "it is as well that you went under such a good escort & I am glad you are so much pleased. I am sure, if you conduct yourself as a lady should do, you will meet with every kindness."

Arlington, situated as it was on the main-traveled road from the South to Washington, was a favorite place for relatives and friends to stop for a few days. Its hospitable doors were always open to such guests. The mansion seemed lonely now without its builder and its gracious mistress. Colonel Lee was now with his regiment, as was also Custis. Rooney married and in his own home, Mildred and Robert at boarding school, and the older girls frequently away on visits, friends were urged to come and stay. The days were not so full of merriment for these cousins and friends as had been their girlhood days; now there was a quieter enjoyment of each other. There were many reminiscences of those joyous times, kindly inquiry about each other's children, and stories concerning their grandchildren. The gay and dancing music of bygone years had changed to deeper and more tranquil tones; but for each there was a refrain of happy memories.

## Mrs. Robert E. Lee

While the wives, seated on the broad portico, talked of the happy past, their husbands were frequently absent on business in Alexandria or Washington. The talk of the future, which they brought back, was not so happy; there were clouds, dark clouds, on the horizon.

As Christmas drew near, Mildred, who had been so eager to go off to school, was begging to be allowed to come home for the holidays. Though anxious to have her at home, her mother wrote that "for many reasons it would be best for you not to come." However, if the holidays were going to be long enough to justify the trip and a suitable escort could be found, her mother would not object. Evidently the conditions were met, and "Milly," to the delight of the family, spent Christmas at Arlington. But there was anxiety in the air, and in January Mrs. Lee writes Mildred: "I do not feel like going anywhere, viewing constantly the sad state of my country. We must be more earnest in supplication to that Almighty Power who alone can save us. . . . There is no such thing as an indolent Christian."

## CHAPTER V

# *War*

THE darkest year in the history of the United States had come. From the birth of the American people, long before the line which stretched from east to west received its baptismal name of Mason and Dixon, the two sections of the country were known as the North and the South, their people representing two essentially diverse civilizations.

In the North life was compact, cohesive, and commercial; that of the South was diffusive and agrarian, which resulted in the development of the individual and the guarding of his rights. The Southerner bore with him wherever he went the cardinal doctrine of the rights, privileges, and franchises of the individual. The New Englander was docile to authorized power, spiritual and temporal.

With the establishment of the Union, the divergent interests of the two sections almost immediately became evident. The antagonism which had existed between the Cavalier and the Puritan manifested itself now in sectional rivalry.

All that great country of which Virginia had stripped herself to cede it to the general government

## Mrs. Robert E. Lee

became Northern in sympathy, largely because the states carved from this territory were settled by a Northern population. Every effort on the part of the South to balance the power which was taken from her by Virginia's gift to the general government was met and resisted by the North as tending to Southern aggrandizement and as being a blow to the rights and privileges of the North.

Now for months in Washington the battle had raged in the Senate between the political giants of both sections. Who was to dictate the policy of the government? Should the conservative South, with its doctrine of state rights, of original sovereignty, rule the country according to a literal interpretation of the Constitution, or should the North govern in accordance with a more liberal construction, adapted, as it claimed, to the new and more advanced condition of the nation? In the heat of the argument between capital and agriculture the real issues were lost sight of, and slavery became the battle cry of both sections.

The many visitors who came and went at Arlington talked of little else than the condition of the country. Newspapers spoke in heated terms of the general dissatisfaction with the result of the election. Party and sectional spirit ran high. Politics had become the affair of everyone.

Mrs. Lee's training and associations had been such that she was a keen student of national affairs.

## War

Though she took little part at this time in the society of Washington, she was aware that in social as in political gatherings there was a constantly widening division between the Northern and Southern elements gathered in the government city. Naturally she was by inheritance a believer in state rights. She was eager for every item of news from the Capitol. To those who came to Arlington from Washington, she said eagerly, "Tell me please what took place today." She knew from them, from letters from friends, and from the papers that the very air was filled with the words "secession" and "war."

Over in Washington, women whose husbands were in public life went daily to the Senate gallery to listen to the angry debates. Every sentence uttered in the Senate or House was full of hot feeling. So fearful were Senators and Representatives of losing their vote on some vital question that they kept their seats all through the night. By the side of Senators, drowsy with long vigils, stood pages ready to awaken them at the calling of the roll.

Monday, January 21, 1861, was the day privately agreed upon by a number of Senators for their public declaration of secession. The day dawned. The galleries of the Senate chamber were densely packed. One by one Senators David Yulee, Stephen K. Mallory, Clement C. Clay, Benjamin Fitzpatrick, and Jefferson Davis, each in turn, rose and an-

## Mrs. Robert E. Lee

nounced that the people of their respective states "had adopted an ordinance whereby they withdrew from the Union formed under a compact styled the United States, resumed the powers delegated to it, and assumed their separate station as a sovereign and independent people." As each of the Senators concluded for his state the solemn renunciation of allegiance to the United States, the women in the galleries grew hysterical. Men embraced each other and wept. As each Senator took up his portfolio and gravely left the Senate chamber, sympathetic cheers rang from many of those in the galleries.

It had been the custom of Mr. Custis to attend the parade held in Washington yearly on the twenty-second of February in honor of the birthday of his adopted father. Mrs. Lee had kept up the custom, and whenever possible had gone over to Washington on that day. This year was to be no exception. On reaching Washington she found there was great excitement as well as disappointment. Because of the great number of soldiers gathered in the capital of the United States, the President had ordered that the parade be omitted. But later reconsidering, he rescinded his order, and the parade was held, so Mrs. Lee wrote Mildred. Writing again a few days later, she said:

The papers are now filled with Mr. Lincoln's arrival in Washington & this week will, I presume, decide our

## War

fate as a nation. . . . I pray that the Almighty may listen to the prayers of the faithful in the land & direct their counsels for good & that the designs of ambitious & selfish politicians who would dismember our glorious country may be frustrated, especially that our own State may act right & obtain the mead promised in the Bible to the peace maker.

A bright note in the life of Arlington at this time was the unexpected arrival of "Charlotte, Rooney & the Boy . . . without a nurse." Much to the delight of his grandmother, the "sweet little fellow" slept in her room. His father and mother going to Baltimore for a visit, he was entirely in the care of his grandmother. Thus occupied she could for a while at least forget her anxieties and the clouds which were gathering.

From his post in far-off Texas Colonel Lee had written his wife of the great excitement in that state, and finally of the secession. Pondering all these things, Mrs. Lee asked herself what this might mean to her husband, an officer in the army of the United States. If it should mean war, what then? Her heart was heavy.

Shortly after the secession of Texas Lee was ordered to report to General Winfield Scott, commander in chief of the United States army. In compliance with this order he immediately set out for Washington, reaching Arlington on March 1,

## Mrs. Robert E. Lee

1861. Though the air was tense, there was no outward change in the life at Arlington. The family met as usual for breakfast, and afterward went into the family sitting room, where Colonel Lee read family prayers.

"Arlington," Mrs. Lee writes, "was never more beautiful than it was that spring." It was a joy to the family to be together, and no mention was made of the gathering clouds. "When," she writes, "my husband was summoned to Washington, where every motive and argument was used to induce him to accept the command of the Army destined to invade the South, he was enabled to resist them all, even the sad parting words of his old Commander."

When he returned to Arlington from Washington on the afternoon of April 14, it was evident to Mrs. Lee that he was greatly disturbed even before he told her of the fall of Fort Sumter.

From Richmond there came shortly enthusiastic letters from friends telling of the wild demonstrations of delight with which the news had been received there. But there was no joy at Arlington. Lee knew what this portended. The day after the fall of Fort Sumter Lincoln issued his proclamation calling on the several states for seventy-five thousand militia for ninety days' service. The wording of this proclamation was such that an immediate decision was forced on the border states. These states had

# *War*

*When the Guns at Fort Sumter Spoke*

held off from the conflict, hoping there would be no war.

But the guns of Fort Sumter had spoken, and the President had answered with his proclamation. Virginia no longer hesitated. Her answer was not a compliance with Lincoln's call for militia; it was secession. With the secession of Virginia the hour had struck for Colonel Robert E. Lee, U. S. A. On the morning of April 19 he went on business to Alexandria, where he heard the news which he had hoped never to hear. As he rode back to Arlington over the route he had traveled so often, up the quiet hills to his home, he knew that, much as he loved the

## Mrs. Robert E. Lee

Union, if it were true that Virginia had seceded he could take no part in the invasion of the Southern states. Entering the room in which his wife was seated, he handed her a copy of the *Alexandria Gazette*, which contained the fateful news. Even then he voiced the hope that there might be some mistake. By nightfall there was no alternative but to believe it. After supper and the usual evening prayers Colonel Lee left the family sitting room and went to his room upstairs.

In the room below sat his wife, mistress of Arlington in her own right. She had prayed earnestly that the politicians might be frustrated in their efforts to disrupt the nation. She had hoped that Virginia by some God-given faculty might be a peacemaker. But those prayers had not been answered. She had made no effort to influence her husband in the decision he was now called upon to make. This she felt was something between him and his God. Now her thoughts and prayers were all with him, as she heard him pace the floor in the room above. She finally heard him fall on his knees, and she silently joined her prayers with his. It was after midnight when her husband finally joined her and handed her his letter of resignation and also a letter he had written to General Scott. If she had any regrets for her husband's decision, neither then nor later did she ever utter them. Months later she wrote a friend, "My

*Christ Church, Alexandria, Virginia*
[Virginia Conservation Commission]

## Mrs. Robert E. Lee

husband has wept tears of blood over this terrible war, but as a man of honor and a Virginian, he must follow the destiny of his State." Yes, she understood. She loved these United States, but she could think of no necessity great enough to cause a man to draw his sword against his native state. Long afterward she wrote, "It was the severest struggle of his life, to resign a commission he had held for 30 years." To Mildred Mrs. Lee wrote:

> With a sad heavy heart, my dear child, I write, for the prospects before us are sad indeed & as I think both parties are wrong in this fratricidal war, there is nothing comforting even in the hope that God may prosper the right, for I see no *right* in the matter. We can only pray that in his mercy he will spare us.

On Sunday morning, April 21, Lee, accompanied by one of his daughters, went into Alexandria to attend service at Christ Church. At Arlington Mrs. Lee, as was her custom when unable to attend church, gathered members of the family and some of the house servants around her. She read the Order of the Morning Service from the Episcopal prayer book, and the psalm in which her mother had found such comfort.

That Sunday afternoon was the last that Lee was ever to spend at Arlington. On Monday morning, at the request of the governor of Virginia, he went into Alexandria and took the train for Richmond.

# War

As he kissed his wife good-by that morning, little did either of them realize that fifteen months must pass before they would meet again.

Lee knew that if hostilities came a war would bring Arlington into the Union lines—that was inevitable. Still, such was his confidence in the ability of his wife that he left it for her to take the necessary action in case of war. It was one of the highest tributes he ever paid her. All around her were the things of hallowed memory which, during the days of General and Mrs. Washington, had graced Mount Vernon. What of them? Would they be destroyed and Arlington confiscated? Though Mary Custis Lee thought much of her forebears and held many loving traditions of them, she gave no thought to the toll war might require of her.

Mrs. Lee stayed on at Arlington with her daughters, and she was joined by Custis, who had been stationed at Fort Washington. She was loath to leave her home; indeed, she would not allow herself to feel that it would be necessary for her to leave, and she busied herself with her flowers and her garden. Her letters to her husband said nothing of anxiety, but spoke of what her daughters were doing and the beauties of the spring at Arlington, with no mention of an impending war. But her husband's letters to her were begging her to leave. From Richmond, on April 26, he wrote: "I am very anxious

# Mrs. Robert E. Lee

*The "Long Bridge," Which Extended from the District of Columbia to the Virginia Side of the Potomac*
[Photograph by United States Army Signal Corps]

about you. You will have to move and make arrangements to go to some point of safety which you must select. The Mount Vernon plate and pictures ought to be secured.... War is inevitable and there is no telling when it will burst around you."

Though her husband had tried to prepare her for the worst, Mrs. Lee seemed unable to realize the actual state of affairs. But she was rudely aroused one morning by the unexpected arrival of a young cousin, William Orton Williams. He was attached to General Scott's office in Washington and was a frequent visitor at Arlington, where he was treated as a son of the house. When he entered the room where Mrs. Lee sat quietly painting, she was startled by his expression. Almost without a greeting he told

# War

her the enemy was preparing to cross the "long bridge" on the next day and take possession of the heights around Arlington. Never doubting that General Scott had sent the young messenger, though he did not say so, she now felt that immediate action was necessary.

The family plate, the Washington letters and papers, some Washington jewelry, and especially prized mementos were packed and sent into Alexandria to be forwarded to Richmond.

After a sleepless night Mrs. Lee began to consider the movements of herself and her daughters. The idea of leaving Arlington "could scarcely be endured." Looking from her window upon scenes so dear to her, she was surprised to see young Orton approaching the house. Entering her room he told her that the movement of the troops was postponed, that there was no need for haste, though the movement would certainly be made, and that she had best prepare for it. Though Mrs. Lee's "sanguine spirit hoped the evil day would not come," yet she commenced to set her house in order.

The portraits and other paintings of value were taken from their frames and sent to Ravensworth, together with the camp bed and equipment which had belonged to Washington. In the garret, as was customary, were laid away the blankets, curtains, and carpets. The more valuable books were placed in two locked closets, and in another closet on the stairway were packed the engravings and various other treasures. The Cincinnati and State china from Mount Vernon was carefully packed in boxes and stored in the cellar.

Of what she had done Mrs. Lee wrote her husband on May 9:

I suppose ere this, dear Robert, you have heard of the arrival of our valuables in Richmond. We have sent many others to Ravensworth & all our wine & stores, pictures, piano etc. I was very unwilling to do this; but Orton was *so* urgent & even intimated that the day was fixed to take possession of these heights, that I did not feel it was prudent to risk articles that could never be replaced. Aunt Maria has been very kind in offering us an asylum there & in taking care of all our things.... I sent the girls up last evening.... I thought they could return if all was quiet. Custis was not ready to go; so I determined to remain with him, being very uneasy lest he should be arrested. I begin now to think, though it is all suspicion, that Orton was made the tool of some of the authorities in Washington to alarm us, either to bring you out to defend your home or get us out of the house. They are anxious at present to keep up appearances & would gladly, I believe, have a pretext to invade.... All day yesterday Gov. steamers were going up to Georgetown—transports, steam tugs & all kinds of crafts. Rumor Harpers Ferry is to be taken. Custis astonishes me with his calmness; with a possibility of having his early & beautiful home destroyed, [and with] the present necessity of abandoning it, he never indulges

## War

in invectives or a word of reflection on the cruel course of the Administration. He leaves that for his Mamma & sisters.

May 12 finds her still at Arlington: "This is a lovely morning, I never saw the country more beautiful, perfectly radiant. The yellow jessamine in full bloom & perfuming all the air, but a deathlike stillness prevails everywhere, you hear no sounds from Washington."

But she was not to enjoy the beauty of Arlington for long. The Federals came now and occupied the hills of Arlington. Leave she must; but, as she wrote to General Winfield Scott, "Were it not that I would not add one feather to his load of care, nothing would induce me to abandon my home. Yours in sorrow and sadness." Bidding good-by to the weeping servants, especially Nurse, she left not as one in flight, but rather did she go as a *grande dame* starting on a round of visits. There was no haste, though the first battalions of the army of the North had swept into the District of Columbia, and the first campfires had been lighted among the oaks of Arlington.

What were her thoughts as she stood on the portico at Arlington, ready to enter the carriage which was to take her to Ravensworth? Distinctly now she could hear the beating of the drums across the river in Washington. As she cast a fleeting glance across the Potomac to the capital of the United States did

# Mrs. Robert E. Lee

*Washington, D.C., as Seen from the Grounds of Arlington*
[Photograph by United States Army Signal Corps]

she remember that the man who had reared her father as his own son was called the "Father of his Country"? Did she call to mind that it was largely through his efforts that these United States had come into being; that it was the grandmother of her father who had given largely of her personal fortune that the soldiers of the Revolutionary army might be clothed and fed?

Arlington never looked lovelier than when she turned for a last glance. Lilacs, crocuses, lilies of the valley, and other spring flowers in luxuriant bloom filled the air with their sweet perfume; the first roses of the season were just appearing; the peonies were in all their splendor. All had been planted by her

# War

mother and for years nourished by her, in a garden laid out by her father's hand.

The house and grounds were left in charge of the faithful overseer. Every morning the great bar was removed and the door flung open in hospitable welcome. At night the door was again barred with the same scrupulous care that had attended this formal ceremony when the family had retired to their rooms in the uneventful days before the clarion trumpet of war had sounded the death of tranquillity and domesticity in Virginia.

The walks were cleaned, the gardens cleared and trimmed, as if in preparation for the return of the mistress.

But this was for a time all too brief. Shortly the stately mansion that had formerly known no harsher sounds than the strains of sweet music or the voices of children in innocent frolic resounded to the clank of saber and accouterments and the heavy tread of cavalry-booted officers. The quiet, gentle life which the place had formerly known gave way to the roughness of a military camp.

Rumors of all this reached Mrs. Lee; and now her greatest anxiety was for the servants, who had been a responsibility of her father and mother, and later hers. She knew them all by name. Because they had never made decisions for themselves, she thought of them now as helpless. So she dispatched a letter

## Mrs. Robert E. Lee

to the commander of the Federal forces at Arlington and received the following courteous answer:

>Headquarters, Department Northeastern Virginia,
>Arlington, May 30, 1861.

Mrs. R. E. Lee.

Madam: Having been ordered by the Government to relieve Major-General Sanford in command of this Department, I had the honor to receive this morning your letter of today addressed to him at this place. With respect to the occupation of Arlington by the United States troops I beg to say it has been done by my predecessor with every regard for the preservation of the place. I am here temporarily in camp on the grounds, preferring this to sleeping in the house under the circumstances which the painful state of the country places me in with respect to these properties. I assure you it will be my earnest endeavor to have all things so ordered that on your return you will find things as little disturbed as possible. In this I have the hearty concurrence of the courteous, kind-hearted gentleman in the immediate command of the troops quartered here who lives in the lower part of the house to insure its being respected. Everything has been done as you desire with respect to your servants, and your wishes, so far as they have been known or could have been understood, have been complied with. When you desire to return, every facility will be given you to do so. I trust, Madam, you will not consider it an intrusion when I say I have the most sincere sympathy for your distress, and so far as compatible with my duty, I shall always be ready to do whatever may alleviate it. I have the honor to be, very respectfully,

>Your most obedient servant, I. McDowell.

# *War*

P.S. I am informed it was the order of the general in chief if the troops on coming here should have found the family in the house, that no one should enter it, but that a guard should be placed for its protection.

Mrs. Lee's stay at Ravensworth was not for long. Her cousin Mr. John Goldsborough, being most anxious about her safety, had telegraphed Lee, urging that arrangements be made for Mrs. Lee to go south. He felt that as the wife of General Lee she and her daughters were in danger while they were in such close proximity to the enemy's lines. Lee felt, too, that Mrs. Fitzhugh might be in danger of reprisals if it were known by the Federal government that Mrs. Lee was her guest; he therefore urged her to go to the "upper country," which she did. Leaving Ravensworth she stopped for a few days at Chantilly, the home of the widow of her uncle Calvert Stuart. Another refugee at Chantilly at this time wrote in her diary:

June 6. . . . Mrs. Genl. Lee has been with us for several days. She is on her way to the lower country, and feels that she has left Arlington for an indefinite period. They removed their valuables, silver, etc., but the furniture is left behind. I never saw her more cheerful, and seems to have no doubt of our success.

Mrs. Lee did not go to the "lower country"; but just two months after her husband had bidden her

## Mrs. Robert E. Lee

good-by she arrived at Kinloch, the home of her cousin Mr. Edward Turner in Fauquier County, the "upper country." Notwithstanding her husband's relief at knowing that she was safely within the Southern lines, he was distressed, as he wrote her, because "Your future arrangements are the source of much anxiety to me. . . . There is no saying when you can return to our home or what may be its condition when you return. What, then, can you do in the meantime? To remain with friends may be incumbent, and where can you go?" Thus the heiress of Arlington became a wanderer, with no place to call home. Such are the exigencies of war! But there was no lack of invitations from friends, urging her to come to them.

Early in August Mrs. Lee crossed the Blue Ridge into Clarke County. She stopped for a few days with her cousin Miss Mary Meade, whose home was near White Post, and finally found sanctuary at Audley, the home of the widow of her cousin Lorenzo Lewis. Mrs. Lee had many friends and relatives in Clarke County—some whose homes were there; others refugeeing from the "low country." All were eager to see her, not only for the love they bore her, but also because of the admiration they felt for her husband, who was indeed glad, as he wrote, that "you are enabled to see so many of your friends."

# War

During the months since Mrs. Lee had left Arlington her arthritis had greatly increased; but brave, unselfish Christian that she was, she minimized her sufferings in her letters to her husband and made no mention of them to those around her. She talked often, though, of her wish to go from Audley to the Hot Springs in Bath County, and finally mentioned her desire to her husband in one of her letters. He rather advised against it, as he felt that it would be cool and damp in the mountains and past the season when she could be comfortable. But Mrs. Lee was not to be daunted. She remembered how in the past she had benefited by her trip to the mineral springs in Virginia, and she was most anxious now to do everything possible for the improvement of her health. So she went ahead with her plans, awaiting only the arrival at Audley of her youngest son, Robert; for General Lee felt that if she were determined to make the trip, Robert should accompany his mother and his sister Mary. The summer had passed into September before the final arrangements for the trip were completed.

While visiting among her friends Mrs. Lee had busied herself knitting cotton socks for her husband. Now, as cold weather approached, hearing from General Lee of the scant clothing of many of the men, who were sleeping on the ground in the rain, she began knitting woolen socks for these needy

## Mrs. Robert E. Lee

Confederate soldiers. The first of the many she was to knit were sent early in October, and on October 7, 1861, General Lee wrote:

> Your letter of the 2nd, with the yarn socks, four pairs, was handed to me.... As I found Perry in desperate need, I bestowed a couple of pairs on him as a present from you.... The others I suppose will fall to the lot of Meredith, into the state of whose hose I have not yet enquired.

Perry was one of the Arlington servants who had formerly waited in the dining room; Meredith, now Lee's cook, was a servant from the "White House."

As the autumn days grew colder Mrs. Lee realized that she must soon leave the springs and make some plans for the winter. Her husband thought that it might be advisable "to try a warm climate for your rheumatism," and suggested that she and the girls go to the Carolinas or Georgia. Mrs. Lee very naturally wished to go to Richmond that she might be near her husband; but this the General discouraged, fearing that "our enemies will make a vigorous move against Richmond."

It was finally decided that she should go to Shirley, that home of the Carters on the James River, where she and her daughters had been urged to come. This, however, was considered only a temporary arrangement until more definite plans could be made for the winter. Early in November Mrs. Lee was

## War

cheered by hearing that General Lee was in Richmond, and that he was planning a visit of a night and a day at Shirley. But she was not to see him. Instead she received his letter saying

> Saturday evening I tried to get down to you to spend Sunday, but could find no government boat going down. . . . I then went to the stable and got out my horse, but it was near night then and I was ignorant both of the road and distance and I gave it up. . . . I was obliged to be here Monday, and as it would have consumed all Sunday to go and come, I have remained for better times. . . . I will come, however, wherever you are, either Shirley or the "White House."

The day after this letter was written, Lee was ordered to South Carolina; and Mary Lee, who had come to Shirley with hopes high at the thought of seeing her husband, had no sight of him, instead only a letter bidding her good-by. Writing to his daughter Mildred, who was at school in Winchester, he says: "I was unable to see your poor Mother when in Richmond. Before I could get down I was sent off here."

Christmas found Mrs. Lee and her daughters at the "White House," the plantation belonging to her son Fitzhugh. This first Christmas away from Arlington, her beloved home in the clutches of the enemy, found her heart heavy indeed, with her husband and son at the battle front. But her letter to

# Mrs. Robert E. Lee

*"White House," Virginia, as It Looked in 1861
before Its Destruction during the Civil War*
[Virginia Historical Society]

her husband told how the day had been spent, of her joy that Fitzhugh was able to be at home for the holiday, and of others of the family circle who were there, for Mary and Robert had joined the family.

Early in March General Lee was recalled to Richmond "and was assigned, on the 13th of March under the direction of the President, to the conduct of the military operations of all the armies of the Confederate States." Mrs. Lee was still at the "White House," with no definite plans. General Lee, being very anxious about her, writes: "Write me your views. If you think it best for you to come to Richmond, I can soon make arrangements for your com-

# War

fort and shall be very glad of your company and your presence."

Mrs. Lee's youngest son, Robert, early in 1861, had wished to join the army. To this his father would not consent, feeling that the boy was far too young and that he should continue his studies at the University of Virginia. Now, a year later, he no longer withheld his consent, and Robert went off to join the Rockbridge Artillery. "I hope our son will do his duty and make a good soldier," Lee wrote to his wife.

Mrs. Lee decided to continue at the "White House"; but on May 11 and even before this the Federals had come dangerously close to the plantation, and her friends had urged her to leave. It had been necessary for her to abandon Arlington to the enemy, and now her son's plantation was threatened also. Such was her courage that, left to her own devices, she would doubtless have stayed and held the plantation against McClellan and his army; but realizing the embarrassment that such action on her part would cause her husband she consented to leave the "White House" and seek refuge at the home of a neighbor. Before going she wrote and had attached to the front door the appeal:

Northern soldiers who profess to reverence Washington, forbear to desecrate the home of his first married life, the property of his wife, now owned by her descendants.

A Granddaughter of Mrs. Washington.

## Mrs. Robert E. Lee

Shortly after her arrival at the house where she was to take refuge, a Federal officer with a detachment was sent to search the house. This Mrs. Lee regarded as a great indignity. While the party searched, she wrote to "the General in Command":

> Sir: I have patiently & humbly submitted to the search of my house by men under your command, who are satisfied that there is nothing here which they want; all the plate & other valuables have long since been removed to Richmond & are now beyond the reach of Northern marauders who may wish for their possession.
>
> Wife of Robert Lee, General C. S. A.

This letter she sent by the officer in command of the searching party.

A few days later two Federal officers rode to the house where Mrs. Lee was visiting and asked to see her. They had come, they said, with a message from General Porter, who desired that they tell her of "his desire to assure her proper care and protection with as little of constraint to her wishes and movements as might be compatible with her position inside the Federal lines."

That the granddaughter of Martha Washington and the daughter of the adopted son of Washington should be offered care and protection on her native heath by Federal officers was regarded by Mrs. Lee as an indignity, and her feelings were expressed to the officers in no uncertain terms. They were

# War

somewhat abashed by both her manner and her words, but they assured her that it was the desire of McClellan that she be given every possible protection until she could get through the lines. Mrs. Lee had no desire to get through the lines at this time; her desire was to return to the "White House." This the officers told her she was free to do, provided that she had an escort. The idea of being escorted by Federal soldiers was most abhorrent to Mrs. Lee; she wished no sight of them. The officers explained to her that the country was full of ignorant soldiers who would respect neither her sex nor her station and might cause her great embarrassment. This was a phase of war with which Mrs. Lee had not reckoned; when she realized its possible dangers, she very willingly consented to the posting of a guard. This situation became so irksome to her that she finally left the vicinity of the Federal camps and journeyed up the Pamunkey to Marlbourne, the estate of Edmund Ruffin, the famous agriculturist, the soldier who fired the first gun at Fort Sumter. It was not long before the Federal camps, by reason of their changing line, were in close proximity to Marlbourne. The situation was far more unpleasant than it had been before, as the colonel in command was suspicious and very confident that Mrs. Lee would find some means to report to the Confederates concerning movements of his command.

## Mrs. Robert E. Lee

The decision as to when she should come to Richmond had been left to her. She now decided that she would no longer remain within the enemy's lines. It was, of course, necessary that General Lee secure permission from the Union commander for her to pass through the lines. As soon as it could be arranged, the permission was granted by McClellan. Major W. Roy Mason was sent by General Lee to McClellan's headquarters to meet her. McClellan himself awaited her there, receiving her with due honor and treating her with every courtesy. In the carriage in which Major Mason had come, she drove with him to Gooch's farm, where General Lee was waiting to welcome her. He found that in the fifteen months that had passed since he had kissed her good-by that April day, her physical condition had grown much worse. Continual moving from place to place, arthritis, and suspense had aged and crippled her. It was only with the greatest difficulty that she was able to walk at all.

Now for a short time the Lees enjoyed such happiness as they had not enjoyed for many months. They were together, And how thankful Mrs. Lee was! A husband and three sons had all been spared to her! With what satisfaction General Lee tasted the joys of domestic life, which he loved so well! The girls were all there; also Robert, who, because of some minor sickness, was at home on furlough.

# War

But only for a short time did this happy state continue. Robert, being much better, returned to his command. The army moved northward, and Lee must lead it. So again he and his wife said good-by, leaving "the rest in the hands of God."

The homes of her friends were always open to Mrs. Lee. Now, with her husband away, there was no longer any reason for her to remain in Richmond; so in a few days she was out in Hanover County at Hickory Hill, the home of the Wickhams. After a short visit there Mrs. Lee and her daughters went to Warren County springs in North Carolina. It was while she was there that the family circle was broken; for Anne Custis Lee, then twenty-three years old, and the daughter to whom General Lee was especially devoted, died at the springs on October 20, 1862. General Lee was unable to come to his wife; he could only write:

I cannot express the anguish I feel at the death of our dear Annie. To know that I shall never see her again on earth, that her place in our circle, which I always hoped one day to enjoy, is forever vacant, is agonizing in the extreme. But God, in this as in all things, has mingled mercy with the blow, in selecting the one best prepared to leave us. May you be able to join me in saying "His will be done." . . . I know how much you will be grieved and how much she will be mourned. I wish I could give you any comfort, but beyond our hope in the great mercy of God, and the belief that he takes her at the time and place

## Mrs. Robert E. Lee

when it is best for her to go, there is none. May that same mercy be extended to us all, and may we be prepared for his summons.

Mrs. Lee did not remain long in North Carolina after the death of Annie. She was anxious to be in Richmond, feeling that there might be an opportunity to see her husband and knowing that it would be a comfort to both of them to be together in this great sorrow which had come to them. Mrs. Lee had no home to which to come. She therefore accepted the very urgent invitation of Mr. and Mrs. James Caskie to become their guest until she could make arrangements about a house and furniture. Norvell Caskie was the devoted friend of Agnes Lee, and the two young girls had delightful times together. Mrs. Lee's heart was often very heavy when she thought of the life of her daughters now, so different from that to which they had been born. No home to call their own, Mary was now visiting at Cedar Grove, the plantation of Doctor and Mrs. Richard Stuart in King George County, and Mildred had remained in North Carolina and was at boarding school in Raleigh. It was therefore a great pleasure to Mrs. Lee to see how thoroughly Agnes was enjoying her visit with Norvell Caskie.

Her greatest joy at this time was the fact that her husband was able to join her for a short while at the Caskies'. In the society of Agnes and Norvell and

# *War*

the admiring circle of young people who flocked to the house when he was there, General Lee, who greatly enjoyed young people, found relaxation from the terrific strain he was under.

At Christmas Mrs. Lee and Agnes went to Hickory Hill, the home of Mr. W. F. Wickham, in Hanover County, where they were joined by several other members of the family. Mrs. Lee, in an effort to hide her own mental and physical suffering, threw herself wholeheartedly into the preparations for Christmas and asked that she might be allowed to make a dessert which she knew to be a favorite with the master of the house. She did not meet with complete success; for Mr. Wickham, used to a more generous table than Mrs. Lee had allowed herself, secretly confided to a member of the family that "Mary had been too sparing with the sugar." After Christmas Mrs. Lee and Agnes returned to the Caskies'. Here they remained until June, when they again went to Hickory Hill to be with Fitzhugh (Rooney), who had been wounded at the battle of Brandy Station. Robert, the youngest son, now a private in the company of his brother, had been detailed to travel with his brother to Hickory Hill and to care for him during his convalescence. It was a solace to General Lee, who was on his way to Gettysburg, to know that Mrs. Lee was surrounded by so many members of the family.

## Mrs. Robert E. Lee

But any peace or enjoyment that the family might have felt was rudely dispelled by the capture of Rooney. Notwithstanding the remonstrance of both his wife and his mother, he was taken from his sick bed by a Federal raiding party which had come to Hickory Hill for that purpose. The carriage and horses of Mr. Wickham were also commandeered; and Rooney, on a mattress, was placed in the carriage and taken to Fort Monroe, where he was imprisoned. Though deeply distressed and greatly worried over the condition of her wounded son, Mrs. Lee forgot herself in her efforts to comfort the young wife of Rooney. But the shock of her son's capture and her anxiety about his health greatly impaired her own health, and she was now so crippled that she could move about only on crutches. Her friends felt that a visit to one of the mineral springs of Virginia might prove beneficial to her. She was anxious to go, but not for herself alone. She was greatly worried about the health of Charlotte Wickham Lee. Charlotte, never strong, was now in wretched health owing to her great anxiety about her husband. Seeking to arouse her interest, Mrs. Lee suggested that Charlotte select the springs to which they should go, and her choice was the Hot Springs in Alleghany County. Travel, difficult for anyone at this time, was especially so for Mrs. Lee, crippled as she was. It was therefore decided that the most

## *War*

comfortable way for her to make the trip would be in a boxcar fitted up as a bedroom. While the arrangements were being made, she went to Ashland to spend a few days with her old friend Mrs. John Peyton McGuire. In those happy days, which now seemed so long ago, they had been neighbors; for the Episcopal High School, of which the Reverend John Peyton McGuire was the head, was near Arlington.

The trip to Hot Springs was made in great comfort, the train traveling slowly. Since engines at that time had not attained any great speed, the sliding doors were kept open, framing pictures of great natural beauty.

Charlotte showed no improvement, and the doctor who was attending her, Mrs. Lee wrote, "pronounced the Hot a bad place for her, so she has gone to the Bath Alum with Annie Leigh and has been sick ever since she got there."

Although she "took the baths most faithfully every day," there was no visible improvement in Mrs. Lee's condition, and she therefore decided to "try the Warm" Springs. From there she wrote: ". . . have taken rooms here for a month. We have a delightful cottage with a portico all around, covered with beautiful vines & roses & looking upon a meadow full of haycocks & a clear stream running thro it & very near the bath, which is one of the finest in the world . . . mountains all around."

# Mrs. Robert E. Lee

Mrs. Lee was greatly cheered by the news she had about Rooney. Writing Mildred, she says:

We have heard from Custis that Rooney was doing very well, walking about on crutches & there is some prospect of his being exchanged. Indeed, I wish he could be, on Charlotte's account, as her health is very delicate. . . . Rob has gone back to the army & is very well; he went on horseback & called at Hickory Hill. . . . They write word they miss us all dreadfully there & long for our return, only hoping the young ladies will not have as much work to do next time.

Though only the middle of August, there was "a sudden change in the weather & it is now as cool here as October, but bright & delightful." But there were open fires in their rooms, and Mrs. Lee and Agnes busied themselves sewing. "Agnes has just finished her domestic; she made it in the garibaldi style, only very close around the neck & it looks very well."

Late in October Mrs. Lee and her daughters returned to Richmond. Mrs. Lee rented a house on Leigh Street, far too small to accommodate the entire family, but the only one available. It was a source of genuine regret to both General and Mrs. Lee that the house was so small that there was room only for Mrs. Lee and her two daughters, Agnes and Mildred, and that Charlotte had to find quarters elsewhere, at least half a mile distant. General Lee, hearing of the arrangement, wrote on October 28, 1863:

# War

I am glad you are so pleased with your house and am truly grateful to the kind friends who have aided you in possessing & furnishing it. I am very sorry that it is too small to accommodate Charlotte. It takes from me half the pleasure of your accommodation, as I wish to think of you all together; and in her feeble condition and separation from her Fitzhugh, none can sympathize or attend to her as yourself. . . . I am glad you have some socks for the army, send them to me. . . . Tell the girls to send all they can. I wish they could make some shoes too. We have thousands of barefooted men.

General Lee's friends were greatly worried that his family should be so uncomfortably located; but the capital of the Confederacy was so crowded that it was almost impossible to find a house of any kind. Mrs. Lee, knowing the difficulty that others were experiencing, considered herself fortunate in having obtained a dwelling place of any sort. The city council, hearing of the limited quarters of the Lees, proposed to buy a house and present it to General Lee; but to this the General would not consent. Although the house was small and the furnishings scant, the family found enjoyment in having a place to call home. There was great pride on Agnes's part that there were "enough glasses to go around" when company came to dinner.

Custis was also in Richmond, occupying a post of honor as one of the aids to the President. Though it was something of a comfort to his mother to know

## Mrs. Robert E. Lee

that he was not in danger, he was very unhappy. His desire was to see field service, and he envied his brothers and kinsmen who had participated in the battles of the Army of Northern Virginia. During one of the rare visits that he was able to pay his mother, he told her of his feeling of frustration. Although she sympathized with him, her sympathy was not for him alone, but also for the many others who, she knew, felt as Custis did.

Rooney was still in prison. Even as she prayed for him she remembered all those other mothers whose sons were in prison.

The family circle had been broken during the past years. Her daughter Annie was in a grave in North Carolina; but her soldier husband and sons had been spared. Each day brought news of some relative or friend fallen in battle. Though eager to express her sympathy, it was not always easy to get a message to those whose husbands and sons had paid the supreme sacrifice; but whenever a messenger was found to carry a letter, a word of sympathy was sent.

It was at this time that Mrs. Lee realized that Arlington was lost to her and to her son Custis, to whom her father had meant it to go after her death. Never again could the family expect to return to it. Under a law passed by Congress in June, 1862, Arlington had been confiscated by the Federal government. This law levied a direct tax on real estate

## *War*

"in the insurrectionary districts within the United States," and required that such a tax be paid by the owner in person. It was, of course, impossible for either General or Mrs. Lee to appear before the Commission "in person." If Mrs. Lee's health had been better and she had been physically able to make the trip to Alexandria, it is possible that she would have made the effort to pass through the enemy's lines, and appear before the Commission; for she was a woman of undaunted courage, fearing neither officer nor private of the Federal forces. She felt that as the grandchild of Martha Washington, whose money had done so much for the country in its infancy, her property rights should be respected. But as the trip was impossible, a cousin appeared before the Commission in her behalf and tendered the taxes imposed on Arlington. The Commissioners refused to accept the money, and were now, so Mrs. Lee was informed, prepared to issue a tax title to the United States. So the war took another toll.

But none of these things were mentioned by Mrs. Lee to her husband when he returned to Richmond on December 7, 1863. This was not a time, she felt, to dwell on family troubles. She was shocked to see how her husband had aged. He had entered the war in the full vigor of robust manhood, and now his hair and beard were white; and although he tried to hide his suffering from Mrs. Lee, sharp

## Mrs. Robert E. Lee

paroxysms of pain wrenched his left side. She was well-nigh desperate about his condition, her anxiety for him overshadowing any poignancy of grief she might have felt from the loss of Arlington.

The question which had brought General Lee to Richmond was one which required long conferences with President Davis. During his stay in Richmond he received every possible honor. The Confederate House of Representatives passed a resolution inviting him to have a seat on the floor. Because Mrs. Lee knew that such marks of esteem gratified him in his quiet way, she was glad to hear of any honors accorded. But it was the tribute paid him when he attended service at Saint Paul's that touched her most deeply. It was just a week after his arrival in Richmond, when he was attending Saint Paul's, that the congregation, at the conclusion of the service, remained in their pews, giving him a silent ovation as he walked slowly down the aisle bowing to friends and returning the salute of officers and soldiers.

General Lee's conferences with the President were drawn out until almost Christmas, and Mrs. Lee prayed that her husband would remain in Richmond until after yuletide. It was just ten days before Christmas when final decisions were reached. No battle was imminent. Surely, thought Mrs. Lee and many of his friends, General Lee will spend Christmas Day with his family, the first since 1859. But

# *War*

he deliberately sacrificed his desire to be with his wife that holyday in order to set an example of obedience to duty, and returned to camp. On Christmas Day a woman ravaged by sorrow and suffering, confined to a wheel chair, sat and knitted that she might add to the comfort of somebody's boy, and as she knitted she wondered . . .

The day following Christmas, war took another toll; and to Rooney, behind prison bars, went the message that Charlotte had been unable to fight longer and, as a candle flickers out, had gone to her reward on December 26.

In the early months of 1864 both armies were mud-bound. All was quiet in both camps; and though this temporary cessation of hostilities may have proved irksome to the soldiers in camp, the "women who remembered in the night" thought of it as a time of thanksgiving.

To Mary Custis Lee it was a time of some contentment; her husband was called frequently to Richmond for conferences with the President, and there were hours between when he could be at home.

A visitor to Mrs. Lee in February says: "Her room was like an industrial school—everyone was busy. Her daughters were all there plying their needles, with several other ladies. . . . When we came out, someone said, 'Did you see how the Lees spend their time? What a rebuke to taffy parties!'"

## Mrs. Robert E. Lee

"Taffy parties" and "starvation parties" were the popular form of entertainment among the young people in Richmond at this time. The taffy parties were considered an extravagance by some, but the starvation parties were heartily approved. A group of young society women had organized a Starvation Club, the principal rule being that no refreshments should be served at the entertainments, which were held at private houses. Of these entertainments General Lee heartily approved. He is reported to have said, when told of them, "My boys must be entertained."

When General Lee came to Richmond in March, it was the Lenten season. Each morning at seven o'clock the rector of Saint Paul's held services in the lecture room of the church. The room was always crowded; old and young, grave and gay, collecting here soon after sunrise. It was impossible, of course, for Mrs. Lee to attend these services; but the Lee girls were always there, and so at this time they were accompanied each morning by their father. At home Mrs. Lee followed the services in the prayer book of the Episcopal Church. On their return from these early morning services the family would gather round the breakfast table. Though the coffee was "Confederate coffee," taken without sugar or cream because there was none, and the corn bread was eaten without butter, these meals were times of apparent

## *War*

cheerfulness. It meant so much to have husband and father at the foot of the table, and as yet war had caused no chairs to be counted empty around this table; for though father and brothers were in constant danger, so far they had all been spared. The talk dealt with pleasant things. There was the discussion of the address which had been delivered by the rector, of which Mrs. Lee wanted to hear, and there were inquiries about which of their friends and kinsmen they had seen among the officers and soldiers who had attended the service.

Before General Lee returned to the army he told Mrs. Lee something of the storm which he feared would soon burst upon Richmond. He was using every means in his power to increase and strengthen his army to meet the storm.

It would have been a relief to Mrs. Lee at this time if it had been possible for her to take part in the work of the women of the Confederacy; but with the same fortitude with which she had met every other emergency in life, she met this challenge and answered it. Though confined to a wheel chair, her hands were never idle. They seemed dedicated to the cause of the Confederate soldier. She was constantly occupied with knitting socks for the army. During the months of March, April, and May she sent over two hundred pairs of socks for distribution to the Stonewall Brigade.

## *Mrs. Robert E. Lee*

The Lees had been married thirty-three years. Even in the thick of battle Mrs. Lee's husband did not forget the anniversary. On June 30 he wrote his wife:

Do you recollect what a happy day thirty-three years ago this was? How many hopes and pleasures it gave birth to. God has been very merciful and kind to us.... I pray that he may continue his mercy and blessings to us and give us a little peace and rest together in this world, and finally gather us and all he has given us around His throne in the world to come.

In spite of the loving ministrations of her daughters and every possible attention from her friends, Mrs. Lee was very ill during the summer of 1864. General Lee, unable to come to her, was greatly worried and most anxious for her comfort and welfare. This was a period of universal scarcity of medicine in the Confederacy, and the sick suffered for want of even the simplest remedies. All medicine that could be procured must be for the use of the hospitals. Thus Mrs. Lee was unable to have the remedies which might have helped her. Not only was she in need of medicine, but she also needed nourishing food, such as fresh fruits, vegetables, pure milk, and butter. Food of all kinds was growing very scarce in Richmond, and General Lee was most anxious for Mrs. Lee to leave. "I do not see how you will be able to live in Richmond; you had better be

# War

looking out for some part of the country where there are some provisions. How Custis, yourself, 3 girls, Billy, and Sally can live long on ¼ lb. of bacon and 1½ pt. of meal I cannot see." He felt not only that she was in need of food but also that she needed the bracing and healthful mountain air and the healing waters of some mineral spring; but she dared not leave Richmond for fear that she might be cut off and subjected to insurmountable difficulties in getting back home. To those friends who urged her to go she would ask, where but in Richmond was there any possibility of her seeing her husband.

She was finally prevailed upon to go to her friends the Cockes, whose home was beautiful Bremo on the James. It was a great relief to General Lee to know that she was there. He wrote:

"I am charmed with your description of the family at Bremo. I have always heard their hospitality etc. extolled; Gen'l Cocke has been proverbial for it all his life." Mary and Mildred were with their mother, and their father expressed his pleasure at their "enjoyment of the pure country air and the association of such kind friends."

With the coming of autumn Mrs. Lee's health showed great improvement, and against the wishes of her husband she returned to Richmond. He realized something of what the future held and feared that Richmond would be a very unsafe place

## Mrs. Robert E. Lee

for her; but she, knowing that only there was there a possibility of her seeing her husband, would not consider going elsewhere. She was able again to take up her knitting, and she was constantly occupied in knitting socks for the soldiers and induced all around her to do the same. In November she wrote her husband of the large supply she had ready to send. In acknowledgment, he wrote, "If two or three hundred would send an equal number, we should have a sufficiency."

Fitzhugh Lee, a nephew of General Lee's and a frequent visitor to the Lee home in Richmond, remembered Mrs. Lee seated in her chair busily knitting. In his book *General Lee* he says, in speaking of his uncle's wedding: "It is difficult to say whether she was more lovely on that memorable day . . . or after many years had passed, and she was seated in her large armchair in Richmond, almost unable to move . . . but busily engaged in knitting socks for sockless Southern soldiers." By December she had another supply of socks ready, and these were sent to her husband with a barrel of apples which had been sent to her by a friend in the country.

In 1861 Mr. John Stewart had offered a house which he owned on Franklin Street to General Lee for his military home. The offer was accepted, and the house was occupied by the General whenever he was in town and before Mrs. Lee came to make her

# War

*The Lee House on Franklin Street, Richmond, Virginia*
[Virginia Historical Society]

home in Richmond. The residence was also for a time occupied by General Custis Lee and "a merry party of young officers," who called it "The Mess." Sometime during 1864 General R. E. Lee leased the house as a home for Mrs. Lee. General Lee's office had been the small hall room on the second floor; this he continued to use as such after Mrs. Lee came to occupy the house. Mrs. Lee chose for her room the back room on the second floor, which opened out on a broad veranda.

## Mrs. Robert E. Lee

A very pretty story is told about the rent for this house. After the surrender, when General Lee gave up the house, he prepared to send to Mr. Stewart the rental; but before he could do this Mrs. Lee received a letter from Mr. Stewart, in which he said:

> I am not presuming upon your good opinion when I feel that you will believe me, first, that you and yours are heartily welcome to the house as long as your convenience leads you to stay in Richmond; and, next, that you owe me nothing, but if you insist on paying, that the payment must be in Confederate money, for which alone it was rented to your son. You must know how much gratification it is, and will afford me and my whole family during the remainder of our lives, to reflect that we have been brought into contact, and to know and appreciate you and all that are dear to you.

Christmas came. With a brave attempt at cheerfulness the Lee daughters decked the house with evergreens, arborvitae, cedar, and holly which had been brought to them by friends from their plantations. There was a great want of fuel in Richmond at this time; only in Mrs. Lee's sitting room was a fire kept burning.

Instead of the bountiful board around which the family had been accustomed to gather, they sat down to a scantily supplied Christmas table; but the same blessing which had preceded every meal in the days of bounty was asked now by Mrs. Lee: "God bless

## War

us and make us truly grateful for these and all thy mercies, and be pleased to continue them to us."

The house on Franklin Street was a veritable haven of hope for those who found their way there, and they were many. Though the furnishings were almost meager when compared with those in the homes of many of the Lees' friends and relatives in Richmond, and though the fare was of the simplest, people forgot such physical things in the presence of Mary Custis Lee; for her keen interest and sympathy proved an inspiration to many who were discouraged. From her lips there was never a word of regret for the sacrifices she had been called upon to make, nor a word of doubt as to the final outcome of the war. Though she never doubted the ability of the Confederate army to defend Richmond, she was heartsick when she thought of the lives that must be sacrificed. As she thought, she murmured a prayer for each of her soldiers, spared so far, but for how long she knew not.

For three long years, with more than a soldier's courage, Mrs. Lee had borne the hardest part—waiting at home. She had listened to the noise of guns, awaiting with blanched face but undaunted heart the news of battle after battle.

Those who came to Franklin Street in those anxious days of January found a woman of dauntless spirit, a woman trusting in a merciful God. She

## *Mrs. Robert E. Lee*

made no plans for the future; she relied on a higher power for guidance and protection.

While Mary Custis Lee sat in her wheel chair, knitting, or writing letters on any scraps of paper which might be available, or telling friends and relatives of their young sons whom she had seen, or writing some word of comfort to a family who had been called upon to sacrifice a loved one on the field of battle, near by, in the Capitol, the Congress discussed the creation of a new office—that of general in chief of all the armies of the Confederacy.

At the Presidential Mansion in Richmond Mrs. Jefferson Davis expressed bitter resentment at the proposed centralized command. She construed it as an attack on her husband, who, by virtue of his office as President, was the proper constitutional commander in chief.

The act creating the office was passed and approved by the President on January 23, 1864. Mr. Davis immediately named Robert E. Lee as commander in chief, and the Senate promptly confirmed his appointment.

Mrs. Lee heard the news of her husband's appointment with mingled emotions. She knew that his health was breaking under exposure and strain. Now this new office would make even greater demands upon an already overtaxed mind and body. General Lee faced a country denuded of men, swept

# *War*

*The Confederate Capitol at Richmond before the Civil War*
[Virginia Historical Society]

clean of supplies. The seed corn of the Confederacy had all been ground.

From her husband's letters Mrs. Lee realized that he was very apprehensive, expecting Grant to move against him at any time. Late in February he wrote her: "Should it be necessary to abandon our position to prevent surrender, what will you do? You must consider the question and make up your mind."

It seemed that Mary Custis Lee was always called upon to face alone the great revolutions in her life. But she did not think of herself as alone, but rather

## Mrs. Robert E. Lee

as treading the path of life with a simple reliance on divine guidance. No misfortune ever dimmed this light. The composure with which she faced the cataclysms of her life sprang from her abiding confidence in divine wisdom and trust in divine goodness.

She was deeply appreciative of any attentions bestowed on her husband. However simple the act, she considered only the impulse which prompted it. In January General Lee, while fronting the Army of the Potomac, wrote her:

> Yesterday afternoon three little girls walked into my room, each with a small basket. The eldest . . . carried some fresh eggs, laid by her own hens; the second, some pickles made by her Mother; the third, some popcorn grown in her own garden. They were accompanied by a young maid, with a block of soap made by her Mother. They were the daughters of Mrs. Nottingham, a refugee from Northampton County, who lived near Eastville, not far from "Old Arlington." The eldest of the girls, whose age did not exceed eight years, had a small wheel on which she spun for her Mother, who wove all the cloth for her two brothers—boys of twelve and fourteen years.

As soon as Mrs. Lee found someone who was going to Petersburg she sent the eldest of the little girls a package and wrote:

Richmond, March, 1865.

My dear little friend:

General Lee gives me such a fine account of your industry that I am tempted to send you this little basket of

## *War*

working materials, which I hope you will find useful in these hard times.

I have put in it a handkerchief for your Mamma, which she must use for my sake & I must thank you both for your kind attention to my husband.

>Yrs most truly,
>
>M. C. Lee.

In June, 1864, General Hunter, himself a Virginian, had bombarded and burned the Virginia Military Institute, the "West Point of the Confederacy." "V.M.I. shall never die" proved no idle boast; for although the results of twenty-five years of progress—buildings, equipment, a technical library second to none in the South, and the personal equipment and clothing of the corps—had gone up in smoke, the corps of cadets reassembled at Camp Lee, Richmond, Virginia, on October 1, 1864, since the buildings at Lexington, which were being rebuilt, were not yet completed. The corps was engaged only in military duties until December 28, 1864, when it was housed in the almshouse of Richmond, a structure which had been secured and remodeled. Academic duties were resumed, though under great difficulties. Among the cadets enrolled were sons of friends and relatives of the Lees. Mrs. Lee, hearing of the homesickness of two of her young friends, wrote to the superintendent, Colonel Francis Smith:

## *Mrs. Robert E. Lee*

Richmond, March 30th.

My dear Sir:

I write to beg the favour of you to allow my two young friends Peyton Skipwith & John Cocke of Bremo, if still with you, to visit us sometimes on Sunday, being the only day when we dine sufficiently early for them to return in time to the Institute. I shall take care that they attend church & shall be most happy if you will grant them permission to visit us.

I will also take this occasion to thank you for your care of our silver & papers & to enquire if you think they can remain perfectly safe where they are until the close of the war, as I should like to preserve the only relicks left us of our once happy home. It would give me great pleasure if you could call & see me when you come to town.

Yrs most truly & respectfully,

M. C. Lee.

The "relicks" to which Mrs. Lee referred were the "valuables" that, as she had written her husband, had been sent from Arlington to Richmond at the beginning of the war. Because of fear for their safety in Richmond, they had been sent to Lexington, where they had been buried.

In March General Lee was in Richmond for a short time. He had come to discuss with President Davis and the civil authorities the situation of the Confederacy. Of the three courses possible Lee felt that only one offered any possibility of military suc-

*Virginia Military Institute before and after Hunter's Raid during the Civil War*

[Courtesy of Colonel William Couper]

## Mrs. Robert E. Lee

cess, however slight. That was the abandonment of Richmond. But the President and his advisers regarded Richmond as a symbol: to lose the capital would mean the end.

The will of the civil authorities must be obeyed, so her husband told Mrs. Lee. There was now only one course left to the Army of Northern Virginia: they must fight where they stood. Mrs. Lee knew that her husband felt that the chance of holding Richmond was a forlorn hope, indeed. Heartsick at the thought of the lives which must be sacrificed, of the widows and orphans who would be the toll, she bade her husband good-by. In her bosom she bore the knowledge of the exhausted resources of the Confederacy, and that this would possibly be the last stand of the Army of Northern Virginia.

There was an increasing and often expressed doubt among those who came to visit her as to whether Richmond could hold against such increasing odds. Whatever feeling may have occupied the recesses of Mrs. Lee's heart, her answer was, "We have no right to doubt the mercy of God."

Sunday, April 2, dawned brightly. A soft haze rested over the city. No sound disturbed the stillness of the Sabbath morn save the music of the church bells. The story of that day has been repeated countless times. In St. Paul's Church, morning prayer over, the rector had started the celebration of the

## War

solemn communion service. A messenger was observed to enter and make his way up the aisle to the pew of President Davis, who was attending the service. He handed Mr. Davis a sealed package. The President rose and walked out of the church. What did it mean? No one in the congregation knew the secret of that sealed package. An uneasy whisper ran through the congregation. They seemed intuitively to feel what the message portended. General Lee's daughters, who were among the congregation, hurried home. They told their mother that rumor said Richmond could no longer be defended, that General Lee's lines had been broken. At first Mrs. Lee would give no credence to the rumor; later when friends brought her the news that the government was moving, that Richmond was indeed being evacuated, she realized that the worst had come. Through the day of excitement and anxiety, with friends asking where she would go and when, Mrs. Lee had no thought for herself nor of any danger in which she might be; her only thought was

*Jefferson Davis*

## Mrs. Robert E. Lee

for her husband. At this time she could give no thought to the symbols of glory and honor which were her husband's. Now she could count only the toll the years of war had taken.

There was no sleep for anyone in Richmond that night. Loud explosions rent the air; the sky was illuminated by burning houses; the sick and dying were carried into the streets. The gutters were filled with liquid fire where liquor had been emptied that it might not be available for invading troops; and the penitentiary opened its doors to its striped inmates. Through the windows of Mrs. Lee's room came the ribald song and the sobs of anguish; but through the sleepless nights and days that followed, Mary Custis Lee showed only a patient endurance and a noble calm, expressing anxiety only for "the brave soldiers who were fighting against such odds."

The next day, on looking from her window, she saw flying over the Capitol the flag of the United States, the flag of a country which owed its being to Washington. She had been brought up to love that flag. It was symbolic of so much to the family at Arlington. Now flying over what had been the capital of the Confederacy, it proclaimed to Mrs. Lee that there was little hope remaining of success for the Southern cause. Her heart was sad, for she could not then foresee the future in which there would be once more a united nation under that flag.

# *War*

*Northern Troops Entering Richmond*
[Courtesy of Virginia Historical Society

The army of occupation entered a burning city on Monday while a stricken people watched in terror for their coming. Richmond was in mourning. The shutters at 707 Franklin Street were barred. All over Richmond a brokenhearted people closed their windows and doors that they might shut out, as far as possible, all sights and sounds of a victorious enemy. Every house was as a house of death.

Mary Custis Lee was stunned. It was as if the way of her life had come to a blank wall. There seemed no path to travel on. Although she gave no thought to possible danger for herself, her friends were anxious lest the fires sweeping through Richmond should reach her home. An appeal was made

## Mrs. Robert E. Lee

by Miss Emily Mason to General Weitzel for an ambulance in which to move Mrs. Robert E. Lee to a place of safety, who, she said, "was an invalid, unable to walk, and that her house . . . was in danger of fire."

The request was readily granted, but Mrs. Lee refused to leave her home. Friends calling on her a few days after the evacuation found her busily engaged in her invalid chair, and very cheerful and hopeful. "The end is not yet," she said, as if to cheer those around her; "Richmond is not the Confederacy."

From her husband and sons she had had no word; for after the occupation all tidings from the Confederacy were cut off. Another Sabbath dawned: the church bells rang; the congregations gathered; the day passed quietly. Many had gone to bed; then suddenly the stillness of the evening was broken by the report of a cannon. From the window which looked toward Fort Jackson, Mrs. Lee could see the flash and smoke of cannon. Through the window came the sound of rapid footsteps and excited voices. "What do those guns mean?" Sad and almost hopeless voices would answer, "I do not know"; and then a voice sobbed as if from a broken heart, "They say General Lee has surrendered." Those who came to Franklin Street to offer sympathy, after authentic news of the surrender had reached Richmond,

# War

found a brave and patriotic woman whose mien was such that sympathy would have been an insult. To one of her visitors she is reported to have said, "General Lee is not the Confederacy; there is life in the old land yet."

It was the background and the middle distance which now made so fine the foreground of the life of Mary Custis Lee. As in painting, so in life: it is the middle distance which gives strength.

A few days after the surrender General Lee arrived in Richmond on Traveller, who had carried him so well

*General Lee at Home after the Surrender*
[Virginia Historical Society]

through the war. He came unattended save by five members of his staff. He had hoped to reach his home unnoticed and without parade, but he could not come unobserved. The news of his arrival

## Mrs. Robert E. Lee

quickly spread through the city, and crowds gathered in front of the house to receive him, cheering and waving their handkerchiefs.

As he dismounted from Traveller the crowd pressed around him, eager to shake his hand. It was more that of a welcome to a conqueror than to a defeated prisoner on parole. Mounting the steps to his home, General Lee raised his hat in response to the greeting of the crowd; then he entered the door, on the other side of which his wife and daughters were anxiously waiting to greet him.

Mrs. Lee's spirit had trod the way of General Lee's Gethsemane with him. Seated in her chair, she raised her eyes to her husband's, thinking she might read in them something of his inner thoughts. But if he suffered, no one could tell. His countenance wore the habitual calm, grave expression she had become accustomed to. As the first excitement of his return wore off, Mrs. Lee realized how her husband had aged under the strain to which he had been subjected. He seemed physically well, but he was quieter and more reserved with his friends. She realized, as she watched him, that he would require time and quiet in which to regain his strength. He who had always ministered to her now needed her gentle ministrations.

Two weeks after the surrender Mrs. Lee wrote to her cousin Miss Mary Meade:

# *War*

Richmond 23rd.

I have just heard, my dear cousin Mary, of an opportunity to Clarke [County] & write to tell you we are all well as usual, and thro' the mercy of God all spared thro' the terrible ordeal thro' which we have passed. I feel that I could have blessed God if those who were prepared had filled a soldier's grave. I bless Him that they are spared I trust for future usefulness to their poor unhappy country. My little Rob has not yet come in, but we have reason to think he is safe. Tho' it has not pleased Almighty God to crown our exertions with success in the way & manner we expected, yet we must still trust & pray not that *our will* but His may be done in Heaven & in earth. I could not begin to tell you of the startling events that have been crowded into the last few weeks. But I want you all to know that when Gen'l Lee surrendered, he had only 8 thousand 7 hundred muskets; that the enemy by their own account had nearly 80 thousand men well provisioned & equipped, while ours had been out 7 days with only 2 days rations; that they were fighting by day & marching all night without even time to parch their corn, their only food for several days; that even in this exhausted state they drove back hosts of the enemy, but could not follow up their advantage; that had Grant demanded *unconditional* surrender, they had determined to sell their lives as dearly as possible & cut their way thro' his encircling hosts; but the conditions he offered were so honourable, that Gen'l Lee decided it was wrong to sacrifice the lives of these brave men when no object could be gained by it. For my part it will always be a source of pride & consolation to me to know that all mine have perilled their lives, fortune & even fame in so holy a cause. We can hear nothing *certain*

# Mrs. Robert E. Lee

from the rest of the army or from our President. May God help and protect them. We can only pray for them. Our plans are all unsettled. Gen'l Lee is very busy settling up his army matters & then we shall *all* probably go to some of those empty places in the vicinity of the White House. Fitzhugh has gone on there to see what we can do; but this place is an utter scene of desolation. So is our whole country & the cruel policy of the enemy has accomplished its work too well. They have achieved by *starvation* what they never could win by their valor; nor have they taken a *single town* in the South, except Vicksburg, that we have not *evacuated*. Dear cousin, write me about you *all* & how you manage to *exist*. Would that I were able to help you. I do not think we shall be here very long; therefore, unless you can write *at once*, you had better wait till you hear from me again. The girls & the General unite in love. He is wonderfully well considering all he has endured. Nannie, Smith's wife is here & several of her boys who have come in.

Love to all friends Ever & affectionately yrs,

M. C. Lee.

# CHAPTER VI

# *Peace — at a Price*

Now that the war was over, General Lee was anxious to get away from Richmond, feeling that he should set an example by going to work. He wrote to General Long: "I am looking for some little, quiet home in the woods, where I can procure shelter and my daily bread, if permitted by the visitor. I wish to get Mrs. Lee out of the city as soon as practicable."

The opportunity for a quiet home was soon offered him by Mrs. Elizabeth Randolph Cocke, of Cumberland and Powhatan counties, a granddaughter of Edmund Randolph. On her estate Derwent, in Powhatan, there was a small cottage. This, with the land attached, she placed at the disposal of General Lee, who, she had heard, was anxious for a retired place in which to rest. She wrote him, offering him the home. Her letter was followed by a visit to Mrs. Lee. Her invitation was most gratefully accepted, the more readily because the trip could be made by canalboat, an easy mode of travel for Mrs. Lee. Early in June General and Mrs. Lee, with their daughters, left Richmond on the packet.

## Mrs. Robert E. Lee

They had left about sunset, and just about sunrise the boat reached Pemberton Landing. They were met there by Custis Lee, who had ridden Traveller from Richmond, and the son of their hostess, Captain Randolph Cocke.

Oakland, the home of their hostess, was reached in time for breakfast. Mrs. Cocke insisted that the Lees remain at Oakland for a visit before removing to Derwent. After a stay of a week they moved to the four-room cottage which was now to be their home. Only Agnes and Mildred were now with their parents. Following the bombardment of Richmond, with its days of unceasing noise, the absolute stillness seemed the most blessed part of this refuge. "A quiet so profound," wrote Mrs. Lee, "that I could even number the acorns falling from the splendid oaks that overshadowed the cottage." The entire neighborhood extended its hospitality to the Lees. Mrs. Lee, writing to Miss Emily Mason, says: "The kindness of the people of Virginia to us has been truly great & they seem never to tire. The settlement of Palmore's, which surrounds us, does not suffer us to want for anything their gardens or farms can furnish. My heart sinks when I hear of the destitution and misery which abound for the South."

It was a joy past words to General Lee to be in the country again. Here he had what he most needed: quiet and an opportunity to rest. That sufficed for

## Peace — at a Price

the present. Offers of places of honor with generous emoluments came to him from those who realized his straightened circumstances, but all these he refused. "They are offering my Father everything," said one of his daughters, "but the thing he will accept; a place to earn honest bread while engaged in some useful work." It was this remark, made to a trustee of Washington College, which resulted in the unanimous election of General Lee as president of the college, at a meeting of the trustees on August 4, 1865.

On a later day in August the rector of the college, Judge John W. Brockenborough, came up the road to Derwent and presented a letter to General Lee. This was the formal invitation to him to become president of Washington College at a salary of $1500 with a house and garden. Judge Brockenborough had also brought with him a letter from John Letcher, former governor of Virginia, whose home was now in Lexington. He wrote: "The salary now increased to $1500 and fees will provide the means of easy support in a country like this, where everything is usually abundant and easily obtained."

While General Lee was considering the invitation, he received a letter from his old chief of artillery, Brigadier General W. N. Pendleton, now rector of the Episcopal church in Lexington. General Pendleton urged him to accept the offer.

# Mrs. Robert E. Lee

*Washington College (Later Washington and Lee University) as It Looked When General Lee Became President*
[Courtesy of Washington and Lee University]

It was not until August 24, 1865, however, that General Lee finally wrote from his home in Powhatan County:

Gentlemen:

I have delayed for some days replying to your letter of the 5th inst. informing me of my election by the Board of Trustees to the Presidency of Washington College, from a desire to give the subject due consideration. Fully impressed with the responsibilities of the office I have feared that I should be unable to discharge its duties to the satisfaction of the trustees or to the benefit of the Country. The proper education of youth requires not only great ability, but, I fear, more strength than I now possess, for I do not

## Peace — at a Price

feel able to undergo the labour of conducting classes in regular courses of instruction. I could not, therefore, undertake more than the general administration and supervision of the institution. There is another subject which has caused me serious reflection, and is, I think, worthy of the consideration of the Board. Being excluded from the terms of amnesty in the proclamation of the President of the U. S. of the 29th May last, and an object of censure to a portion of the Country, I have thought it probable that my occupation of the position of President might draw upon the College a feeling of hostility; and I should, therefore, cause injury to an Institution which it would be my highest desire to advance. I think it the duty of every citizen, in the present condition of the Country, to do all in his power to aid in the restoration of peace and harmony, and in no way to oppose the policy of the State or General Government directed to that object. It is particularly incumbent on those charged with the instruction of the young to set them an example of submission to authority, and I could not consent to be the cause of animadversion upon the College.

Should you, however, take a different view, and think that my services in the position tendered me by the Board will be advantageous to the College and Country, I will yield to your judgement and accept it; otherwise, I must most respectfully decline the office.

Begging you to express to the trustees of the College my heartfelt gratitude for the honor conferred upon me, and requesting you to accept my cordial thanks for the kind manner in which you have communicated their decision,

I am, gentlemen, with great respect,

                Your most ob't serv't,

                          R. E. Lee.

## Mrs. Robert E. Lee

This letter was not written, however, until he had ridden over to Albemarle County to consult his old friend the Reverend Joseph P. B. Wilmer. Lee considered that Providence had given him this opportunity to improve his personal resources; but he doubted his own ability, and he wished to hear from the lips of his friend whether he considered him competent to undertake the work.

Competent? Yes. And so General Lee decided to dedicate his life to the cause of education, hoping that he might thus be of use to others.

From Derwent Mrs. Lee wrote Miss Emily Mason:

> The papers will have told you that the Gen'l has decided to accept the position at Lexington. I do not think that he is very fond of teaching, but he is willing to do anything that will give him honorable support. He starts tomorrow *en cheval* for Lexington. He prefers that way, and besides, does not like to part even for a time from his beloved steed, the companion of many a hard-fought battle.

Mrs. Lee was deeply concerned at this time about the fate of Mr. Davis. General Lee was a prisoner on parole. With Jefferson Davis and others he had been indicted in June for treason by a grand jury in Norfolk. Now the former President of the Confederate States was behind prison bars in a gun casement at Fort Monroe, under constant guard and surveillance. He was not allowed to write to his

## Peace — at a Price

*General Lee and Traveller* (*Autographed*)
[Courtesy of the Honorable Henry Wickham]

wife, who wrote Mrs. Lee in September that she knew "nothing whatever of her husband, except what she had seen in the papers." Mrs. Lee, writing to Miss Mason of Mrs. Davis, says, "She writes very sadly, as well she may, for I know of no one so much to be pitied."

## Mrs. Robert E. Lee

When it was known in Lexington that General Lee had accepted the presidency of Washington College, it was as if the little college town had received an infusion of new life.

A war had drained it of its lifeblood. Hunter had entered Lexington with hatred in his heart and a torch in his hands. The ruins of what had once been the "West Point of the South," the Virginia Military Institute, bore mute testimony to his work. But now the news had come that General Lee would dedicate "his future life to the holy work of educating the youth of his country."

The announcement had gone forth from the board of trustees that "the college, under the administration and supervision of General Lee, will resume its exercises on the 14th inst."

The exact time of Lee's arrival was unknown, and he entered the town unheralded on the afternoon of September 18. In a diary is recorded that

Gen'l Lee, having been invited to take the presidency of Washington College and having accepted it, was daily expected. One afternoon Allen came into my room in an excited manner and announced his arrival. I went to the window and saw riding by on his old war-horse Traveller, the great soldier.... Slowly he passed, raising his brown slouch hat to those on the pavement who recognized him, and not appearing conscious that he more than anybody else was the center of attention.

## Peace — at a Price

*General Lee's First Home in Lexington
at Washington and Lee University*
[Washington and Lee University]

He wore his military coat divested of all marks of rank; even the military buttons had been removed. He doubtless would have laid it aside altogether, but it was the only one he had, and he was too poor to buy another.

Mrs. Lee remained at Derwent temporarily; for in Lexington the house which was to be the home of the president was rented and would need many repairs when it was vacated.

When the house was finally vacated, about the

## Mrs. Robert E. Lee

middle of October, General Lee pushed the repairs as rapidly as possible, his first thought being Mrs. Lee's room.

The dwelling, known as the "president's house," was one of the charming, white-pillared houses which today grace the campus of Washington and Lee.

The necessary repairs proved so numerous that General Lee wrote Mrs. Lee: "The scenery is beautiful here, but I fear it will be locked up in winter by the time you come. Nothing could be more beautiful than the mountains now."

In November Mrs. Lee and her daughters, accompanied by her youngest son, Robert, left Derwent and went by canalboat to Bremo, some twenty-five miles up the James River. The president of the James River and Kanawha Canal Co., Colonel Ellis, placed at Mrs. Lee's disposal his private boat, which enabled her to reach Bremo with great ease.

She had chosen the canal route to Lexington; for Lexington, though beautifully situated, was remote. There was no railroad, the nearest station being Staunton. From there the journey to Lexington must be continued by stagecoach through Goshen Pass. Or the trip could be made from Richmond by the James River and Kanawha Canal. Mrs. Lee, having chosen this route and hearing that the house in Lexington was now ready for occupancy, accepted the offer of Colonel Ellis to make the trip in his

## Peace — at a Price

*James River Canal Terminal*
[Old Virginia Gentleman]

private boat. It was an ideal way for her to travel,—slow but sure,—and no mode of travel could have suited her better. The boat was roomy and comfortable and was well fitted up with sleeping quarters, not to mention a dining room with a cook in attendance. Though not so luxurious as the modern private car of the president of a railroad, it was more roomy and comfortable.

Several days were required for the trip. On the eventful morning of December 2 the packet boat reached Lexington, and there the first sight which met Mrs. Lee's eyes was General Lee seated on

# Mrs. Robert E. Lee

Traveller. A carriage was there for Mrs. Lee and the other members of the family. With the family in the carriage General Lee, riding beside the vehicle, escorted them to the house which was to be their home. Soon the family, excited and happy, were seated around the breakfast table. A thoughtful wife of a member of the faculty had told General Lee that she would have this first breakfast prepared in her kitchen and sent in as soon as the family arrived. It was a little attention long to be remembered. When the meal was over, the General enthusiastically showed his family over the house, Robert carrying his mother up the stairs.

The ladies of Lexington had vied with one another in making the house as attractive as possible. They had put down the carpets and had made the beds. Only Mrs. Lee's room was completely furnished. The furniture for this room had been made by a one-armed Confederate soldier from plans drawn by Mrs. Margaret Preston. As Mrs. Lee entered her room she realized the love and admiration for her husband which had gone into the preparation of a home for his family by the ladies of Lexington. So Mary Custis Lee, who had left Arlington filled with the finest of furnishings, much of which had once graced the mansion at Mount Vernon, brought to her sparsely furnished new home a heart lifted up in thanksgiving.

## *Peace—at a Price*

In the parlor there stood, almost alone in its glory, a handsomely carved grand piano, which had been sent as a gift from the maker, Stieff of Baltimore. The floor was covered by the carpet once used at Arlington, and at the windows hung the curtains which had framed the well-loved and oft-remembered views from the windows of her old home.

After Mrs. Lee had left Arlington, Mrs. Britannia Peter Kennon of Tudor Place, her first cousin, who had been one of her bridesmaids, hearing that the personal belongings of the Lees were being carried away by marauding Federal soldiers, asked and received permission to remove some of the furnishings from Arlington. General Lee had written to Mrs. Lee while she was at Bremo: "I think you better write at once to Brit to send the curtains you speak of and the carpets." These had come and had added greatly to the comfort of the new home. As Mrs. Lee gazed on them, however, she was overcome for a moment by a flood of memories; but she quickly recovered herself.

If she remembered the past years, of what they had robbed her, she remembered also that she had great cause for thanksgiving. Not only her husband but her three sons had seen active service in the Army of the Confederacy, and they had all been spared. Now she was grateful and happy to be once again in a home of her own, surrounded by an atmosphere of kindliness.

## Mrs. Robert E. Lee

Mrs. Lee found that these new friends had stocked her pantry with pickles, preserves, and brandied peaches. Almost daily some gift was brought. Even the poor mountaineers, anxious to do something, came with bags of walnuts, potatoes, and game. These tributes of admiration and sympathy deeply touched Mrs. Lee. If she was sometimes tempted to live in memories, neither her family nor her friends in Lexington knew it. They knew her to be an invalid; but they saw her always bright, sunny-tempered, and uncomplaining, constantly occupied with her books, letters, knitting, and painting.

Reared as she had been in an atmosphere of hospitality and generosity, Mrs. Lee was always most eager to share with others. Now, in these days after the war, there was little for anyone to share; but never were the generosity, the unselfishness, the *noblesse oblige* of the gentry of Virginia shown in bolder relief than at that time. Many were the baskets and trays that went in and out of the Lee home. These qualities were not confined to any one group. A young professor at the Virginia Military Institute, writing at that time, says: "I went hunting the other day and sent my game to Mrs. Lee—she suffers a great deal, but bears it all patiently and is always planning for the comfort and happiness of others." Thus did she win all who came in contact with her by her wonderful personality.

*"The Home-Coming, 1865"*
[Courtesy of the Confederate Museum, Richmond]

## Mrs. Robert E. Lee

In Mary Custis Lee were found no superficial marks of culture. Her charm went deeper. It was woven into her life and spirit. Neither four years of dreadful war, nor her failing health, nor the loss of her home had destroyed her gentleness, generosity, and unselfishness.

It was not only those around her for whose "comfort and happiness" she might be found planning. Hearing of the reduced circumstances of a family who had been most attentive to General Lee during the siege of Petersburg, she took advantage of an opportunity and wrote, wishing she

... had something to send you all by Mr. Bolling worthy of your acceptance. But as it might inconvenience him to take anything besides this letter, I enclose $5.00 which you must lay out in your judicious manner. It is part of some funds given me by kind friends for the South & to none could I give it more worthy than those who have so bravely borne up under all the sufferings inflicted on them by a cruel foe & who are preparing themselves for future usefulness.

Some months later she sent to a little girl in the same family ". . . the last $5.00 of the money entrusted to me & you & your sister must get something nice and pretty for Xmas. I am sure that you will spend it wisely."

Though there were two colleges in the town, Presbyterian Lexington took its social life very seri-

## Peace — at a Price

ously, approving neither dancing nor card-playing. It was a difficult atmosphere for the Lee girls. A young professor, writing at that time, says:

> I have been recently to call on the Miss Lees, and found them exceedingly agreeable. They don't seem to like Lexington much, think the people stiff and formal, which is very much the case. I only saw Miss Mary and Miss Agnes. Miss Agnes I like very much, her seeming haughtiness and reserve which offend the Lexingtonians so much, I particularly admire.

It was hard for the Miss Lees to adjust themselves to the life in Lexington. In Tidewater Virginia, the region in which they had been reared, there was a oneness of feeling among neighbors, friends, and kinsfolk, with interests and tastes in common. The society was like that of one big family, much going on among friends and kinsfolk—simple, friendly intercourse, with true elegance, but with no desire for show.

During the autumn of 1866 "the ladies," we are told, had "gotten up a reading club. They meet weekly on Wednesday evening and read a little and talk a great deal, so it must be pleasant. I think I will attend the next." The Lees were among "the ladies, who, together with such gentlemen as can be secured for the occasion, make up the club."

The Miss Lees, returning from regular meetings of the club, were always questioned by Mrs. Lee as

## Mrs. Robert E. Lee

to what they had read. From what she gathered, the club appeared more social than literary. Writing of a meeting early in December a member says:

I attended the last meeting of the Reading Club.... There was quite a gathering of the belles and gongs; the Lees were there.... The Lees are charming. Miss Mary is bright and willful, intelligent and cultivated; Miss Agnes has a little haughty way about her that seems to give offense here, but I think charming. They are more like our lower valley girls than any others I meet here.

General Lee, writing to Mildred on a visit to the Eastern Shore of Maryland, said of the Reading Club: "As far as I can judge, it is a great institution for the discussion of apples and chestnuts, but it is quite innocent of the pleasures of literature. It however brings the young people together and promotes sociability and conversation." The club meetings evidently grew in popularity, and there was a certain pleasant rivalry on the part of the hostesses. Agnes, writing to Mildred, says:

The reading is usually a small matter, and they are becoming right pleasant since people know each other better. Ours, everyone said, was a real success. It was several weeks ago & was less stiff than those had been before it.... We had cake, apples, nuts, and iced punch which seemed very palatable. There were sixteen men, a doz. ladies & some wd [would] stay in the corner. Mary and I worked hard.

# Peace—at a Price

*Agnes Lee*      *Mildred Lee*

The Reading Club kept up the regular meetings, and skating also became a popular pastime, as the river was now frozen over. Heretofore it had been said in Lexington, "No lady skates; if she does, it is a Yankee lady." Now the Lees, who loved to skate, had made it quite the thing, until it was said: "The ladies are having a gay time skating. . . . The ladies and the students in their gay costumes and the cadets in their uniforms formed a very animated picture. . . . I have an engagement to go skating with Miss Mary Lee on Thursday morning."

Not satisfied with skating, the Miss Lees accepted the invitation of a professor for a sleigh ride. "In

## Mrs. Robert E. Lee

the evening we astonished the natives," he writes, "by a genuine old-fashioned sleighing party. The party was composed of Miss Mary and Agnes Lee, Captain Henderson, and myself. We drove out about six miles into the country and got back about eight o'clock P. M. We all enjoyed it very much."

Mrs. Lee was greatly amused that the innocent pastimes of the young people should so shock the good people of Lexington. She and General Lee were most anxious that the young people, who had been deprived of their social heritage by a cruel war, should grasp every opportunity for pleasant intercourse. They were therefore almost as greatly interested as their daughters when they heard that the

> bachelor professors propose to entertain the Reading Club at the Institute. The Engineering Academy will be used as the Assembly room, the Laboratory for the supper room, and my special sanctum will be for the time converted into a ladies' boudoir. We shall do everything to make it, and hope it will be, a success.

Evidently it was a success, for the same bachelor writes: "The party was delightful, all the ladies said. ... The dancing was kept up until three o'clock, and then I could only get them to leave by having the reel played and having the music sent away."

The dances so merrily stepped were, besides the Virginia reel, the lancers and the quadrille; for the

# Peace — at a Price

Reading Club would have brought down upon its heads "phials of wrath" indeed from Presbyterian Lexington if any of the members had indulged in "round" dancing. So, however much the Lee girls would have liked "to dare" the band to play a waltz or polka, Custis Lee, their brother, who was one of the bachelor professors, would have forbidden it.

# CHAPTER VII

# *Reminiscences*

IN DECEMBER, 1867, there came to Lexington a bride, and there began for her a friendship with the Lees which was to be cherished through many years and severed only by death. Little notes bearing her name and no other address than "E. V.," "At Home," or "Present," were frequently sent from the Lees' home to the house at the "Second Limit Gate," which in time came to be the home of the bride.

There is always a fascination about memories. Perhaps these little notes will help to convey some idea of the atmosphere of that shrine of the South, the home of Robert E. Lee. Amusements were simple in those days, as is so clearly illustrated by the following acknowledgment of an invitation by Agnes Lee, in which she says:

> I will enjoy very much going with you & Mary H. But is it not right *raw* for two ladies of your *strength* & *prudence* to "wander by the brook" such a day as this? I suppose you want me to take care of you! So I will be ready & if you do not come, will understand it is too cold today. It will make no difference to me. I will take a little walk

# *Reminiscences*

as I do every morning. I was going to send the moss-from-the-wood I promised Mrs. H. & avail myself of yr. messenger.

The day proved to be bright, and the three ladies wandered over the cliffs and by the little brook. There came another day when the weather was not so propitious, and in place of an invitation for a walk was substituted an invitation to dinner by Marietta [Mary Lee]:

I see the weather, in other words the fates, are still against us & as the weather is unpropitious-looking at least & we have a turkey for dinner, cannot you and the Col. dine with us *en famille*, at half past two? Please come. In spite of the clouds I am obliged to go off to my dressmaker this morning; so be prepared to amuse me after dinner. Yrs. Marietta.

Saturday afternoon is holiday I think, so the Colonel is free, is he not?

Shortly after the arrival of the bridal pair in Lexington, the Lees arranged a reception for them, the first entertainment given by them since the surrender. The refreshments were light; but no one thought of that, so great was the charm of the Lee home.

The bride always cherished the memory of Mrs. Lee as she saw her that evening seated in her wheel chair, immaculate in her attire, her silver hair almost covered with a dainty lace-trimmed organdy cap, her

## Mrs. Robert E. Lee

face framed with silver curls. A bright word of greeting was on her lips for all who came.

Some years before her marriage the bride's husband, now a professor at Virginia Military Institute, but a former Confederate soldier, had written her:

> I trust there will be no more war yet awhile. I trust there will not be any unless there is a prospect of a happy result to us. I trouble myself very little about the progress of events. I have General Lee to think for me, and when he acts, I will follow in his steps.

So now this bride, whose home had been in the Shenandoah Valley which had been devastated by Sheridan, saw in Mrs. Lee one in whose footsteps the women of the South should follow. In Mrs. Lee she saw displayed the true heroism of life; for Mrs. Lee had accepted her fate and met it bravely, had cherished her affections, had performed her duties, and had shown that duties faithfully discharged bring a dearer recompense than any circumstance of ease and luxury can supply.

The bride, when once established in her own home at the "Second Limit Gate," was anxious to show Mrs. Lee some little attention and incidentally prove her ability as a housekeeper; so she sent her a basket in which were dainty dishes, such as wine jelly, custard, brandied peaches, and cake. Mrs. Lee wrote:

## Reminiscences

Many thanks, my dear Mary, for the nice things which came very safely. Only a *little* custard spilled in the basket. If you would like some sprout turnip tops, we have plenty; send Harrison any time with a basket & he can get some. Won't you come to the meeting [of the sewing society] tomorrow? I write in great haste not wishing to keep your valet waiting.

Yrs. Affectionately,

M. C. Lee.

The meeting to which Mary was invited was that of the Grace Church sewing society, of which Mrs. Lee was president. Because of Mrs. Lee's health the meetings were always held in her room. General Lee, writing to his son Robert, says: "There is to be a great fete in our Mother's room today. The Grace Church sewing society is to meet there at 10 A.M., that is, if the members are impervious to water. I charged the two Mildreds to be seated with their white aprons on and with scissors and thimbles at hand."

The purpose of the society was to aid in raising money for the building fund of the Episcopal church. The church was a small and very indifferent structure, sadly in need of repairs. "The Episcopalians," wrote General Lee to his daughter Mildred, "are few in number and light in purse and must be resigned to small returns."

But they were not lacking in energy, and they were greatly inspired by Mrs. Lee's enthusiasm. The

## Mrs. Robert E. Lee

meeting of the society hummed not only with conversation but also with industry; for it was at this time that various fancy as well as useful articles were made. The results of these labors were priced, and as Christmas approached they were carefully packed in baskets. Ladies offered the services of some trusty servant, by whom the baskets were carried from house to house. In the house the articles were carefully examined and selections made, and the man or maid who carried the basket was paid. Sometimes a bazaar was held; then many of the students would write home asking for donations. On one occasion a very handsome pincushion was sent by the mother of one of the students. This the ladies thought should be priced beyond the pocketbook of any Lexington Episcopalian. "Why not raffle it off?" someone suggested. General Lee, coming in while the discussion was under way, said: "No, don't raffle things for the church. What would you hope to raise by such a plan?" On being told the amount, he asked who the treasurer of the society was and immediately purchased the pincushion at the hoped-for amount.

Suppers and strawberry festivals were also among the means resorted to for raising money. "This is the night for the supper for the repairs to the Episcopal Church," wrote General Lee to his daughter Mildred. "Your Mother and sisters are busy with

# Reminiscences

their contributions. It is to take place at the hotel, and your brother, cousins, and Father are to attend."

Mrs. Lee, reared as she had been in an Episcopal atmosphere, where the churches were among the most attractive buildings of the neighborhood, was most eager for improvement in the Lexington church. Being rather gifted with her brush, she put this talent to work for the cause. The portraits of General and Mrs. Washington, which had once hung on the walls at Arlington, were now in the Lee home in Lexington. These Mrs. Lee had had photographed, and then she busied herself coloring them in the same tones as the portraits. General Lee, writing to his son, says: "Your Mother is becoming interested in her painting again, and is employing her brush for the benefit of our little church, which is very poor." These colored photographs were in great demand and proved a considerable source of revenue to the church. While Mrs. Lee busied herself on behalf of the building fund of the church, Mary and Agnes were endeavoring to build up a Sunday school. Colonel M. of the faculty of the Virginia Military Institute had been appointed superintendent, and Mary and Agnes were teachers.

A library was greatly needed for the use of the pupils. Such libraries as had once lined the shelves in Lexington homes had been scattered and destroyed during the war, and now, for the children

## Mrs. Robert E. Lee

anxious to read, there was nothing to read. Mrs. Lee felt that one of the greatest contributions the Sunday school could give the children of the congregation was to make it possible for them to have books to take home to read. This hope was frequently expressed in her letters. In consequence a number of her friends became interested and sent donations. Mary Lee writes to Colonel M., the superintendent: "I have received from New York about 70 or 80 volumes for the Sunday school. Thought it might influence somewhat your contemplated purchase of books."

The "contemplated purchase" was to be made from funds "which were the proceeds of a bazaar." For this bazaar the children of the Sunday school had made a number of articles which had apparently sold readily; for Agnes, unable to execute a commission, wrote: "Papa bought the little houses, and as there was nothing left that the children had made, I am obliged to tell you of my inability to execute even a fraction of yr. commission."

As Christmas drew near, the Lees began to make elaborate preparations for the Sunday-school celebration. There were no Christmas-tree ornaments to be found in the stores; and even had there been, there was no money with which to buy any. But the children had been promised a tree, and it must not only be a tree, but it must be a beautiful tree, and the occasion must be one long to be remembered. The talents

# *Reminiscences*

of everyone were pressed into service. Mary Lee writes to Colonel M., whose stepmother was quite a talented artist:

> Would your Mother have time to make an angel for the top of the Christmas tree? Of pastels with the conventional blue eyes and golden curls, with draperies of white gauze and wings of gold or silver paper? Also a crown? If she can and will, send one of the boys for what she requires. I will send it to her. It ought to be tolerably large. Let me know how many cornucopias N. can make of that paper, as I want to know how many we have. We made fourteen yesterday, and L. W. is making some.
>
> Mamma, of course, takes advantage of this opportunity to ask for the apron for which she sends a box.

A few days before Christmas the Lees and their friends gathered at the church to help "make wreaths for the church"; and when, on the twenty-fourth of December, the Christmas celebration was held, the congregation found the church decorated as never before. The gallery was festooned all around with a heavy wreath of evergreens, and around each of the pillars was twisted a spiral of evergreens. Around the walls and in each panel of the gallery was a shield, with some scripture text upon it, each trimmed with evergreens—all the work of members of the congregation. One who attended the celebration tells us:

> The chancel was fringed around with pine and the reading desk and pulpit with spruce and ivy. On the blank

# Mrs. Robert E. Lee

wall behind the pulpit there was in the center I. H. S. in large gold letters bordered with evergreen. Upon each side [was] a cross of gold, and above, a scripture motto in gold letters. The general effect was beautiful.

The Christmas tree (a large cedar) stood by the font & was decorated with flowers, wax candles, and bon bons, and was loaded down with fruits, cornucopias, and presents & prizes for the children. Something for every child in the congregation and presents for the scholars. It began with the singing by the children of a Christmas anthem, during which the wax candles were lighted and the lamps turned low—the tree was perfectly beautiful. While the candles were blazing, we had a short service; and then the presents were distributed by General Pendleton. Mrs. Lee came over, or rather was brought over in her chair, and sat in the middle aisle. She seemed to enjoy it so much and had something to say to each of the children. General Lee gave N. a beautiful apron. Everything passed off very pleasantly, and I trust the effect will be very good.

Sharing was prevalent in Virginia in the days following the war. That the faculty at the Virginia Military Institute were frequently without their salaries was no secret, and as it was difficult for them to secure things which required cash their wants must frequently be satisfied at the commissary, where the selection was limited; so when Mrs. Lee knew that a baby was expected in the house at the "Second Limit Gate," she sent a gift selected from clothes which had been so lovingly made for the baby of

# Reminiscences

Charlotte and Rooney. But this little baby had lived only a short time, and now Mrs. Lee hoped that these little dresses and petticoats might be of use to the child of another Confederate soldier. But neither was this baby to live to wear the clothes, and the young mother, ill and greatly distressed at the loss of her baby, returned to her father's home in Clarke County to recuperate. Journeying from Lexington to Clarke County was long and circuitous, and therefore expensive. There was no railroad at Lexington, the nearest point at which a train might be taken being Goshen, twenty-three miles away over a wretched road. The alternative for the traveler was the James River and Kanawha Canal, along which the packet crept to Lynchburg, fifty miles away.

The state of Virginia was having great difficulty in finding the money with which to pay the members of the faculty at Virginia Military Institute, who therefore found ready cash hard to secure; so, in order to save expenses, the young wife decided that even though her health was much better she would remain at her old home until her husband could join her there for his vacation. Thus for some months her husband was alone. When she finally returned, she one day saw General Lee ride to her gate and dismount. Hitching Traveller to the fence, the General came in and paid a long call. In leaving he said, in the whimsical way he often had with the

## *Mrs. Robert E. Lee*

friends of his daughters: "Don't ever stay away from your husband so long again. It is not right for a husband and wife to be separated." Her pride did not permit her to say that it was scarcity of funds which had kept them separated. Her husband was often at the Lees' home during her absence, and he frequently made mention of these visits in his letters to her:

> Last night General D. H. Hill lectured at the Franklin. I started to go, but stopped at the Lees' to call and spent the entire evening with General and Mrs. Lee. . . . Mrs. Lee and I talked politics and gardening. General Lee sat by drawing plans for Robert's improvements, occasionally joining in the conversation.

It was very natural that Mary Custis Lee should take the greatest interest in the political situation of the country. From her father she had often heard the story of the birth of the nation which she had seen rent in twain. In these reconstruction days she was filled with apprehension for the future. She felt that Virginia was "being flooded by men who have none of the traditional regard for the honor and credit of the State."

When, on March 13, 1867, the first Reconstruction Act was proclaimed and the Old Dominion became Military District No. 1, Mrs. Lee had written to Mrs. Chilton:

## *Reminiscences*

It is bad enough to be the victims of tyranny, but when it is wielded by such cowards and base men as Butler, Thaddeus Stevens, and Turner, it is indeed intolerable. The country that allows such scum to rule them must fast be going to destruction, and we shall care little if we are not involved in a crash.

Her regrets were not for the sacrifices she had personally been called upon to make, but for the South.

They still desire to grind [the South] to dust & wish to effect this purpose by working on the feelings of the low and ignorant negroes many of whom do not even comprehend what a *vote* means. My indignation cannot be controlled and I wonder how our people, helpless and disarmed as they are, can bear it. Oh God, how long?

When there were guests staying at the house it was a very charming custom of Mrs. Lee's to invite friends with whom she felt they would be congenial to come in after tea to meet them. So Colonel M., during the absence of his wife, "received a message from Mrs. Lee to come up and spend the evening with General Hampton. . . ." He went with Mrs. Taylor and "spent a very pleasant evening."

Mrs. Taylor was a friend of the Lees from New York—a Northern woman of intense Southern proclivities. She had come to Lexington to board, that she might be near the Lees. Upon meeting the Colonel she had greatly embarrassed him by saying, "I have heard General Lee speak so often of the gal-

## Mrs. Robert E. Lee

lantry of all of you, that I have come to look upon you as a race of heroes." To which he replied, "Bravery was a necessity, for a man to be brave was a matter of course, to be otherwise was a disgrace and degradation."

For the first year of General Lee's presidency of the college the Lees lived in the greatest simplicity. Simple living had been a virtue during the days of the Confederacy; now it was a necessity. Mrs. Lee made no excuses for the plain fare found on her table. Those who knew the Lees in Lexington remembered vividly their simple and unassuming way of life. The family was content in living modestly and sharing the hardships of the times. Mrs. Lee, who had been reared in even greater luxury than her husband or children, never complained of the plain way of living and the lack of money.

A very familiar picture to callers at the Lee home in the evening was Mrs. Lee seated before the fire in the dining room mending her husband's and son's socks and underclothing, while General Lee by the light of a lamp read aloud to her.

The Lees' home was popular, and there were usually callers; but Mrs. Lee did not always join the group of young people in the parlor. A caller at that time writes:

I went up to call at General Lee's this evening and saw them all.... Mrs. Lee sent for me to come to the dining

*Reminiscences*

room, and I sat there for half an hour, when it was announced Colonel Massie had called to see Mrs. Lee and I wheeled her out into the parlor which I found thronged with visitors. . . . Mrs. Lee is still busy with her paintings and is continually adding to the fund.

With the return of the mistress to the house at the "Second Limit Gate," there was a renewal of the amenities which had so frequently been exchanged between this house and the Lee home in the past. Agnes, who was the housekeeper at that time, wrote:

Find that at least one wagon hasn't been to yr. house today, I send you a basket by way of remembrance. The pears of course are to ripen in a drawer. Tell Colonel M. the roses are rather imperfect examples of some of the roses I want him to take cuttings from & the remarkable stranger I found on one of them this morning goes with them.

Of course in a hurry,

Affec. A. Lee.

Baskets were never returned empty. Mildred, who had not been well, having received one, wrote:

I enjoyed yr. nice ice cream and cake so much the other evening. It was so sweet of you to think of me in the midst of yr. many cares, for you have had a sick house I hear.

I hope you are all better now; do let me know if I can aid you in any way. The cook has just sent in some fresh biscuits which I send, with a wee bottle of champagne for dear Col. M. You don't know how much I love you both.

Ever aff'ly, Mildred Lee.

## Mrs. Robert E. Lee

If the bushes were full of currants and the house was full of guests, and there was no time for jelly-making, from the house at the "Second Limit Gate" would go an offer to see to the matter of having the jelly made. Agnes replies to the offer:

I send two jars wh. came to me filled with your nice pickles before I left home in Nov. I kept one of them for "Commencement," and it has been most useful these last few days. I have not forgotten your very kind offer to have some currant jelly made for me & if you still find it entirely convenient, I will send you some any day you wish to have them just for the pleasure of having some of yr. jelly, wh. we know will be very nice. I still look forward to seeing you all soon. Mamma says send an answer to her note at yr. convenience.

Evidently the jelly was a great success; for Agnes writes:

A thousand thanks for the elegant jelly. Won't you make Aunt Hannah sensible of our appreciation of her share in it by giving her this handkerchief "all the way from Balt."?
Let Lina bring back the large basket.
With good-bye to you all,

Affec. Agnes Lee.

On a trip to Baltimore in 1869 General Lee purchased for Mrs. Lee "a little carriage, the best I could find, which I hope will enable you to take some pleasant rides." The carriage was ordered in the spring,

## *Reminiscences*

but it was not until the autumn that it reached Lexington. General Lee was frequently the driver when the carriage finally arrived and was put to use. He would often take the roads which carried them over the beautiful hills around Lexington. When her husband was unable to go with Mrs. Lee, she would choose that afternoon for calls, frequently asking some friend to join her. So a little note, folded into a cocked hat, went to "Dear Mary" at the "Second Limit Gate":

Since you admire the grandeur of my equipage and it is so mild this afternoon, would you like to take a drive with me, possibly to Colonel Johnston's? I will call for you at four, or even earlier if possible. There is a seat for R. if you would like to take her & I shall be glad of her company.

In haste, Affec. yours,

Mary Custis Lee.

## CHAPTER VIII

# The Home of the College President

THE white-pillared house which was now the home of the president of Washington College had once been the home of Doctor William Junkin, a former president. It was his daughter who had become the wife of Thomas Jonathan Jackson ("Stonewall" Jackson), "Professor of Natural and Experimental Philosophy and Military Tactics" in the Virginia Military Institute.

In the charming circle of the Junkin home Stonewall Jackson and his wife spent the few brief years of their married life. In those antebellum days a lovely old-fashioned yard surrounded the home of the president. It was amidst the beauty and fragrance of this garden that the grave professor had wooed and won the lovely Eleanor Junkin. War and neglect had laid a devastating hand upon this garden. When the Lees came, there was little evidence of one; but Mrs. Lee, who loved flowers and gardens, had the weeds and all signs of neglect removed, and General Lee busied himself supervising the making of a vegetable garden and the careful

## The Home of the College President

transplanting into it of many of the plants he had grown from seed in his hotbed.

Throughout her first spring in Lexington Mrs. Lee eagerly watched to see what hidden flowers would bloom. Jonquils (resurrection flowers she called them), snowdrops, star-of-Bethlehem, and lily of the valley had come. In May she writes to a friend in "lower" Virginia, "We have a few rosebushes in our yard, but they have not bloomed yet & the Gen'l is very busy with his vegetable garden; but the season here is very late."

Though Mrs. Lee was deeply interested in the many improvements her husband was making in the president's home, of far greater moment to her were his plans and hopes for the college. His often-expressed belief that of all human efforts education was the most prophetic had inspired her. Now she began to wonder about the education of the daughters of Confederate soldiers. She had belonged to a generation of Virginia gentry, part of their daughters' heritage being a fine classical education. She realized that now there were few educational opportunities offered to the girls of Virginia. War had closed the doors of many of the schools for girls, and there were no funds with which to open them. The schoolhouses on the plantations no longer rang with the voices of children, for there was no money with which to employ tutors.

## Mrs. Robert E. Lee

Charming and cultured women, many of them widows of Confederate soldiers, were now anxiously seeking positions as governesses as the only means of livelihood open to them. Even if the salary was small, or if, perhaps, there was no salary at all, such a position at least provided a home. Mrs. Lee, having been appealed to on behalf of one young woman, replied: "Tell your Mamma I have enquired particularly about a situation for your Aunt, but have not heard of one. Very few people about here can afford to employ teachers." Evidently she did not dismiss the request from her mind, for some months later she again referred to it:

> Your Aunt wrote or sent me a message sometime since about obtaining a situation to teach in this vicinity & when I returned from the Springs, I wrote to some of you . . . as I had heard of a situation in which music, especially playing on the guitar, was a requisite. As I never heard from her, I suppose she did not receive the letter & the situation is, I presume, now filled. It was down on the James River near City Point & perhaps would not have suited her.

Between the lines may be read an implied rebuke to a young friend for a courtesy unacknowledged; for both by birth and by training Mrs. Lee was a believer in the social amenities.

Hearing from a little girl of the arrangements her parents had made for the education of herself and

# The Home of the College President

her younger sister, Mrs. Lee replied: "I am glad . . . that you all have an opportunity for improving yourselves, for a good education is something that fortune cannot deprive you of. . . ."

This same little girl, whose home was in Petersburg, anxious to send Mrs. Lee a gift, chose from her scanty possessions a pair of young chickens. Mrs. Lee wrote:

> I am sure, my dear Fannie, you are anxious to learn of the safe arrival of your pretty fowls, which I value most highly at the same time that I must scold you for parting with them. You ought to have kept them to raise from, they are so beautiful. Your white cock is a beauty and reigns supreme in our yard, as we have gotten rid of the old one which rejoiced in the name of Garibaldi. I have not decided yet what to call this one. You did not tell me his name. We have also gotten lately a pretty yellow cat, which is a great pet & we call him after one we had at my dear old Arlington "Tom Tita." He kills a large rat every day for his dinner and breakfasts on mice; so you see he is quite well employed.

Mrs. Lee's health had shown no improvement during the first winter in Lexington. In June she wrote:

> I have not been so well this winter and spring. We are soon going to the Warm & Hot Springs, tho' I have little hope of any permanent benefit. The Gen'l was not well this spring, but is better now. . . . Lexington has been quite gay recently with the two commencements,

## *Mrs. Robert E. Lee*

Washington College & the Institute; but I am unable to mix in anything that is going on & am often very sad & lonely. God knows what is best for us all, yet it often seems to me that my affliction is peculiarly trying to one of my active temperament.

The plans for a trip to the Warm and Hot Springs were evidently abandoned, for on July 4 she writes: "I am still confined mostly to my chair, but I am to go to some Baths near this place which have quite a reputation."

These were the Rockbridge Baths, famous for the medicinal qualities of the waters. To Mrs. Lee the Baths made an added appeal. They were only eleven miles from Lexington, and it would therefore be possible for General Lee frequently to ride over on Traveller. This he did, greatly enjoying the ride and making friends with the people whose cabins he passed each week.

As was characteristic of all Southern matrons, Mrs. Lee held an especially warm place in her heart for "her boys"; but dearest to her of all her sons was Robert, her youngest. He was still to her "my dear little Rob." She had hoped that he would join her at the Baths, and she was disappointed when he felt that he should not leave Romancoke, the plantation which he had inherited from his grandfather and from which he was now trying to make a living. From the Baths she wrote:

[240]

# *The Home of the College President*

Your Papa told me he would leave his letter open that I might write you a little note, dear Rob, & you know I never miss an *opportunity* & therefore I could not refrain from placing those few lines in the bundle of papers even at the risk of Uncle Sam's penitentiary; but as I neither *feel* nor *owe* any allegiance to him, except what is exacted by force, my conscience does not trouble me. We are protected neither in person nor property by his laws; nor do I feel any respect for the military *satraps* who rule us. As soon as I return to Lexington I will send you the papers every week regularly. How I wish you could have come up here, plenty of pretty girls & a great scarcity of beaux; you would have been quite a lion. . . . We shall return to Lexington about the 1st of September & hope you & Fitzhugh will be able to come there. I do so long to see you both.

The college opened the last of September. Mrs. Lee returned and two of her daughters with her. General Lee was "kept very busy now at the College. There are so many students," she wrote, and added, because her letter was to a young girl:

There is also a large girls' school here, called the Ann Smith Academy, quite an old institution; but the girls are not allowed to speak to or even bow to the students when they meet them on the street. I suppose the day scholars are not so particular, but the *boarders* are kept very strict. How would you like that?

Though secretly amused, Mrs. Lee had been a very sympathetic listener to the plaints of young

## Mrs. Robert E. Lee

cousins, students at Washington College, who, believing themselves enamored of certain "Ann Smith girls," were greatly chagrined that they received not so much as a nod as they passed by the girls.

Hearing in the spring of 1867 that the Greenbrier White Sulphur Springs would open its doors for the first time since the war, and having great belief in the waters, General Lee arranged to take Mrs. Lee there that summer.

It was not an easy trip for Mrs. Lee, for it was the days of lumbering stagecoaches; only part of the journey could be made by rail—from Goshen to Covington. Arriving at "the White," the Lees found that the cottage assigned to them was Harrison Cottage in Baltimore Row, only a short distance from the hotel. Seated on the vine-covered porch of her cottage Mrs. Lee had a clear view of the gaieties at the hotel. Milly Howard, her devoted maid, took the greatest pride in Mrs. Lee's appearance, and saw that she was carefully dressed to receive the many guests who found their way to the cottage.

After supper it was the custom to transform the great dining room at the hotel into a ballroom. The Negro waiters made an inspiring orchestra, playing waltzes and polkas; and for those whose family training debarred them from "round" dancing, there were quadrilles, lancers, and the Virginia reel. To Harrison Cottage came the strains of the dance

## *The Home of the College President*

*Greenbrier White Sulphur Springs in 1867,
"Where the Charm of Antebellum Days Lingered"*
[Old Virginia Gentleman]

music and the voices of the young couples as they promenaded up and down the broad veranda. It was a charming life at "the White" in those days. Much of the atmosphere, charm, and simplicity of the antebellum days still lingered. Though socially "the White" left nothing to be desired by the Lees, Mrs. Lee failed to receive any benefit from the waters. General Lee therefore decided that they would try the waters of the Old Sweet Springs. Here Mrs. Lee was made very comfortable. One of the parlors

## Mrs. Robert E. Lee

which opened on the veranda was turned into a bedroom for her; thus her chair could be wheeled through the long French window onto the veranda and into the ballroom. There, surrounded by friends, she could enjoy the simple gaieties and informal intercourse of the young people.

In September the Lees returned to Lexington, General Lee making the trip on Traveller, and Custis Lee accompanying his mother and sister Agnes on their tedious journey by slow train and uncomfortable stagecoach.

During the two years that General Lee had served as president of Washington College the enrollment had greatly increased, and it was found necessary to add a number of professors to the faculty. This necessitated more houses. It was therefore decided by the trustees that a new home be built for the president, and General Lee was authorized to select the plans. These plans were frequently discussed with Mrs. Lee, who was deeply interested in them. The house would be larger than the original president's house, and it would therefore be possible to entertain the many friends who had opened their homes to the Lees during the war.

Without realizing it Mrs. Lee was suffering from intense nostalgia. She longed to see her old friends, to be able to say to someone "Do you remember?" Writing to her cousin Edward Turner, she says:

## *The Home of the College President*

We are expecting to move into a new house by the spring that they are building for the President of the College & hope then to have more room to entertain our friends & that some of you may get to see me. Life is waning away, and with the exception of my own immediate family I am entirely cut off from all I have ever known & loved in my youth & my dear old Arlington I cannot bear to think of that used as it now is & so little hope of my ever getting there again. I do not think I can die in peace till I have seen it once more.

An intimate friend asked Mrs. Lee, "If Arlington came back to you, what would you do with all those Yankee graves around there?" She replied, "My dear, I would smooth them off and plant my flowers."

A young girl visiting in Alexandria had driven out to Arlington. She wrote:

The house is like some grand old castle. . . . We wandered off in the Union Cemetery & here we found the last resting place of some of the supporters of the Lost Cause. . . . Such a pang as went to my heart when I saw some of the graves marked "Unknown Rebel," "Unknown Soldier," "Rebel."

Though greatly distressed about her health Mrs. Lee made no mention of her anxiety to her family; but in letters to old friends she sometimes voiced her anxiety.

I do not improve at all in walking & have to be lifted in & out of a carriage by 2 men & the physicians do not

## *Mrs. Robert E. Lee*

give me hope that I shall be any better—sad is it not to renounce all hope. I can only pray & strive for submission to God's holy will. My general health is good & was much improved by my visit to the springs this summer, but I do not walk any better, though I gave both the Warm & Hot Springs a fair trial.

Mrs. Lee had taken refuge at the Turner home, Kinloch, after her departure from Arlington. She had visited there frequently as a girl and had gone there often with her children, as it was the home of the man who had been Robert E. Lee's guardian. It filled her mind with memories, and now she wrote to her cousin Edward Turner:

I am glad to hear you have decided to remain at dear old Kinloch. I could not bear to think of your leaving it for any other place. I have so many pleasant memories connected with it, the most recent of all your kindness during the war. To think how all our fond hopes are blasted & what a prospect we have, 4 more years of radical rule. Yet what can we do but submit?

Mrs. Lee cherished the secret hope that to her husband might be given the opportunity to deliver the South from its thralldom. Just after his death she wrote: "I was ambitious enough to hope the day might come when, in a political sense at least, he might again be its [our country's] Deliverer from the thralldom which now oppresses it. By our country I mean the South."

## *The Home of the College President*

It was rarely that more than one of the Lee daughters were at home. Frequent invitations were extended to them from friends and relatives to come for long visits. Their letters were eagerly looked forward to by their mother, as they told of the friends they had seen and the homes they had visited. These letters seemed to bring Mrs. Lee's old world nearer to her. But Christmas, 1867, found five of the children at home: Mary, Mildred, Agnes, and Custis were all there; Robert came from his plantation for a stay of two weeks; only Fitzhugh was absent. This

*Mrs. Lee's Christmas Gift to a Little Girl*
[Washington and Lee University]

## *Mrs. Robert E. Lee*

was a happy time for both General and Mrs. Lee; something of the old Arlington spirit seemed to be in the celebration. For each member of the family there were numbers of gifts. After breakfast and before church General Lee set out on Traveller to deliver the gifts that Mrs. Lee had made for the children of the neighborhood. For the little girls there were china dolls, dressed in woolen suits knit by Mrs. Lee, or in a more fancy dress fashioned of some bit of silk or satin remnant of an evening dress of long ago. For the boys there were knitted reins or gay mittens.

Early in the New Year came the news that the case against Jefferson Davis had been nolprossed. Mrs. Lee had deeply sympathized with Mrs. Davis during the years of Mr. Davis's imprisonment and during the months when he was on bail under bond —a bond famous because it represented the first step in the reconciliation of the North and the South. The first to sign the hundred-thousand-dollar bond under which the former President of the Confederate States had been released from prison was Horace Greeley. He was followed in turn by Augustus Schell, who signed for himself and for his friend Cornelius Vanderbilt; Gerrit Smith, the devoted abolitionist; Benjamin Wood of New York; A. Welsh and D. K. Jackson of Philadelphia; and a number of Southern sureties, including the Virginia Unionist leader, John Minor Botts.

# *The Home of the College President*

Mrs. Lee, hearing that the case had been discontinued, wrote to Mrs. Lorenzo Lewis:

I am sure you have all rejoiced in the release of our President, whose misfortunes & heroic endurance of them has endeared him so strongly to every Southern heart & must command the love & respect of Christendom. Those evil spirits who, like their Father the Devil, can rejoice in nothing that is pure or lovely will continue to *howl* even after their hold upon him has been wrenched away. The Gen'l got a letter from a gentleman, formerly high in office in Richmond, who said he *walked* 5 miles before breakfast from a little farm, where he is barely enabled to make bread for his family & had no other means of getting into town, found Mr. Davis and family at breakfast; to which meal, after being most cordially received, he sat down but could not eat a mouthful, his heart was so *full*; he then accompanied him to the Court Room (the particulars there you have seen in the papers). Immediately upon their return, himself and Burton Harrison being alone, and Mr. M. present besides the family, the doors were closed & the Rev. Mr. Minnegerode knelt down with them all, offering up a most fervent prayer of gratitude to Almighty God for their deliverance. That God, whose ears are ever open to our prayers, will still protect & bless them. John Minor Botts who, I suppose, only came forward with some courtesies to Mr. Davis for the sake of recovering some degree of popularity, or rather respectability, now comes out with an apology for it. He certainly is one of the *basest, meanest* of mankind. What did you all think of Judge Underwood's charge? If it were not so wicked, it would be perfectly ridiculous. He is one of

## Mrs. Robert E. Lee

the *blessed mementoes* bequeathed to us by the "Sainted" Lincoln, for which we are expected to be grateful; but unfortunately our Southern hearts are still rebellious.

It was not possible for General Lee to answer the great number of letters received by him as expeditiously as he would have wished to do. A Christmas letter from General E. G. W. Butler, who had married Frances Parke Lewis, a first cousin of Mrs. Lee's, remained unacknowledged until March 2, when he wrote:

My dear Gen'l:

Your kind letter with its greetings & sympathy has been before me a long time, until days have run into weeks and weeks into months. It has, however, been daily appreciated and only unacknowledged for want of ability. My correspondence is very large and my time much occupied, so that I can do little else than perform the routine of my regular duties. I had, as you supposed, a very pleasant visit to Petersburg. I had suffered so much, in body and mind, when our lines enveloped it, on account of its good people, that, since the night I was obliged to abandon it, I had always looked back upon it in sorrow and sadness. But I found the inhabitants bearing their afflictions so cheerfully and struggling so manfully to repair their fortunes, that a heavy weight has been lifted from my mind.

Fitzhugh (Rooney) had been married the previous November, and his father continues his letter to General Butler:

# *The Home of the College President*

I was very much pleased with my new daughter. She is very handsome and seems to be a great favorite with all her acquaintances, old and young; and is captivating in every way. I became acquainted with her when the army was around Petersburg, and she frequently rode out to my camp to see me. I had, then, no idea that she would ever be nearer or dearer to me. I hope that she may be pleased with her new home and life. I fear she will find it both rough and uninviting at first, for we have to depend mainly on our own hands now for all we receive. Young people, however, can make themselves very happy, and we must all be content with the bare necessaries of life, if we can maintain clean hands and clear consciences. I am sorry that ——— has been obliged by the state of the times to dissolve his engagement, for I think the young should now receive every stimulus to exertion and every tie to bind them to their country, and hope that he may soon be in a condition to gratify his inclination. A poor young farmer can do but little by himself, and I should be very glad if my son Robert could secure a proper helpmate and companion through life. He labours under even greater disadvantages than Fitzhugh, for he has not his knowledge and experience and his plantation is not improved. He has so far, however, made his support and been able each year to extend his cultivation.

. . . I am truly sorry to hear that the past season has been so disastrous to the planting interests of the South; for letters from other states besides Louisiana give similar pictures of the condition of things in the vicinity of the writers, as yours do with you. But my dear Gen'l we cannot stand still. We must persevere and continue to labour; and leave the rest to a kind Providence. I think your course

## Mrs. Robert E. Lee

is the true one; go manfully to work, put your own shoulder to the wheel and be sure to cultivate those articles necessary for the support of yourself and family.

With messages of affection to "our dear Cousin Parke" and other members of the family, who "are all the subjects of our thoughts, our conversation, and our prayers," he turns to a slight mention of his own family, who, he says, are only tolerably well.

Mary and Agnes are in Baltimore, and Mildred is therefore our only dependence. Custis and two of my nephews, who attend College, also form part of our household. My niece Mildred (Carter's daughter) has also been with us since Sept. . . . Your friends in Va. are generally well, though we are all full of troubles. Wisdom, prudence, and fortitude will, I hope, carry us through.

General Butler's home was in Louisiana, now part of Military District No. 5. General Phil Sheridan had been the first commander of the District. Under him the course of reconstruction had been so turbulent that the President, becoming exasperated by Sheridan's indiscretion if not insubordination, relieved him of his command on August 17 and ordered him to the command of the Department of the Missouri.

Sheridan was succeeded by General Winfield Hancock, of whom General Lee wrote General Butler:

# *The Home of the College President*

*The President's House at Washington and Lee University
in Which General Robert E. Lee Lived and Died.
The House Was Built under His Supervision*
[Washington and Lee University]

I am very glad that Judge ——— has conceived so good an opinion of Gen'l Hancock. He is the only one of the District Commanders who seems to have taken a right conception of his duties & to understand the necessities of the Country. I knew him very well, in former years, and always had for him a high consideration, which is in no degree diminished by the manner in which he is administering the affairs of his district.

When Mrs. Lee left Arlington in the spring of 1861, it was impossible for her to remove to a place of safety many of the valuable relics of General Washington's which her father had inherited from Mrs. Washington. After the Federal authorities

[253]

## Mrs. Robert E. Lee

took possession of Arlington the most valuable of the Mount Vernon relics found there were taken to Washington and placed in the Patent Office. There they were placed on exhibit, with the label "Captured from Arlington."

About the time that the new home for the president of Washington College was nearing completion, Captain James May, member of Congress from Illinois, and a long-time friend of the Lees, suggested to Mrs. Lee that she should apply to the President to have these articles restored to her. Twenty years later, long after the death of both General and Mrs. Lee, their son General Custis Lee wrote to Colonel Marshall MacDonald:

> Lexington, Va.
> 2 May, 1887.

My dear Colonel:

Your kind letter of the 28th ult. was duly received, but I have not been able to acknowledge it with my own hand before today.

When President Johnson ordered that the "Arlington relics" should be returned to my Mother, to whom they belonged, Congress passed a violent joint resolution that they should not be so disposed of. For this reason, I have always thought that an Act of Congress would be necessary for their restoration to the family. I am none the less obliged to you, however, and to Prof. Baird for your offices in the matter, and only ask that you will not give yourselves too much trouble in my behalf.

# *The Home of the College President*

I have never made application for the removal of my political disabilities, and never expect to do so; nor do I wish to trouble my friends, who doubtless have troubles enough of their own, to trouble themselves on my behalf.

Always very sincerely your friend,

G. W. C. Lee.


So, when the president's house was finished, the move was made without the Mount Vernon relics, valuable to Mrs. Lee because they had belonged to her great-grandmother, Mrs. Washington, but more precious to her, perhaps, because of their associations with her own home, Arlington. But the portraits which had been cared for at Ravensworth, and the silver which had been buried at Lexington during the war, with the furnishings salvaged by Britannia Peter, added much to the charm of the new home. The new home was much larger and very much better adapted to the needs of the family. Mrs. Lee's room was on the first floor and opened out on the veranda, which extended around three sides of the house, and there Mrs. Lee could be rolled in her chair. General Lee claimed this privilege at least once a day; and the students, knowing the hour, would walk slowly by the house, hoping to catch a glimpse of their idol rolling his wife in her wheel chair, stooping at times to see if she was comfortable, and occasionally leaning over to pat her on the cheek.

## Mrs. Robert E. Lee

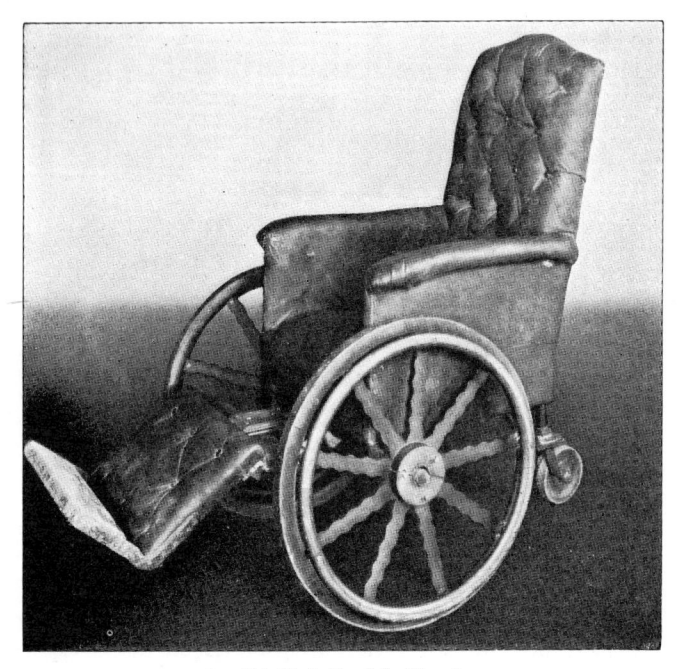

*Invalid Chair Used by Mrs. Lee*
[Virginia Historical Society]

There was something about this picture that deeply impressed these boys, who, sixty-five years later, spoke of it with emotion and reverence.

As the years passed, Mrs. Lee longed more and more for the friends of her earlier life. This is evident from a letter to a cousin, wherein she says: "The people up here are very kind, well educated and excellent; but they are not to me as the friends of my earlier and happier days."

# *The Home of the College President*

Because of arthritis, from which Mrs. Lee suffered, she had been unable to walk or stand on her feet for several years; and now frequently for weeks at a time she was unable to raise a hand to her head. This helplessness on her part and the inaccessibleness of Lexington made the separation from her old friends seem so final.

I fear [she wrote] I must make up my mind to endure this state of helplessness the remainder of my existence on this earth. It is such a deprivation to me to be unable to visit or even to see the friends whom I have known & loved from my youth up. I travel now with so much difficulty that I cannot go anywhere except to the springs. I am not even able to get to see my own children & they are unable to come to see me but once a year. I have never even seen my grandson R. E. Lee III.

This grandson whom she was so anxious to see was the son of Fitzhugh (Rooney) Lee and Mary Tabb Bolling. Fitzhugh's first wife, Charlotte Wickham, had died during the war while he was a prisoner at Fort Monroe. After the surrender Fitzhugh had gone to make his home at the "White House," the plantation willed to him by his grandfather George Washington Parke Custis.

It had been a great delight to both his parents when he had taken Mary Tabb Bolling there in 1867 as his bride. The old house had been burned during the war, and they had started housekeeping

## Mrs. Robert E. Lee

in the new house which he had built. Mrs. Lee was anxious that all her sons should marry and establish homes of their own, and she was disappointed that there were "no weddings or prospects of any."

Custis I fear is a confirmed bachelor & Rob thinks himself too poor to get married yet. As to the girls, they seem to be in the condition of "poor Betty Martin" who, you know the song said, could never "find a husband to suit her mind." I am not in the least anxious to part with them; yet think it quite time, if they intend to change their condition, they were taking the matter under consideration.

Lexington at this time was one of the most inaccessible places in Virginia. Only two routes were available: the one involved a fifty-mile canal journey of some twelve hours to Lynchburg, on a packet offering the most meager accommodations; the other, a journey of twenty-three miles in a lumbering stagecoach, which took from seven to eleven hours to make the trip from Goshen and deposited the bruised and weary traveler about dawn in Lexington. Therefore it was the desire of all interested in the future of the two institutions of learning, Washington College and the Virginia Military Institute, that a railroad be built.

Because it was a matter of importance to her husband, Mrs. Lee was greatly interested in the efforts which were being made. She writes:

## *The Home of the College President*

Robert has been quite sick for a week past with a violent cold, & today, at the urgent solicitation of the people here, has gone with a delegation to Baltimore to solicit aid from that rich city for a railroad. I do hope the ride in the rain will not injure him, for it has been pouring all day.... When we get the R. Road, it will be a great comfort; for this is now the most inaccessible place I know of.

It was while on this trip to Baltimore that General Lee purchased for Mrs. Lee "a little carriage, the best I could find, which I hope will enable you to take some pleasant rides." Upon its arrival some months later it proved a pleasure not only to Mrs. Lee but also to the many friends with whom she shared it; for if her husband was unable to go with her she always invited some friends to accompany her.

Shortly after being settled in the new house, Mrs. Lee decided to publish a revised edition of her father's *Recollections* and to enlarge her *Memoir* of her father. Many of the valuable papers of the Washington family which Mrs. Lee had inherited from her father had been buried during the war. These had recently been restored to her. Now she might be found almost any day seated in her invalid chair before a table on which were spread these papers, faded and discolored, "which," she wrote, "are nearly all that are left to me from a home once abounding in relics of the Father of Our Country." She was attempting the almost impossible task of

## Mrs. Robert E. Lee

deciphering these molded and almost effaced letters of inestimable value. Some of the Washington papers had been inherited by Mr. Lawrence Lewis. These Mrs. Lee had seen when on a visit to Audley. She had written to Mrs. Lorenzo Lewis to verify some notes she had made. On receiving Mrs. Lewis's answer, Mrs. Lee wrote her:

I received your kind letter, my dear Esther & also the enclosure, but do not altogether *understand* the extract. I always thought it was during the winter at Valley Forge, 1777, that Mrs. Washington gave that money. Does it say in the Day Book 1780? Write, when you write again, the *particular* title of *that Day Book* & all about it, as I *hope* another Edition of my "Recollections" may be brought out. The other little scrap of paper enclosed has on it: 6000 Jan from 1772 July 1793. Though it appears to be in my handwriting, I do not know what it means; tho', as I saw the Book once when at Audley, I must have copied these dates from it, I have lost all recollection about it. I do not wish to state anything not exactly correct & think Mrs. Washington's Bounty would be an interesting fact. *Strange* it has never been published. Perhaps her modesty forbade it.

The "president's house," as General Lee designated the new home, was a source of pleasure to the entire family. They were eager to share it with the many friends whose hospitality they had not been able to return when in their first home in Lexington. When the commencement festivities began,

## The Home of the College President

the house was filled, among the guests being six young ladies. Mrs. Lee was no less pleased than her daughters with the air of festivity which pervaded the house. From General Lee his daughters' guests received gallant attentions. He was fond of young people. "No one enjoyed the society of ladies more than himself," wrote Mrs. Lee a short time after his death. "It seemed the greatest recreation in his toilsome life."

It was always in his own house and with his family that General Lee's social graces and charm of manner were most beautifully displayed.

His tenderness to his children, especially his daughters, was mingled with a delicate courtesy which belonged to an older day than ours, a courtesy which recalls the *preux chevalier* of knightly times. He had a pretty way of addressing his daughters in the presence of other people, with a prefix which would seem to belong to the age of lace ruffles & side swords. "Where is my little Miss Mildred?" he would say on coming from his ride or walk at dusk. "She is my lightbearer; the house is never dark if she is in it."

It was a beautiful life in the president's house, characterized by General Lee's devotion as a husband and father and by Mrs. Lee's charm of refinement and culture. Mrs. Lee, heiress of Arlington, and reared in the purple, never expressed a regret. Her beautiful character ran as a sublime refrain

## Mrs. Robert E. Lee

through the daily life of that home where life was lived modestly; but all who entered knew that here were lives dedicated to the unswerving purpose of gathering up the fragments of the shattered South.

Her daughter Mildred wrote many years later of the life in Lexington: "Coming here as we did when all was over — homeless, poor, exiled as we were — we found kindness in every heart and home, and my mother valued everyone according to his real merit and was soon beloved by the whole community as much as my Father."

At Arlington Mrs. Lee had seen the sun set; in Lexington she faced the east, hoping for the sunrise.

## CHAPTER IX

## *The Shadows Lengthen*

GENERAL LEE'S health at this time was a source of great anxiety to Mrs. Lee. He spoke to her often of the fact that he felt that his days were numbered; but she comforted herself with the thought that he was depressed because of the general state of his health, which had been greatly impaired by the hardships he had suffered during the war. She dreaded the strain of the approaching commencement exercises, which would make demands both upon his strength and upon his time, greatly overtaxing him. That ordeal was passed, however, without any appreciable ill effects, though it was evident to Mrs. Lee that her husband was very tired. Thinking that a change would be beneficial, she urged him to go for a visit to his sons Fitzhugh and Robert. Not only would he enjoy being with his sons, she thought, but he would have the additional pleasure of meeting his relatives (to whom he was devoted), many of whom lived in the vicinity of the "White House" and Romancoke. He was eager to go, but it was impossible to arrange the trip at that time because of duties which detained him in Lexington.

## *Mrs. Robert E. Lee*

Mrs. Lee decided that she would go no farther from home that summer than to the Rockbridge Baths. The waters had proved most helpful in the past, and she realized that should her husband take her either to the Hot Springs or to "the White," it would be a tax upon his strength. Therefore, always thoughtful of him, she decided that when she was settled at the Baths he should be free to try the waters of any of the springs which he felt might be beneficial.

Hardly had they arrived at the Baths when General Lee was called to Alexandria by the death of his brother Smith, "a truly sad event to me," he wrote, "and I went from there [Alexandria] to his residence Richland, in Stafford Co. to see my poor sister, his wife; who had been so overwhelmed at his sudden death as to be unable to attend his funeral. The attempt to give consolation is very hard, when you have no words to express it and your own heart requires it."

Robert, who had come to Alexandria to his uncle's funeral, persuaded his father to return home with him by way of the "White House." From there General Lee wrote to his wife that he was bringing his daughter-in-law Mrs. Fitzhugh Lee and her son, Robert E. Lee III, with him. Writing to General Butler, he says:

. . . on my return, proceeded to carry out my pre-arranged plan of visiting the springs [White Sulphur]

# The Shadows Lengthen

by the recommendation of my physician. I left Fitzhugh's wife, her child, and Martha Williams with Mary [Mrs. Lee] and brought Agnes and Mildred with me. My daughter Mary I left with her Aunt Nannie, at Richland....

You have probably learned by the papers that Mr. Peabody is here. He is very feeble; but, I think, has improved since I first saw him. He seems to be very desirous that his munificent donation for education in the South should redound to its benefit, and I trust his aspirations may be realized and his kind intentions fulfilled. His Agent, Dr. Sears, thinks that everything is in a fair way, but that it will take a little time before results become apparent....

I shall have been here three weeks next Monday, 30 Inst., the term appointed for me to drink the waters, and I shall return on that day to Lexington and prepare to collect my scattered family. I hope that we shall be improved in health and refreshed for our duties. I am better than when I came, and the girls, I think, are improved in health. Mrs. Lee writes me that the part with her has been benefited, so we should all be grateful.... I do not recollect ever to have experienced such heat in these mountains. The drought too has been excessive. The cornfields literally parched up, the pastures burned, and the streams dry. I fear no corn will be made in Va., and that there will be much suffering among our people. The wheat crop was good, however,—the oats fair.

Evidently there had been some mention made by General Butler of George Bancroft in a letter written on August 17 from his home in Dumboyne, Bayou Goula, Louisiana, to which General Lee replies:

## Mrs. Robert E. Lee

Mr. Bancroft has given action to many pens in correcting the errors of his *history*. There is one thing that he never fails to do on every occasion, to disparage the South and all things belonging to it. I have ceased to read him or to care for his words.

The "scattered family" all returned to Lexington early in September, Mrs. Fitzhugh Lee and her son returning from the Baths with Mrs. Lee. The baby proved a veritable tonic to both General and Mrs. Lee. The grandmother busied herself with knitting afghans, sacks, and socks, and Agnes wrote to the mistress of the house at the "Second Limit Gate":

Dear Mary,

Could you get Miss Campbell to sew for us for a few days? That is, if you have not engaged her or wish her; for if you do want her, don't hesitate to tell us so. If not, we wd. like her Thursday, Friday & Saturday, or Monday, or any one of those days. And where can we find her?

A seamstress was needed to help in making the dainty little linen shirts and short dresses that Mrs. Lee wished for her grandson.

The house seemed very lonely after the baby left. As Christmas approached, Fitzhugh wrote, urging his parents to come and help in celebrating Christmas for their grandson. Mrs. Lee, realizing that the trip would be impossible for her in the winter, urged her husband to go; but this he would not do.

# The Shadows Lengthen

Perhaps he realized that it would be their last Christmas together; but if he felt any sadness, there was no evidence of it in the very cheerful letters he wrote to his sons.

On New Year's Day the Lees kept open house. The reception was a brilliant one. The daughters of the house had asked several of their friends to assist them in the dining room. It was General Lee who received the guests that crowded the house. Many of the callers found their way into Mrs. Lee's room. In the evening she was rolled in her chair out into the drawing room, where she greeted the late-comers in her charming manner; and for those who had assisted her daughters she had a most gracious word of thanks for their kindness. Those who were there treasured her words and repeated them many times later to their children.

Many of the students who came to Washington College brought with them letters of introduction to the Lees. Once introduced into that home, they were likely afterward to be frequent visitors. One of the loveliest features of the Lee home to these frequently homesick boys was the motherly attitude of Mrs. Lee toward the student body. She missed them when they did not come. During her first year in Lexington she wrote: "There are so many students. I suppose they are studying very hard, as they never seem to find time to visit me." As the years passed, she

## Mrs. Robert E. Lee

could no longer complain that the students did not visit her; and when she found among her visitors a boy who was far from home she would take a special interest in him, frequently telling him to bring to her any of his clothing which might need mending.

As the winter wore on, it was very evident to Mrs. Lee that there was no improvement in her husband's health. Even had she wished to blind herself to his condition, it would have been brought home to her very forcibly by the action of the faculty in a letter to General Lee in which he was urged to take a vacation and spend it in travel for the benefit of his health. Mrs. Lee knew that her husband's physicians had been urging him to escape the rigors of a Lexington March and to try the effect of a Southern climate. Upon the receipt of the letter from the faculty she and other members of the family added their importunities to those of the physicians. General Lee, though reluctant, finally consented to take the advice of his doctors; but it was the last of March before he was able to get away. He was accompanied by his daughter Agnes, who had been his devoted nurse all winter.

Though those who loved him best had urged the trip because of the benefits which they hoped he might derive from it, it probably hastened his death. The trip proved a triumphant progress, filled with

# The Shadows Lengthen

*Mrs. Lee and Her Friends at Ravensworth.*
*Left to right, Miss Minnie Lloyd, Mrs. Robert E. Lee,*
*Mrs. Sidney Smith Lee, Mrs. William Henry Fitzhugh*
[Virginia Historical Society]

excitement and with no opportunity for rest. Rest is what his doctors had hoped for, but he did not find it.

While General Lee was in the South, Mrs. Lee carried out a long-cherished plan to visit her son Fitzhugh. Though she had talked often of going, none of her family thought that she would attempt it. In the past December, when Fitzhugh had urged his parents to come to him for Christmas, General Lee had written him:

It is too cold for your Mother to travel now. She says she will go down in the spring; but you know what an exertion it is for her to leave home, and the inconvenience,

## Mrs. Robert E. Lee

if not the suffering, is great. The anticipation, however, is pleasing to her and encourages hope, and I like her to enjoy it, though am not sanguine that she will realize it.

Though she still continued to talk of going, she appeared to be making no preparations. When her husband, in a teasing way which he often had with his family, asked why, if she were going, she did not make some preparations, she replied rather disdainfully that she had "none to make, they had been made years ago." Shortly after her husband left she completed her plans, as there were still some things she wished finished before she went away. Deeply interested in the building fund of the Episcopal church, in addition to coloring the photographs of General and Mrs. Washington, she was now busy making "housewives," or sewing cases, which were sold to the cadets of the Virginia Military Institute. At this time there was no tailor at the Virginia Military Institute. A cadet must bring with him a "housewife" if he wished to keep his clothes in proper repair. Many of them, used to a mother's attention at home and not knowing that they must be their own tailors at school, came unequipped. Mrs. Lee, hearing of this dilemma from a member of the building committee who was also a member of the faculty of the Institute, suggested that she would make sewing cases if he would agree to sell them to the cadets. The sewing cases found a ready

## The Shadows Lengthen

sale, not only because they filled a need of the cadets but also because the letters which went home telling of the purchase of Mrs. Lee's handiwork were likely to bring orders from parents, more anxious to have something made by Mrs. Lee than in need of sewing cases. It was Colonel M. who procured for her from the commissary at the Institute the supplies needed to equip the sewing cases. Anxious to finish a supply before starting on her trip, she writes:

My dear Col.

I propose to leave on the boat tomorrow wk. *Deo volente*, and would like to close up the financial concerns of the Society before I go, and would like too to finish all the needle books I have in the house; for which end will you be kind enough the first opportunity convenient to you to get me 6 dozen pants & drawers buttons, about 4 doz. of the first & 3 doz. of the last & also 3 spools of cotton no's 30, 40, & 50 ? I think this will be all I shall need. I send $5.00 & you can make up your account & let me settle it. Also, if you have collected anything on that paper for the poor soldiers, I would like to send that. I have about $10.00, including the $5.00 Col. Allen sent me. Ask Mrs. Mac. to see about the bonnets & what material is left.

Yours in haste,

M. C. Lee.

The "White House" plantation, situated on the Pamunkey River, New Kent County, had been a gift of the Honorable John Custis to his son Daniel Parke

## Mrs. Robert E. Lee

Custis upon the marriage of the latter to Martha Dandridge, afterward the wife of George Washington. George Washington Parke Custis, having inherited the plantation from his grandmother Martha Washington, willed it to his grandson William Fitzhugh Lee. But the old house, filled with so many memories and associations, had been burned by the Federals during the war. The house to which Mary Custis Lee now came was the new one built by her son Fitzhugh.

Mrs. Lee had loved Charlotte Wickham as a daughter, the last to reign as mistress in the house once graced by Martha Washington. Now she found many changes: "The locust trees are in full bloom, and the polonia, the only tree left of all that were planted by poor Charlotte and myself. How all our labours have come to naught!"

Notwithstanding the many changes which she found, she thoroughly enjoyed her visit to the "White House." Long drives were taken, with Fitzhugh as the driver. She wrote her daughter:

The road was fine, with the exception of a few mud-holes, and the woods lovely with wild flowers and dogwood blossoms, and with all the fragrance of early spring, the dark holly and pine intermingling with the delicate leaves just brought out by the genial season, daisies, wild violets, and heart's-ease. I have not seen so many wild flowers since I left Arlington.

# The Shadows Lengthen

Always interested in any effort to increase the building fund of the church, she was anxious to know more of the details of a church fair than a letter from Mildred had told her; so she wrote:

I was so glad to receive yrs & your sister's letter, my dear Mildred & to learn you were all well & that the Fair had been such a success; but I would like to learn more particulars—as to who bought certain things, the shawl for instance, the little bedsteads, what chicken salad you had & how nice it was &c &c.

Nor was she unmindful of the difficulties Mildred was having about servants. She continues her letter:

I wish you had been equally successful in getting a cook, but hope you will find one as the time approaches for Louisa to leave; you will find perhaps that she was of more use than you supposed. I have not yet heard from Mary Cocke; but as soon as I do, if she has not been successful, will try to find a maid in this country. I am truly sorry to learn of poor Sam's sickness; that spell of rainy weather was enough to lay anyone up who was exposed to it. Perhaps Louisa will not be in such a hurry to leave him now. You must not forget to give Esther a chance to go out of evenings sometimes.

General Lee and Agnes arrived at the "White House" from their Southern trip on May 12. The following day Mrs. Lee wrote to Mildred:

Your Papa arrived last evening with Agnes. He looks fatter, but I do not like his complexion, and seems still

## Mrs. Robert E. Lee

stiff. Agnes looks thin, but I think it was partly owing to the *immense chignon* which seems to weigh her down and absorb everything. I have not yet had time to hear much of her tour, except a grand dinner given them by Mr. B. Papa sends his love & says he will be in Lexington somewhere about the 24th, but will write to you soon.

Speaking of the servants she inquires for Sam, who, she hopes, is better:

Did he have inflammatory rheumatism & how does Henry perform his duties? . . . Remember me to all enquiring friends & to the servants. Louisa, of course, cannot leave Sam while he is so ill; but by the first of June you may find someone. I shall be very sorry to lose Esther. . . . Will try and get a maid, but the prospects are not very encouraging. I suppose the girls are all crowded in the cities, which they are unwilling to leave. There is no news except that the country becomes more lovely each day.

Mildred was evidently proving herself a most economical housekeeper, some mention of which was made in Mary's letter to her mother; so Mrs. Lee writes: "You must not starve your brother & sister. I suppose the garden now furnishes you with plenty of spinach & lettuce & you must get plenty of eggs."

Anxious to have some of the spring house-cleaning done before General Lee returns, she asks that "if practicable," she "would like to have" her "carpet taken up and the floor oiled before your Papa returns, and also the kitchen floor & when my

## The Shadows Lengthen

carpet is taken up, do have my breastpin again searched for; its disappearance is very remarkable. I wrote a note to Mr. Charlton the painter, which he had best see before he oils the rooms. The kitchen might be done any afternoon & the tea kettle could be boiled in my room or dining room. It would be dry enough the next morning to use & there would be no occasion for Esther going in there at all; so the carpet would be in no danger of being tracked."

It was not until the last of May that Mrs. Lee started on her journey home. She first went to Bremo, where she remained for a short visit. The trip from Bremo to Lexington was made in comparative comfort on the packet boat. Mrs. Lee was not only greatly refreshed by her journey but was also highly elated to feel that she had accomplished in comparative ease a trip which her family had considered almost impossible. Heretofore she had felt as if she were separated from her sons and friends of former days by an insurmountable barrier. Even if the barriers still remained, she had proved to her own satisfaction that they were no longer insurmountable.

Shortly after Mrs. Lee returned home the General left for the Hot Springs, hoping that he might receive from the waters there benefits which he had failed to derive from his Southern trip. Early in

## Mrs. Robert E. Lee

September he returned to Lexington. Shortly after his return Mr. Valentine, the famous Virginia sculptor, arrived to model a bust of him. It was suggested by Mrs. Lee that the sculptor establish his studio in the president's house; but Mr. Valentine felt that this arrangement would disturb the regular routine of the family. Arrangements were therefore made for him to have his studio elsewhere. Thus Mrs. Lee did not see the bust until it was carried to her for criticism and approval; for without her approval no likeness of General Lee, whether portrait, or photograph, or work in plastic art, could go forth officially.

The judging of the bust was to be something of an occasion. Mrs. Lee invited several of her friends to come and serve as her advisers. But the real critic was Mrs. Lee. As the sculptor moved the bust, now in profile, now with full face, General Lee, standing by the bust, did likewise, under orders from his wife. After a most careful scrutiny Mrs. Lee announced herself as delighted.

It had been very evident to Mrs. Lee upon General Lee's return from the springs that he had failed to derive any benefit from his trip. There was so much she wished to do for him; but in her crippled state there seemed so little she could do. It was Agnes, therefore, who was her father's nurse. However, Mrs. Lee took upon herself the duties of amanuensis

# The Shadows Lengthen

*The Dining Room, in the Background, Was Where General Lee Died.
The Room in the Foreground Was the Parlor.
This Picture Was Taken during General Lee's Occupancy of the House*
[Washington and Lee University]

for her husband. Writing to a cousin, whose letter she had seemed dilatory in answering, she says:

> It is long, my dear Edward, since I have written to you. But if you knew how many letters I had to answer, you would pity me; especially of late when my husband has thrown some of his correspondence upon me, as his Doctors have thought it was not well for him to sit so long at his desk as he has been doing for years past.

Almost immediately upon his arrival in Lexington General Lee had been elected a member of the

## Mrs. Robert E. Lee

vestry of Grace Episcopal Church. He and his family had been actively engaged in working for the church, even interesting friends at a distance, who made most generous contributions to the building fund. General Lee was a member of the building committee and was greatly interested in the plans for the proposed new church. On September 28 was held the regular monthly meeting of the vestry. It was a chilly, rainy day. Mrs. Lee begged her husband not to go; but he felt the meeting to be a most important one, and one from which he should not absent himself. He left the open fire, before which he had dozed after dinner, and walked across the campus to the church. The church was cold, the meeting long. Of General Lee's return home Mrs. Lee wrote to her cousin Edward Turner:

No doubt the newspapers have told you of his alarming and sudden attack on the evening of the 29th, when also the terrible storm commenced which has desolated this whole country & carried off every bridge for miles & miles around. Robert had been unusually well the last 4 or 5 weeks & had been riding out regularly since the cool weather commenced; but that day he was detained at the College till about half past one o'clock. He looked very tired when he came in; but ate, as usual, a plate of grapes & then his ordinary dinner, always a very moderate one; his little doze in his arm chair after dinner & then went to church, being the usual evening for week services; then there was a vestry meeting of not a very pleasant

# The Shadows Lengthen

nature & at 7 o'clock, when I went into tea, he was not there. I waited about an hour, when I heard him come in as usual, lay down his hat & coat & enter the dining room. As he came in, I remarked, "You have kept us waiting a long time, where have you been?" He stood up at the foot of the table without replying as if to say grace, but did not utter a word & sank back in his chair. I said, "You seem very tired, let me pour you out a cup of tea." He tried to speak, but muttered something unintelligible. This alarmed me & Custis came to him & in the course of 10 minutes we had both Doctors who had been at the same meeting & had not reached home. They put cold applications to his head & hot ones to his feet & wrists & after a short time had a bed brought down into which they lifted him. He seemed perfectly conscious of what they were doing & assisted in taking off his clothes, tho' he did not speak. He slept continuously for 2 days and nights, only rousing to take a little drink & turn over in his bed, which he accomplished without any difficulty.

The Doctors finding that he did not recuperate as rapidly as they had hoped, cupped him and gave him some medicine. Since then he has been roused & taken more nourishment; but still does not speak, except occasionally a few words, tho' I think it is more from disinclination to make the effort than from inability to do so. Welcomes me always with a pressure of the hand, but never says anything & sleeps still a good deal. The Drs. think he will now recover, tho' it seems to us very slow, & that he has no symptoms either of paralysis or apoplexy. God grant they may be right in their view of his case, for I cannot help still feeling very anxious about him. . . . We never leave him alone a moment either night or day; tho'

## Mrs. Robert E. Lee

he does not require much, yet as he does not *speak* to make known his wants, he must be watched.

The anxiety which Mrs. Lee felt for the ultimate recovery of her husband she did not express to those who came daily to inquire, but rather spoke often of "when Robert gets well."

It was a trying ordeal to her that she could not actively nurse her husband, and she was eager to find things that she might do for him. On October 10, 1870, she writes to General Smith, superintendent of the Virginia Military Institute:

My dear Gen'l:

The Drs. think it would be well for Gen'l Lee to have some beef tea at once & as I cannot get it at market before night I send to beg a small piece, if it can be found at the Institute, lean & juicy if possible; a pound would answer for the present, as I can get some more tonight.

In great haste Yrs.

M. C. Lee.

All Lexington felt General Lee's life to be hanging on the event of a moment. Superstitious persons began to read signs in the sky. For several nights an aurora had illumined the heavens. They interpreted the lurid streamers of light, which were like great curtains waving backward and forward, as waiting only the appointed time to open for the pass-

*Recumbent Statue of General Lee over His Tomb in Lee Chapel
on the Campus of Washington and Lee University, Lexington, Virginia.
It Is the Work of the Celebrated Sculptor Valentine*

[Virginia Conservation Commission]

ing of a soul into eternity. One Lexingtonian of Scotch descent, who often read *Lays of the Scottish Cavaliers*, remembered and pointed to the quatrain

> All night long the northern streamers
>   Shot across the trembling sky:
> Fearful lights that never beckon
>   Save when kings or heroes die.

But to Mrs. Lee no one mentioned the omen which superstition saw written in the skies; and she, who belonged to a generation which believed that the falling of a portrait portended a death, refused to acknowledge that she felt any anxiety when such an accident occurred in the president's house, and said to a caller: "If I were superstitious, I would feel disturbed at an accident that happened this morning. Robert's large portrait fell from the wall where it hung and injured the frame very much."

Then came the day when the doctors told Mrs. Lee that there was no hope. The prayers that she had so fervently offered that the life of her husband be spared were now "Thy will be done for me and mine." All through the night she kept her vigil by his side. She knew now that he was awaiting only the summons of One whose commands he had always obeyed. She leaned closer in order to catch the words he was so faintly whispering. Then clearly to all those gathered round his bed came his voice,

## *The Shadows Lengthen*

"Strike the tent," and a great soul passed through the curtain now opened wide for him.

That evening Mrs. Lee wrote to her very dear cousin Miss Mary Meade:

We all prayed God so fervently to prolong a life so important to his family & country; but *He*, in his mysterious Providence, thought best to call him to those mansions of Rest which he has prepared for those who love and serve him & Oh what a rest to his toilsome and eventful life. So humble was he as a Christian, that he said not long ago to me he wished he felt sure of his acceptance. I said all who love and trust in the Savior need not fear. He did not reply, but a more upright & conscientious Christian never lived . . . so long has the will of God been the guiding star of his actions. I have never so truly felt the purity of his character as now, when I have nothing left me but its memory, a memory which I know will be cherished in many hearts besides mine. I may soon follow him; but his children—what a loss to them! I pray his death may be blessed to them, for dearly they all loved him.

Writing later and speaking of the storm which occurred during his illness she says:

Nature seemed to grieve with convulsive throbs and the windows of Heaven to be opened and all the next day & night the storm raged unceasingly . . . yet all our thoughts & aspirations were centered on that noble form lying so helpless . . . but ere long his spirit passed away, the skies brightened and more lovely weather I have never seen & ever since it has seemed at times to mock our grief, it has been so beautiful.

## CHAPTER X

## Sunset

MRS. LEE'S simple unselfishness shone in the days following her husband's death. She talked without bitterness to those who came to offer their sympathy. Writing to a friend, she says:

> God knows the best time for us to leave this world & we must never question either His love or wisdom. This is my comfort in my great sorrow, to know that had my husband lived a thousand years he could not have died more honoured & lamented even had he accomplished all we desired and hoped.

She was lonely now indeed; for "everything in the house was always done with reference to his comfort, his wishes & now there seems to be no object in having anything done."

During General Lee's trip to the South in the spring of 1870 the trustees of Washington College, at their April meeting, had recorded in the minutes that "in order that the President's mind be relieved of any concern for the support and comfort of his family" they conveyed to Mrs. Lee for her life the use of the president's house, and upon the death or

## Sunset

disability of General Lee she was to receive an annuity of three thousand dollars. General Lee must have been informed of the action of the trustees before his return to Lexington and had evidently discussed it with Mrs. Lee when he met her at the "White House"; for the day following his return to Lexington he wrote to the trustees:

*Mrs. Robert E. Lee*
[From a photograph belonging to Mrs. James Oliver of Shirley]

Though fully sensible of the kindness of the Board, and justly appreciating the manner in which they sought to administer to my relief, I am unwilling that my family should become a tax to the College, but desire that all its funds should be devoted to the purpose of education. I know that my wishes on this subject are equally shared by my wife, and therefore request that the provisions of the fourth and fifth resolution (conveying the house and annuity to Mrs. Lee) . . . not be carried into effect. I feel assurance that, in case a competency should not be left to my wife, her children would not suffer her to want.

Notwithstanding General Lee's letter, which was presented to the trustees at the meeting on June 21, they made no change in the resolution regarding the annuity, and had the life-term lease of the president's house to Mrs. Lee recorded.

Mrs. Lee knew of the action of the trustees, and though deeply appreciative of their thoughtfulness for her she notified them a short time after her husband's death that she would not consider the president's house as hers and that she would remain there only until she and her daughters had decided upon their future home. She had no desire now to leave Lexington, where she found "the kindness of everyone is unceasing."

However, any hesitancy she might have felt in occupying the president's house was removed by the election of Custis Lee as president of the college in succession to his father. The house built for General Lee and occupied by him for only a little over a year became the house in which Mrs. Lee was to spend the remainder of her life; but she steadfastly declined to accept the annuity.

For some time after General Lee's death Mrs. Lee was buoyed up by the letters and tributes paid to her husband. Many of the letters she answered herself, but it was a slow and trying task for her. To one near relative she wrote:

> I should have answered your kind letter sooner, my dear Edward, but have been too unwell to write & since I have been able to sit up, have injured myself by attempting to reply to too many of the kind letters that have been

*Washington and Lee University, Lexington, Virginia. Endowed by George Washington*
[Virginia Conservation Commission]

# Mrs. Robert E. Lee

sent to me; but will take advantage of Mrs. Washington's return to your neighborhood to send you a sermon, one of the best, I think, of the many which have been delivered on the occasion, by a Presbyterian clergyman whom we saw frequently in Richmond during the war. I suppose you have seen Mr. McKim's or I would send it to you.

She writes:

If anything can alleviate sorrow like mine, it is the knowledge of the many true tears that have been mingled with mine & the prayers that have been offered up for me and my husband. Could he have been more lamented & honoured had he obtained for our beloved South the Independence to the attainment of which he devoted his life & renounced all ease & comfort? The fame so unsought & never desired will follow his name through ages to come.

She who had never criticized any act of her husband, uttering no reproach for the ease and comfort which she had been forced to renounce, now found comfort in the encomiums of praise showered upon him. It was an elixir to her tired heart. Her often-expressed wish now was "that his noble example may inspire our youth to the course of uprightness which never wavers from the path of duty at the sacrifice of ease or pleasure."

In December she wrote to General Butler:

You speak of my husband's "*untimely* death." We must not deem that untimely which God ordains. He

# Sunset

knows the best time to take us from this world; and can we question either his love or wisdom? How often are we taken from the evil to come.

How much of care and sorrows are those spared who die young. Even the heathen considers such the favorites of the gods; and to the Christian what is death but a translation to eternal life. Pray that we may all live so that death will have no terrors for us.

The great storm which at the time of General Lee's death "raged unceasingly, carrying away in its fury houses, bridges, men & cattle, so that for 8 days" Lexington was entirely isolated from the rest of the world, had so damaged the canal that several months passed before navigation was resumed on it. Fitzhugh had written, begging his mother to come to the "White House" for a visit. As the spring approached, Mrs. Lee found life without her husband increasingly hard. She was restless and anxious to be once again at the "White House." Having found that she could make the trip in comfort on the packet, she awaited only the opening of the canal to start on her journey. To Mildred, who was already at the "White House," she wrote:

I hope to leave this day week on the Packet *Marshall*, Captain Wilkerson, the same Captain; but he leaves Tuesday evening instead of Sunday & will reach Richmond, I suppose, on Friday morning. I wrote the Captain to know but he did not tell me. We are very quiet here & miss you all greatly. The canal is just open & we are getting our first load of coal. The house will be much warmer. I shall reserve all news till I come & hope I shall find you at the "White House." Your darlings are all well. Fritz is enormous & often comes to see his Grandma, but Love rarely comes in the house. Many mice & rats have been caught in traps & I *believe* the cats have condescended to eat a few, which accounts for their size. . . . Your sister [Mary] will write soon; she is quite a housekeeper, tho' I am the dessert maker. We are expecting the trustees the 30th. I do not think they will have much except turkeys. . . ."

Not only Mrs. Lee's family but also her intimate friends were anxious to have her make the trip. She was eager to go; for not only did she wish to be with Fitzhugh and his family at the "White House," but she hoped that her proximity to Robert's plantation would enable her to see something of him and to hear of his plans. For Robert was taking a bride to Romancoke in November, and he was now busy getting his "bachelor hall" in order.

But the early summer found her once again at home. She had not realized when she left how hard would be the return to the "president's house" without her husband's welcome, which had for so long greeted her upon her return from every journey. All Lexington was filled with sympathy for her, a sympathy expressed in the many little attentions paid her. Any little delicacy which graced the table of a Lexington housewife was likely to be shared

## Sunset

with Mrs. Lee. True to a Virginia custom, she always sought some little thing to place in the basket when returning it. She writes:

> I have long intended, my dear Mrs. Smith, to return your little basket, but have been delayed with the hope of filling it with something that would be acceptable to you. But it seems that I have waited in vain, for I have nothing but a few poor flowers, scarcely worth your acceptance; yet I will send them & hope to get a rose bud, the last on a bush planted and cherished by Gen'l Lee, which you might value.

In the early autumn, before General Lee's death, Robert had written to tell his parents of his engagement to Charlotte Haxall, an intimate friend of Mildred's and a great favorite with the entire family. General Lee had written of his delight "to hear of Rob's engagement to my beautiful Lottie Haxall." Mrs. Lee had a specially tender feeling for Robert. He was her youngest; his happiness was her happiness. But this happiness was short-lived. Before a year had passed, Romancoke was again without a mistress, and the mother mingled her tears with those of her son.

Agnes and Mildred had attended Robert's wedding and had then gone on to the "White House" for a visit. When Christmas came, only Custis and Mary were with their mother. Mary busied herself in helping to decorate the church and arranging a

## Mrs. Robert E. Lee

Christmas celebration for the Sunday school, and Mrs. Lee, thinking of those friends with whom she might share the delicacies which had come to her, wrote:

My dear Mrs. Smith:

I can only write you a few lines, as I can scarcely mark with my pen, to offer you some Richmond oysters which I hope you all will enjoy & some ginger which the young ones too may enjoy. The weather prevents our meeting, but my heart is with you & yours. You have heard of the loss of our dear little baby. I can scarcely bear it, but God is good. I cannot write more.

Yrs. affectionately,

Mary C. Lee.

And to the Colonel and his lady at the "Second Limit Gate," there went with "some Richmond oysters" a bottle of rare old wine.

Christmas had been saddened for Mrs. Lee because "during that time Fitzhugh lost his youngest child of whooping cough, a lovely little girl of one year old, whom I had been looking forward to enjoy so much this winter when I expected to go down."

The greatest incentive that Mrs. Lee might have had for making the trip was to see her grandson, now three years old. Letters coming from the "White House" were largely taken up with details about him. Answering one, his grandmother says:

## *Sunset*

I am glad to hear my darling little Rob is becoming so sweet & good. Don't spoil him. I fear he will have too many indulgences to make a great & self-controlled spirit essential to a great & good man; but we must pray that God will direct him in all his ways & teach him early to love & serve Him. Kiss him for his Gran, who is now looking forward to seeing him next summer, when he will no doubt be able to ride Lucy, with Fritz behind & Love before.

Fritz and Love were two of the cats which were pets in the president's house. There were always cats to be found as pets in the Lees' home. There had been a constant procession of them at Arlington; some of their progeny had gone to Old Point and some to West Point. Mildred, especially, had inherited her father's fondness for cats, and those now in the Lee home were regarded as her special pets. Her mother was therefore likely to make some mention of them in her letters. In a letter enclosed in one to Fitzhugh she says:

Fritz, altho' never welcome to the parlor, slips in to see me, jumps in my lap & on my chair to fondle me, tho' I never have a mouthful to give him. Love rarely comes in, looking very subdued; but is often in the kitchen in Linda's arms. They are both as fat as possible & sometimes come in my room & have a tussle.

In a later letter she says:

I rarely see the cats, except sometimes when I make a morning visit into the kitchen, when Love is usually in

## Mrs. Robert E. Lee

Linda's lap eating bits of bread & Fritz, poor fellow, drawing something out of the *slop bucket* & they are both very fat & Love has had no new kittens. I saw her flirting with a strange yellow cat not near as handsome as old Fritz; the old black & white has deserted her. Where they sleep these cold nights is not known, tho' your brother George thinks it is with the cow.

Always interested in her housekeeping, she wishes Fitzhugh, when he writes again, to tell what he gives "for good brown sugar by the barrel, such as will answer for servants' use & for nice *crushed* not *cut* white sugar, which latter is more expensive. As soon as navigation is well open, we would like to get a supply."

Mrs. Lee had written: "My dear old Arlington ... so little hope of my ever getting there again. I do not think I can die in peace till I have seen it once more." She felt the shadows lengthening, and knew that if she were to see her old home once again she must no longer delay. Her daughter wrote: "My mother's heart was ever turned to Arlington, the fair scene of her life's best happiness."

There were those who told her that she would not find Arlington greatly changed; that the War Department, regretting the devastation, had done everything possible to restore it to its natural beauty and former grandeur of forested hills and sloping lawns. The terraces, which had been battered down

## Sunset

by the constant tramping of man and horse and utterly denuded of turf, had been built up and re-sodded. Drives had been restored, and emerald lawns again stretched away in velvety beauty from the mansion.

There came a day in June when the former mistress of Arlington while staying with her aunt Maria Fitzhugh at Ravensworth, came to visit scenes so dear to her memory. Of this visit Mrs. Lee wrote:

> I rode out to my dear old home but so changed it seemed but as a dream of the past—I could not have realised that it was Arlington but for the few old oaks they had spared & the trees planted on the lawn by the Genl & myself which are raising their tall branches to the Heaven which seems to smile on the desecration around them.

The devastating scythe of war had spared the splendid oak grove immediately surrounding the mansion. Thus the natural beauty and the familiar setting of the place had been preserved. But Mrs. Lee saw a house deserted by its own, never again to bear the loved title of "home": empty rooms, and the loved garden, made by her mother and cherished by her, marked now by long lines of white headboards. Her cup of sorrow was indeed full. There were no tears. Those who watched saw only a gallant soul, of mien so proud that no one dared offer sympathy.

## Mrs. Robert E. Lee

> I rode out to my
> dear old home but so changed it seemed
> but as a dream of the past — I could not
> have realised that it was Arlington but
> for the old oaks they had spared, & the trees
> planted on the lawn by the Genl & myself
> which are raising their tall branches to the
> Heaven which seems to smile on the
> desecration around them — I did not
> get out of the carriage but the young
> friends who were with me went all over

*Part of a Letter Written by Mrs. Robert E. Lee to a Friend after Her Last Visit to Arlington*
[Miss Betty Cocke]

Her daughter wrote many years later:

Her heart ever turned to Arlington. She visited it once not long before her death. After this visit, she said she never wished to see it again. The cruel change sank deep in her soul.

Of this visit the *New York World* said:

There are few modern incidents more full of simple pathos than the quiet visit which Mrs. Mary Custis Lee paid to her old homestead of Arlington about three weeks [months] before her death. Mrs. Lee had not put in words her heart's longing for the place endeared to her by so many bright associations. During the General's lifetime she had

## Sunset

said not a word about her confiscated estate, and after his death she did no more than consent that a modest petition should be sent to Congress asking that the judgment which deprived her of her ancient home for no fault of her own, should at any rate be examined into, even if it could not be revised. It was thought she took this step for the good of her children, and not because she had any personal feeling in the matter. But when she felt the hand of death begin to tighten upon her, she painfully left the seclusion to which ten years of rheumatic fever had confined her, slowly and with sad interest revisited the old homestead and the scenes of her youth and womanhood, gazed upon that which she had loved so well and longed for in silence and resignation and then went quietly back to Lexington to die. It will add a pang to the sense of loss which her friends have for this gracious lady, of such nobility of character and patience in affliction, to feel that to her other griefs was joined this unavailing yearning for the old home she could not come back to—a yearning not put in words, not suspected until expressed by that most pathetic leave-taking on the eve of death.

The third anniversary of the death of General Lee approached, and Agnes, of all Mrs. Lee's children dearest to her heart, lay ill; she lingered only three days. All Lexington mourned with Mrs. Lee, for Agnes had endeared herself to all those who had learned to know her there.

November came, and Mildred wrote:

Mamma enjoyed yr. nice things very much. She is worse today & my heart is very heavy; but in the midst of

## Mrs. Robert E. Lee

*Lee Memorial Chapel, Lexington, Virginia*
[Washington and Lee University]

all this darkness, the love & sympathy of true & tried friends is very comforting.

I have put aside yr. sweet letter, and if she ever gets well, will show it to her.

      Yrs. with love

       Mildred Lee.

The sons came to join Mildred at the bedside of their mother. Only Mary was absent.

# Sunset

On a clear November day Mary Custis Lee saw the sun set for the last time. By her bed were a few late rosebuds from bushes planted by her husband. As a new day was about to begin, the symphony, which was her life, ended in one triumphant chord, and her spirit went to join his from whom she had never been parted.

In the *Lexington Gazette and General Advertiser* of Friday, November 7, 1873, appeared the following notice:

Mrs. Mary Custis Lee died at her home in Lexington on the night of the 5th of November, near the hour of twelve.

The funeral services will be held in the Lee Memorial Chapel today (Friday) at 12 o'clock, and the remains will be deposited in the vault of the Chapel, in accordance with her wish.

The places of business will be closed during the services.

In the *Southern Collegian* it was said of her:

Tempting as the theme is, we forbear to offer any eulogy on the character of this woman, so venerated and loved by the entire community in which she resided, related to our University—we may say linked to its history and its destiny—by so many strong and tender ties, and around whom there was gathered for years past a degree of public interest and affectionate solicitude that has never attached to any other woman in the history of our country. It is enough to say that in intelligence and in refine-

## Mrs. Robert E. Lee

ment of taste, in kindness of heart and attractiveness of manner, in cheerfulness under the heaviest reverses of fortune and the agonies of bodily pain, in sympathy and in benefactions towards the impoverished and suffering people of her country, in her manifold and ceaseless self-denials and labors on behalf of religion and the church of her fathers and of her choice, in all this she was an ornament to her sex, was worthy of her illustrious husband.

# INDEX

Agricultural Bureau, Washington, establishment of, 106
Alexandria, Virginia, 8, 24, 26, 46, 143, 146, 149
Ambler's School, Mr., 122
American Colonization Society, 48, 88
Analostan Island, Mason estate, 32
Ann Smith Academy, 241
Anne, Queen, 10
Archers, the Miss, 53
Arlington, 6–7, 41, 152–153, 159, 245, 294, 296; confiscated for taxes, 172–173; family life at, 3, 4, 18–19, 20, 54, 55–59, 63–64, 66–67, 81, 82–83, 102, 142; festivities at, 34–35; furnishings of, 211; garden at, 81, 152; guests at, 57, 135–136; improvements at, 105, 106; Mrs. Lee leaves, 151–152; Mrs. Lee visits, after war, 295; occupied by Federal troops, 153; servants at, 19, 91–93, 151, 153–154; Washington relics at, 253–255
Army of the Confederacy, 183
Army of Northern Virginia, 172, 190
Army of Occupation, 193
Army of the Potomac, 31, 186
Ashland, 169
Assembly, Virginia, 17
Audley, Lewis estate, 47, 62, 108, 122, 156, 260
Aunt Eleanor. *See* Lewis, Mrs. Lawrence

Aunt Maria. *See* Fitzhugh, Mrs. William Henry

Baltimore, 40, 53, 68, 94, 141
Baltimore and Ohio Railroad, 64
Bancroft, George, 265, 266
Bazaar, church, 226, 273
Beaumont, Dr. William, 72
Bible, 38, 55
Bible lessons, 54
Billy, servant at Arlington, 132
Blue Ridge Mountains, 122, 156
Bolling, Mary Tabb. *See* Lee, Mrs. William Henry Fitzhugh
Books for Sunday school at Fort Monroe, 53
Bounty, Mrs. Washington's, 260
Brandy Station, battle of, 167
Bremo, Cocke estate, 179, 188, 208, 275
Bridesmaid of Mary Custis, 31–32
Brooklyn Navy Yard, 86
Buchanan, James, 117
Building fund of Grace Episcopal Church, 270
Butler, Frances Parke Lewis (Mrs. Edward G. W. Butler), 27, 130, 250
Butler, General Edward G. W., 27, 130, 250, 264, 265, 288

Calvert, Benedict, 14
Calvert, Eleanor (Mrs. John Parke Custis), 14
Calvert, Julia, 32
Camp Lee, 187
Campbell, Miss, 266

[301]

# Mrs. Robert E. Lee

Capitol, Washington, 6
Capitol of the Confederacy, 184
Carey, Mrs., 90
Carter, Charles Henry, 28
Carter, Shirley, 28
Caskie, Mr. and Mrs. James M., 166
Caskie, Norvell, 166
Cassy, servant at Arlington, 38, 56, 91
*Catechism, Brown's*, 53
Cedar Grove, estate of Richard Stuart, 82, 166
Chantilly, Stuart estate, 62
Chatham, Fitzhugh estate, 8, 25, 26, 81
Childe, Edward, 118
Childe, Mary, 118
Childe, Mildred Lee, 118
"Children's hour," 66
Chilton, Mrs. R. M., 230
Christ Church, Alexandria, Virginia, 19, 84, 146
Christmas, at Arlington, 54, 64, 85, 107–109, 136; at Fort Hamilton, 96–97; at Hickory Hill, 167; at Lexington, 226–228, 247–248, 291–292; at Richmond, 174–175, 182; at the "White House," 159
*Christmas Annual*, 98
Church, attendance at, 19, 51, 97, 108, 176
Church bells, 43
*Churchman*, 74
City life, dangers of, 106
Civil authorities, 190
Clarke, Captain, 94

Clarke, Mrs., 94
Clarke County, Virginia, 8, 156, 228
Clay, Henry, 88
Clay, Senator Clement C., 139
Cochran, Mr. W. W., 117
Cocke, Mrs. Elizabeth Randolph, 199
Cocke, General, 179
Cocke, John, 188
Cocke, Mary, 273
Cocke, Randolph, 200
Colonization Society. *See* American Colonization Society
Confederacy, Capitol of, 192
Courtesies, exchange of, 222, 233, 291
Coxe, Dr., 70
Coxe, Mrs., 70
Crows Nest (mountain), 110
Cumberland County, 199
Cumberland Road, 64
Custis, Daniel Parke, 12
Custis, Edward Hill, 8
Custis, Eleanor Calvert (Mrs. John Parke Custis), 14, 18
Custis, Eleanor Parke. *See* Lewis, Mrs. Lawrence
Custis, Frances Parke (Mrs. John Custis), 10–12
Custis, George Washington Parke, father of Mrs. Lee, 5, 6, 7, 8, 14, 15, 16, 19, 26, 29, 34, 37, 41, 57, 58, 66, 108, 123–124, 140, 257, 272
Custis, John, 10–12
Custis, John Parke, 5, 12, 14, 15, 17, 18

[302]

# Index

Custis, Mrs. Martha Dandridge, 12. *See also* Washington, Martha

Custis, Martha Elizabeth Ann, 8

Custis, Martha Parke, 12, 15

Custis, Mary Anna Randolph. *See* Lee, Mary Anna Randolph Custis

Custis, Mary L. F. (Mrs. George Washington Parke Custis), mother of Mrs. Lee, 3, 8, 19, 20, 23, 26, 29, 37, 39, 41, 53, 57, 66, 77, 95, 104, 111

Custis, Nelly. *See* Lewis, Mrs. Lawrence

Custis estate, 6

Custis Spring, 7

Dancing, 34, 218, 242

Daniel, servant at Arlington, 108

Davis, Jefferson, Senator, 139; President of the Confederacy, 174, 175, 188, 191, 198, 204–205, 248–249

Davis, Mrs. Jefferson, 184

Day Book, General Washington's, 260

Derwent, Cocke property, 199, 200

Dick, servant in the Lee home, 54

Doddridge, 38

Ducachet, Dr., 51

Dumboyne, home of General Butler, 265

Eastern Shore, 6, 10, 216

Education, General Lee's interest in, 237; of Lee children, 94, 106, 110, 116, 122, 134, 166; Mrs. Lee's interest in, 237–238; of Southern girls, 237

Engineering Academy, 218

Engineer's Office, Washington, 56, 64

Enlistments in the Revolutionary War, 17–18

Entertaining, at Arlington, 20–21; at Fort Monroe, 49; at Lexington, 221; at Richmond, 176

Ephraim, servant at Arlington, 132, 133

Episcopal Church, in Alexandria, 19; in Baltimore, 102; at Fort Monroe, 49; in Lexington, 223

Episcopal High School, 169

Episcopal Theological Seminary, 19

Esther, servant in the Lee home, 273, 274

Eustis, Mrs., 42

Evacuation of Richmond, 190–192, 194

Fairfax County, 8, 26

Fairfax Institute, 89

Fashions in dress, 28, 31, 48, 87

"Father of his Country," 32, 129, 152, 259

Fauquier County, Virginia, 3, 32, 156

Fitzhugh, Mary Lee. *See* Custis, Mary L. F. (Mrs. George Washington Parke Custis)

Fitzhugh, William, 8, 25

# Mrs. Robert E. Lee

Fitzhugh, William Henry, 25, 26, 35
Fitzhugh, Mrs. William Henry, 28, 43, 115, 124
Fitzpatrick, Benjamin, 139
Flowers. *See* Garden
Food, shortage of, 176, 178–179
Fort Hamilton, 83
Fort Monroe, 35, 36, 168, 204, 257
Fort Sumter, 142, 143, 163
Fort Washington, 147

Garden, at Arlington, 81–82; at Fort Monroe, 42; at Lexington, 236–237; at West Point, 109–110
George, servant at Arlington, 52
Gerard College, 70
Gettysburgh, Pennsylvania, 167
Goldsborough, Anne Maria. *See* Fitzhugh, Mrs. William Henry
Goldsborough, John, 155
Goldsborough, Mary, 3, 4, 32, 43
Government, policy of, 138
Grace Church, 223
Grant, General U. S., 185
Gratiot, General Charles, 49, 50
*Great Western*, 87–88
Greeley, Horace, 248
Groomsmen of Lee, 32
Gunston, estate of the Masons, 81
Gurley (Ralph Randolph), 48

Hackley, Harriet Randolph. *See* Talcott, Mrs. Andrew
Hampton, General, 231

Hancock, Winfield, 252–253
Harpers Ferry, 150
Harrison Cottage at White Sulphur Springs, 242
Henderson, Captain, 218
Hickory Hill, Wickham estate, 165, 168
Hill, General D. H., 230
Hot Springs, 275
Houston, Sam, 30
Howard, Milly, Mrs. Lee's maid, 242
Huger, Mrs., 45, 46, 47
Hunter, General David, destruction by, 187, 206

Jackson, Andrew, 49, 50
Jackson, Eleanor Junkin (Mrs. Thomas Jonathan Jackson), 236
Jackson, Fort, 194
Jackson, General Thomas Jonathan ("Stonewall"), 236
Jackson, Rachel (Mrs. Andrew Jackson), 50
James River, travel on, 40
James River and Kanawha Canal Co., 208, 229
Johnson, Andrew, 254
Judy, the baby's nurse in the Lee home, 51
Junkin, Dr. William, 236

Keith, Mrs. Ruel, 77
Keith, the Reverend Ruel, 32, 33, 77
Kemper, Bishop, 76
Kennedy, Lieutenant John P., 32

[304]

# Index

Kennon, Britannia Peter (Mrs. Beverly Kennon), 31, 211, 255

Kinloch, estate of the Turners, 3, 32, 62, 156, 246

Kitty, servant at Arlington, 68, 75

Lafayette, George Washington, 23

Lafayette, Marquise de, 21; visits Alexandria, 22–23; visits Arlington, 22

Lee, Anne Carter (Mrs. Henry Lee), mother of Robert E. Lee, 24, 26, 127

Lee, Anne Carter, daughter of Mrs. Robert E. Lee, 79, 94, 106, 132, 133, 165

Lee, Eleanor Agnes, daughter of Mrs. Robert E. Lee, 84, 106, 132, 166, 215, 216, 218, 220, 225, 233, 265, 297

Lee, Fitzhugh, nephew of General Lee, 109, 180

Lee, George Washington Custis, son of Mrs. Robert E. Lee, 46, 47, 48, 49, 56, 60, 63, 66, 76, 89, 120, 181, 200, 218

Lee, General Henry ("Light-Horse Harry"), father of Robert E. Lee, 24, 127

Lee, Marietta. *See* Lee, Mary Custis

Lee, Mary Anna Randolph Custis (Mrs. Robert Edward Lee)
Ancestry, 5–16
Annefield, place of birth, 8
Arlington, leaves, 151–152; life at, 3, 4, 18–19, 20, 54, 55–59, 63–64, 66–67, 81, 82–83, 102, 142; loses, 172–173; visits, after the war, 295–297
As parent, 45, 48, 49, 56, 60–61, 107, 117–118, 120, 135, 240–241, 258
Attention to business, 114
Birth, 8
Character, 4, 214
Cheerfulness, 194, 212
Childhood, 3, 4, 18–19, 26–27
Church interests, 38, 76, 225, 270, 273
Courage, 125–126, 162–163, 173, 192, 193
Courtship, 29–30, 84
Death, 299
Devotion to, of husband, 55, 147, 178, 255; of parents, 4, 27, 37, 41, 112, 125; of servants, 56, 131
Economies, 89–90, 131
Edits Mr. Custis's *Recollections*, 129–130
Education, 29, 237
Faith in God, 183, 186, 190, 197, 283, 284, 288–289
Health, 59, 60, 113, 115, 125–126, 129, 157, 164, 178, 239, 245–257
Heroism, 183–184, 191, 222
Home, at Baltimore 102–103; at Fort Hamilton, 83, 93–94, 95; at Fort Monroe, 36–56; at Lexington, 210–212, 232–233, 260–261; at Richmond, 170–178, 179–184; at St.

[305]

## Mrs. Robert E. Lee

Louis, 72–78; at West Point, 109–110
Housekeeper, 53, 132, 134, 273, 274–275
Industry, 42–43, 44, 175–176, 177, 212, 232
Interest in students, 267–268
Knitting for soldiers, 157–158, 177, 182
Lover of nature, 118
Marriage, 31–35
Painting, 42, 225
Politics, interest in, 58, 139, 140–141, 146, 230
Portrait, sits for, 68–69
Religious practice and belief, 18–19, 51, 54, 97, 99, 107, 108, 117–118, 133, 144, 146, 182
Sense of humor, 218
Sharing, 212, 228
Social life, at Arlington, 21; at Baltimore, 103–104; at Fort Monroe, 49; at Lexington, 221, 231, 266; at Washington, 27–28
Teaches, children, 81, 97; servants, 54
Lee, Mary Custis, daughter of Mrs. Robert E. Lee, 59, 60, 66, 68, 75, 108, 115, 157, 166, 215, 216, 218, 265, 274
Lee, Mary Tabb Bolling. *See* Lee, Mrs. William Henry Fitzhugh
Lee, Mildred Chiles, daughter of Mrs. Robert E. Lee, 98, 115, 134, 135, 136, 159, 166, 170, 216, 220, 225, 226, 233, 261, 265, 274
Lee, Robert Edward, 23, 24–27, 41, 51, 64, 83, 147
Appointed to West Point, 29, 35
Arrives in Lexington, 206–207
As father, 63, 65, 80, 104, 115, 131, 165, 261
At Arlington, 56, 127
Bust of, 276
Church interests, 277–278
Commander in chief, named, 184
Conference with President Davis, 174, 188–190
Custis estate, executor of, 127
Death, 283
Family life, 55, 107–109
Honors, 100, 174, 288
Illness, 263, 268, 278–283
Ordered, to Baltimore, 102; to Fort Hamilton, 83; to Fort Monroe, 36; to Harpers Ferry, 127; to Louisville, 112; to Mexico, 99, 113; to St. Louis, 61, 67; to Washington, 56, 59, 127, 141; to West Point, 109
Religious belief and practice, 165, 176
Residence in Lexington, 207–283
Resigns commission in United States army, 144
Returns from Mexican War, 101–102
Sits for portrait, 68–69

[306]

# Index

Southern trip, 268, 273
Surrender, 194–195, 197
Vestry, member of, 277–278; attends meeting of, 278–279
Washington College, accepts call to, 202–203; elected president of, 201
Wedding of, 31–35
Lee, Robert Edward (II), son of Mrs. Robert E. Lee, 85, 115, 133, 157, 161, 167
Lee, Robert Edward (III), grandson of Mrs. Robert E. Lee, 257, 264, 293
Lee, William Henry Fitzhugh ("Rooney"), 61, 66, 75, 96, 108, 114, 115, 119, 120, 121, 127, 141, 167, 168, 170, 175, 250, 257
Lee, Mrs. William Henry Fitzhugh (Charlotte Wickham), 121, 127–128, 141, 168, 170, 175, 257, 272
Lee, Mrs. William Henry Fitzhugh (Mary Tabb Bolling), 257, 264, 266
Lewis, George Washington (Wassy), 47, 100
Lewis, Lawrence, 57, 100, 260
Lewis, Mrs. Lawrence (Eleanor Parke Custis), 3, 14, 15, 27, 28, 29, 35, 45, 51, 57, 74, 86
Lewis, Lorenzo, 47, 63
Lewis, Mrs. Lorenzo, 47, 122, 156, 249
Lexington, Virginia, 188, 204, 206, 214, 229, 239
Lilly, servant at Arlington, 91
Lincoln, Abraham, 140, 142, 143, 250
Linda, servant in the Lee home, 293
"Long bridge," 116, 149
Lossing, 6, 7
Louisa, servant in the Lee home, 273, 274
"Lower country," 155

McClellan, General, 161, 163, 164
MacDonald, Marshall, 225, 254
McDowell, General Irvin, 154
Margaret, servant in the Lee home, 54
Marshall, Judge William L., 103
Marshalls, the, 40
Mary Eliza, nurse for the Lee children, 108
Mason, Emily, 194, 200, 204
Mason, Major W. Roy, 164
Mason and Dixon's line, 137
Meade, Bishop, 39
Meade, Mary, 156
Meades, the, 39
Meniday, servant in the Lee home, 52, 54
Meredith, Arlington servant, 158
Mexican War, 98–99, 100
Mical, servant at Arlington, 134
Military District, No. 1, 230; No. 5, 252
Morris, Gouverneur, 90
Morris, Pat (Martha Jefferson), 90
Mount Airy, estate of Benedict Calvert, 14
Mount Calvary Church, 103

[307]

## *Mrs. Robert E. Lee*

Mount Vernon, 15, 18, 81, 147; coach of, 39–40; pictures of, 148; plate of, 148; relics of, 8, 188, 254–255
Musicians at Arlington, 34
Myrtle Grove, estate of the Goldsboroughs, 26

Nancy, servant in the Lee family, 42
*National Intelligence*, 128
New Year's reception at Lexington, 267
New York Harbor, 83
*New York World*, 296
Norfolk, Virginia, 46
North, life in the, 137
Nottingham, Mrs., 186
"Nurse," 51–52, 56, 130, 132, 151

*Old Churches and Families of Virginia*, 39

Parke, Colonel Daniel, 9–10
Parke, Frances. *See* Custis, Frances
Pemberton Landing, Virginia, 200
Pendleton, General W. N., 201
Perry, Arlington servant, 158
Pet names: Boo, 45, 98; Booty, 56; Bouse, 45, 47, 48, 50; Bun, 45; Bunny, 45; Daughter, 98; Dunket, 45, 46; Loren, 47; Marietta, 221; Markie, 111, 116, 132, 134; Milly, 136; Precious Life, 115; Rooney, 61, 75, 108, 119, 120; Wassy, 47

Peter, Britannia Wellington (Mrs. Beverly Kennon), 3, 31, 34
Petersburg, Virginia, 31, 186, 250; siege of, 250
Politics, 138
Pompey, servant at Arlington, 10
Porter, General, 162
Prayers, 99
Prentiss, James H., 32
President's house, Lexington, 208, 244–245, 255–256, 261
Preston, Mrs. Margaret, 210
Puritan, the, 137

Raffling opposed by General Lee, 224
Ravensworth, estate of the Fitzhughs, 8, 25, 35, 43, 59, 95, 115, 155
Reading club, Lexington, 216
Reconstruction, 230, 241, 246, 252; Act of, 230
Relics of Mount Vernon, 253–254, 259
Richland, home of Sidney Smith Lee, 264, 265
Richmond, Virginia, 142, 188, 190; city council of, 171
Riggs, Mrs. Elisha, 117
Rip Raps, 50
Rockbridge Artillery, 161
Romancoke, estate of Robert E. Lee (II), 126, 263, 290

Saint John's Church, 84
Saint Paul's Church, Richmond, 174, 176, 190, 191

[308]

# Index

Sally, servant at Arlington, 133
Sam, servant in the Lee home, 273, 274
Sanford, General, 154
Schell, Augustus, 248
Scott, General Winfield, 119, 127, 141, 144, 148, 149, 151
Secession, 139–140
"Second Limit Gate," 220, 222, 266
Sermons, 51
Servants, 42, 131
Sewing Society of Grace Church, 223–224, 271
Sheep-breeding, 123
Shenandoah Valley, 222
Sheridan, General Phil, 252
Shirley, estate of the Carters, 24, 40, 81, 127, 128
Shoal Creek, estate of the Goldsboroughs, 4
Slavery, 138
Smith, Colonel Francis, 187, 280
Smith, Mrs. Francis, 291, 292
Smithsonian Institution, 6
South, life in the, 137, 251–252
*Southern Collegian*, 299
Starvation parties in Richmond, 176
State rights, 138
Stevens, Thaddeus, 231
Stewart, John, 180–182
Stewart house, Richmond, 180–182
Stonewall Brigade, 177
Storm at Lexington, 278, 283
Stratford, Lee estate, 24
Stuart, Calvert, 155

Stuart, Gilbert, 15
Stuart, Julia, 82
Stuart, Rosalie, 115
Sunday, observance of, 19
Surrender of Lee, 194

Taffy parties, 175, 176
Talcott, Captain, 94
Talcott, Colonel Andrew, 36
Talcott, Mrs. Andrew (Harriet R. Hackley), 36, 60, 78, 116, 117
Tayloe, Elizabeth, 28
Texas, secession of, 141
Totten, General, 121
Traveller, 195, 196, 210, 229, 240
Trundle bed, 4
Tudor Place, home of the Peter family, 3, 31, 34
Turner, Edward Carter, 80, 156, 245, 246, 286–287
Turner, Marietta, 3, 4, 32, 33
Turner, Thomas, 32, 34, 62
Tyler, President, reception to, 86

"Uncle" Charles, servant at Arlington, 133
Underwood, Judge John G., 249
Union, the, 137, 140
Union Bank, the, 76
University of Virginia, 115
"Upper country," 155

Valentine (sculptor), 276
Valley Forge, 261
Vanderbilt, Cornelius, 248
Virginia, state of, 137–138, 143, 144

[309]

# Mrs. Robert E. Lee

Virginia Military Institute, 100, 187, 206, 212, 218, 222, 228, 229, 258
Virginia reel, 34
Visiting at Arlington, 3, 4
Volunteers in Revolutionary War, 17

War, 139, 141, 148
Washington, D. C., 5, 135, 138, 139
Washington College, 201, 244, 258; Lee called to, 201; Lee becomes president of, 206
Washington, George, 5, 12, 128, 161; papers of, 16–17, 149, 259
Washington, Martha (Mrs. George Washington), 5, 7, 8, 12, 14, 58; bounty of, 173, 260; will of, 8–9
Washington Monument, 6
Wedding of Mary Custis, 32–34
Weitzel, General, 192
West, William E., 68, 76

West Point Military Academy, 29
"West Point of the South," 206
"White House," estate of William Henry Fitzhugh Lee, 126, 130–131, 198, 257, 263, 264
Wickham, Charlotte. *See* Lee, Mrs. William Henry Fitzhugh
Williams, Martha (Markie), 111, 116, 132, 135, 265
Williams, William Orton, 148, 149
Wilkerson, Captain, 289
Wilmer, the Reverend Joseph P. B., 204
Winchester, Virginia, 134, 135, 159
Woodlawn, estate of Lawrence Lewis, 3, 31, 35, 100

Yorktown, Virginia, 14
Yule log, 85

PRINTED IN THE UNITED STATES OF AMERICA